HISTORICAL ARCHAEOLOGY

Contributions in
Intercultural and Comparative Studies
SERIES EDITOR: ANN M. PESCATELLO

Power and Pawn: The Female in Iberian Families, Societies, and Cultures
Ann M. Pescatello

Tegotomono: Music for the Japanese Koto
Bonnie C. Wade

Peter R. Schmidt

HISTORICAL ARCHAEOLOGY

A
Structural
Approach in an
African Culture

CONTRIBUTIONS IN INTERCULTURAL AND COMPARATIVE STUDIES, NUMBER 3

GREENWOOD PRESS
WESTPORT, CONNECTICUT • LONDON, ENGLAND

Library of Congress Cataloging in Publication Data

Schmidt, Peter R
  Historical archaeology.

  (Contributions in intercultural and comparative
studies ; no. 3 ISSN 0147-1031)
  Bibliography: p.
  Includes index.
  1. Haya (African tribe)—History. 2. Rugomora
Katuruka site, Tanzania. 3. Archaeology and history—
Tanzania. 4. Oral history. I. Title.
DT443.S29   967.8'27   77-84758
ISBN 0-8371-9849-6

Library of Congress Catalog Card Number: 77-84758
ISBN: 0-8371-9849-6
ISSN: 0147-1031

First published in 1978

Greenwood Press, Inc.
51 Riverside Avenue, Westport, Connecticut 06880

Printed in the United States of America

10 9 8 7 6 5 4 3 2 1

DEDICATED TO THE
PEOPLE OF THE UNITED
REPUBLIC OF TANZANIA

Contents

Preface

This study emphasizes the interplay of historical data derived from a pre-dominantly oral historiography and archaeological data. Research was done among the Bahaya. Today the culture area is in the administrative areas of Bukoba and Muleba in West Lake Region of Tanzania. Research in Buhaya was sponsored by the Program of African Studies of Northwestern University and by the National Science Foundation, Grant #GA 2769.

Twenty months during 1969 and 1970 were devoted to field research. The first half of the study included ethnographic research that concentrated on the oral traditions and the oral historiography of the Bahaya. I conducted this research while residing with my family in villages located in Kiziba and Maruku kingdoms.

The archaeological phase of research began during January 1970. Most of the archaeological data discussed in this book were recovered from excavations conducted at the Rugomora Katuruka site in Maruku. Hereafter I will refer to this site as the Rugomora Mahe site to avoid confusion and to give it a name that duplicates the name of the Bahinda king who allegedly built his royal palace on the site. During excavation of this site, I lived some fifteen miles to the north near Bugabo kingdom. We later moved to Nshambya village in Kyamutwara kingdom immediately to the northwest of Bukoba and remained there for the last six months in Buhaya. Throughout the archaeological phase of research, investigations into the traditional exploitative economy and oral traditions continued.

During the course of my studies in African history, anthropology, and archaeology, I have been fortunate to study with people who have encouraged my work from its inception. I have also had many friends and colleagues who offered me to help and encouragement. Merrick Posnansky first stimulated my interest in oral tradition and African history. I spent two terms of academic year 1966 at Makerere University in Uganda, where he introduced me to some of the exciting problems to be investigated in East Africa. My introduction to Buhaya came during a field trip there with Posnansky and Hamo Sassoon, who was always more than helpful during my occasional trips to Kampala from Buhaya.

I have received every encouragement from John Rowe of Northwestern University; he has always had faith that this was a worthy study. I am indebted to Stuart Struever who was not only responsible for much of my archaeological training, but who also taught me that a rigorous method in archaeology is essential and that anthropological archaeology can occur only with a firm grounding in anthropological method.

I am extremely grateful to the Republic of Tanzania for allowing me to carry out research there. It is my hope that this work is complementary to the goals of its people. There are many Tanzanians to whom I own thanks. Amini Mturi of the Department of Antiquities has continually offered his kind help. Israel Katoke of the National Ministry of Culture and Youth has offered his counsel. John Sutton, now at the University of Ghana, has been a source of encouragement and helpful intellectual exchange.

My real debt lies with the Bahaya, many of whom provided assistance and encouragement. I am especially grateful to Augustine Kaindoa for the many patient hours and days he spent with me, as well as to Bernardo Muhambo, Bayekela Rusinga, Wazee Lugimbana Bandio and Kaijage of Maruku, Mzee Kamurasi of Buyango, and Mwami Mataihwa Lubelwa of Kigarama, Kiziba. There are, of course, many others who directly assisted my research, some of whom are cited in the text. To my archaeological workmen I owe a great deal, especially to Cleophace Kahanantuki and Salvatore Rubagumya. To many others I cannot mention here I remain deeply grateful for their help.

While in the field, I came to know Father Paul Betbeder of the Société des Missionaires d'Afrique (White Fathers), who has lived in Buhaya for forty-two years. His knowledge of Bahaya archaic vocabulary and his deeply abiding interest in Bahaya culture and oral tradition were a great source of stimulation.

Finally, there have been many who helped to fund the project. The History Department at Northwestern University provided a travel grant; the Program of African Studies provided a grant for the oral tradition work and also offered assistance in the analysis phase; and Makerere University provided funds for student assistants. The research could not have been carried out without the kind support of Gwendolen Carter and the Program of African Studies at Northwestern University. The archaeological phase of the research was sponsored by a National Science Foundation predoctoral grant issued to Stuart Struever.

Suzie Zeeman and Mary Hall provided yeoman-like services in handling the drawings, and Mark Hurwitz and Barbara Jones helped in the archaeological analyses. The typing was done by Mary Yde, Helen Shuman, Kitsy Nurmi, and Bertha Robbins—all of whom bore up under much stress and helped immeasurably. Finally, I am blessed by a family that willingly endured much. My wife, Jane, has been a good companion and essential colleague in Africa. She has handled the burden of running a lab in the field.

Two forms of notation are used in this book. For the most part, the conventional form of anthropological citation is used. The exception is the use of end notes in Chapters 4, 5, 6, and 7, which cite primary sources for historical evidence in Buhaya. In most cases, the notes give the name of the individual who provided the historical evidence along with the date and place. Much of the historiography of the Bahaya is held in oral form, and it is convention among historians of Africa to provide a clear citation so that other scholars can investigate similar problems and find the original sources.

I want to emphasize that the discussions about land tenure, political structure, and some aspects of the exploitative economy in Chapter 3 are strictly historical. The *nyarubanja* land tenure system, for example, now abolished under TANU policy, and the much changed political systems experienced their last major change when the Bakama, or kings, were removed from authority in the administrative system several years prior to Independence.

Peter R. Schmidt

HISTORICAL
ARCHAEOLOGY

1 Introduction to Approaches, Problems, and Goals

The primary goals of this study are to develop a methodology that scientifically demonstrates the ties between archaeological materials and oral tradition, and to develop new explanations for change and development of an African Iron Age culture from its earliest beginnings to contemporary times. The broader goals of the study are inherent in the spirit of "new archeology." The work of Binford, Hill, Deetz, Longacre, and Struever in the mid 1960s stressed the perspective of anthropological theory and the development of ethnoarchaeology, where material culture is studied using the methods of cultural anthropology.

One of the most exciting dimensions of new thinking in North American archaeology about anthropological archaeology is the strong emphasis on the anthropological aspect of the archaeological experience. Most archaeologists rarely have the opportunity to step away from their excavations and analyses to explore aspects of culture other than the material culture. Few archaeologists have the time or opportunity to become familiar with the cosmological system and the oral traditions of the people with whom they work and whose ancestors they may be studying.

Bahaya culture provided the opportunity to explore several aspects of culture, especially oral tradition (including mythology), the productive economy—agriculture and iron working—and spirit mediumship, to see how the Bahaya conceptualization of the past related to the patterning of material remains left by Iron Age peoples during the last 2,500 years. This approach is suited to a sedentary people such as the Bahaya, who display significant continuity in settlement patterns and who have related to the same climatic

regime for, perhaps, millennia. So, a basic premise
from the study's inception was that an initial
anthropological-historical study was the foundation
upon which a more fruitful strategy for archaeological
investigation could be developed.

One of the general goals of this study was to collect,
analyze, and use historical oral tradition which was
linked to archaeological sites. The structural study
of these oral traditions, it will be seen, helps to
explain the chronological structuring of dynastic
histories as well as the history of occupation of at
least one major site. The connection between these two
data sources was established by application of structural principles; hence, the title of this book. As I
became familiar with forms of oral tradition among the
Bahaya, I came to realize that the types of oral traditions which I least expected to be useful in combination with archaeology, mythology and folklore, proved
to be far more essential than royal and clan histories.
Such a realization came with the help and understanding
provided by many Bahaya friends and informants. The
value of their introducing me to Bahaya culture is
inestimable.

An important dimension of the following study is its
relevance for the development of new methods for
African history and for the anthropological archaeologist. The intent from the beginning of the study was
to test some long-standing but still incipient notions
about the methodological efficacy and applicability of
archaeology to African history. African historians and
archaeologists (Fagan and Willett, 1967; Willett, 1973)
have been calling for interdisciplinary approaches to
the study of African history. There has been response
to the obvious need to step beyond disciplinary
boundaries, but it has been either very limited in
scope, or it has suffered from the lack of an effective
theoretical model to guide research.

The active development of interdisciplinary studies
among archaeologists of Iron Age Africa can be traced
to Merrick Posnansky, who has long taught the need
for historians to study and understand the methods and
theory of archaeology, if only to avoid misinterpreta-
tion of archaeological explanation. The corollary
of this position is that archaeologists as students of
historiography and process must familiarize themselves
with the methods of the historian and the anthropo-
logist, especially the methods of historians who employ
ethnohistorical techniques (Vansina, 1965). Many
archaeologists intimate with archaeological problems
in African societies are prevented, either by training

(Soper, 1971) or insufficient funds and time, from
pursuing a more comprehensive approach to historical
problems. Several notable exceptions are John Sutton
and Frank Willett. Sutton is an archaeologist who
has grappled with historical problems in western Kenya
while employing ethnographic, linguistic, and
archaeological data. Willett has excavated at the Orun
Oba Ado site in Ife, Nigeria, explicitly because the
site was associated with legends about the foundation
of Benin (Willett, personal communication). Willett's
work bears many affinities to the present study, in
that shrines are often ancient sites tied to oral traditions in Ife.

Posnansky's work at Bweyorere (1968) demonstrates one
of the many possibilities open to the archaeologist-
historian in Africa. Oral tradition about Bweyorere,
an Ankole royal capital site, indicated that the site
had been occupied on three separate occasions during
the last 250 years. Posnansky's excavations indicated
that the site had been occupied, abandoned, and re-
occupied. The evidence from oral sources in the case
of Bweyorere is limited to a dynastic genealogy which
mentions the site as a place of royal occupation during three different generations. The archaeological
evidence at Bweyorere did not allow direct verification
of the oral data. The most an archaeologist can
legitimately claim in this case is that there was
occupation, abandonment, and reoccupation of the site,
presumably by the royal family.

The interpretive problems illustrated by the
Bweyorere excavations suggest that, in interpreting
archaeological evidence discovered in conjunction with
ethnohistoric information, caution must be exercised
until adequately tested methodologies have been
developed. The simple conjunction of archaeological
evidence with ethnohistoric evidence in specific
cases does not ipso facto constitute proof of the oral
tradition, nor does it mean verification of interpretative ideas that might be held in an oral tradition,
such as a discussion about the function of an earthworks
or a technological area.

The conjunction of ethnohistorical evidence and
archaeological evidence when recognized allows the
formulation of hypotheses (some of which may be explicitly suggested by the ethnohistory). These
hypotheses can then be tested in subsequent excavations
where similar phenomena appear. In addition to our
goal of developing a scientific methodology to discover and to verify the relatedness of oral traditions and archaeological phenomena, a further funda-

mental assumption is that the correlation of
archaeological data with oral tradition is more than
ethnography and archaeology; it is also historical
archaeology and African history. A qualification of
this definition is necessary, for one aspect of
historical archaeology is that in which historical
data, usually documentary sources, are employed in
archaeological description and interpretation. Liter-
ary evidence is often absent from African and other non-
Western cultural systems, which often depend on nonliterary forms of historiography. The use of a nonliterary historiography with archaeology is parallel to the
use of documentary sources in historical archaeology.
Problems of interpretation are compounded by the relatively uncharted ground in the utilization of nonliterary history with archaeological sources. Another
goal of this study is to demonstrate that some aspects
of oral tradition, such as mythology, have historical
value. If through archaeological evidence, mythology
can be concretely affirmed to contain an order of
historical reality that has usually been denied it by
most historians, then it is incumbent to develop
methodologies that can continue to test this basic
proposition. Through a consideration of the place
of mythology in Bahaya culture—specifically its role
as an analyzable historical form in the repertoire of
African historians, as a locational device for prehistoric sites, and as an explanatory device for culture change in prehistoric times—we can then argue
that the demonstrated historical value of nonliterary
historiographic forms when employed with archaeology
constitute historical archaeology and African history;
hence, the other half of this book's title.

The latter point, that oral tradition and archaeology
employed together lead to African history, is begging
the question. Many African historiographic systems
stand alone and do not need to be verified by other
sources. But Vansina (1965) argues that a higher
degree of confidence is needed for various oral tradition forms and that archaeological confirmation is
one way to heighten veracity. African historians can
take two basic directions in the future. One is to
develop better methods for analyzing historiographic
systems, their development, and their indigenous
function as a means of expanding our understanding
about the variability of historiography. The second
is to follow Vansina's prescription under the tentative
assumption that forms of oral tradition need verification from archaeology, not because they are inherently
less credible than our own historiography, but because
our traditions deny them veracity. Therefore, verification by archaeological means is a way of influencing

our own traditions, a way of altering our own concepts
about what makes up historical truth.

In the following study, both of the above positions
will be taken into consideration in discussing the
function and structure of myth and the subsequent
proposition that historical archaeology in Buhaya, and
possibly other regions in Africa, touches on all
periods of the Iron Age, the earlier period of which
has heretofore been considered prehistoric. All of
these interrelated theses basically reduce to the
development of new perspectives and new methodologies
for history and archaeology. This approach is very
similar to that advanced by Walter Taylor (1948), whose
conjunctive approach basically seeks to integrate all
possible functionally interrelated cultural phenomena.
This perspective takes shape in this book when
archaeological data are correlated with ethnographic
information, such as local historiography, which in
Buhaya is closely tied to religious and political life.

Binford (1968:269) has stressed similar concerns. He
recognizes that greater confidence can be created for
archaeological explanation as well as better conditions
for hypothesis testing if an integrated approach is
adopted: "The archaeologist must then develop models
that will allow him to relate the archaeologically
observed phenomena to variables which, although observ-
able in different form among living peoples, are
thought to have explanatory value." Explanation in
this form consists simply of demonstrating relatedness
between things which at first sight may appear separate.
Ethnographic data are often important for revealing how
a historiography varies in subsystems of a culture.
For instance, it will be seen that in the Bahaya
religious system content and structure of oral
traditions such as didactic myth, political history,
and tales about the functions of shrines as mnemonic
devices differ considerably from the oral traditions
of praise song singers who formerly related political
history for the kings. Recognition of different
historiographic subsystems according to context helps
to explain the development of different historical
perspectives in Buhaya.

Obviously, there must be some point of limitation, some
selectivity by the archaeologist-historian who inquires
of ethnography to obtain aspects of the culture that
are relevant to archaeology. This book emphasizes
aspects of the Bahaya religious, political, and
technological subsystems as they relate to oral tradition and archaeology. To achieve this goal, we must
consider man's relationship with his environment

(Chapter 2). In this book, analyses of prehistoric
and contemporary settlement-subsistence systems also
touch on aspects of the exploitative technology,
particularly iron production as it related to the
natural and sociocultural environment (Chapter 3).
These considerations emphasize iron production, the
utilization of iron in agricultural production, the
nature of intense agriculture and its possible relationship to high productivity in iron technology. All
of these functional interrelationships are relevant to
the study of change in Buhaya during the Iron Age, and
many of them are directly related to Bahaya historiography which discusses change.

Study of the exploitative aspects of Bahaya culture is
relevant here insofar as they indicate how they came to
be and the adaptive values they express. Essentially,
I suggest an historic sequence that charts a partial
interaction of environmental and cultural factors
through time. Much of the historical construct is
suggested from historical interpretations which the
Bahaya themselves offer in their mythology. (These
constructs are set out in Chapter 11.)

After a discussion of the exploitative economy and
a general introduction to Bahaya culture, the characteristics of oral tradition in Buhaya and the
methodologies employed in collecting and analyzing
oral traditions are described (Chapter 4). Differences in the structure of royal genealogies in Kiziba
and Kyamutwara kingdoms are also analyzed in order to
explicate the different histories of royal sanctions
against independent versions of oral traditions in the
two kingdoms. (See Figure 1.)

Chapter 5 develops a detailed discussion of the
historiography in Kiziba kingdom. The origins of the
Babito dynasty are traced from Bunyoro, but particular
attention is focused on oral traditions about Mugasha,
the Bahaya god of the waters and storms. Mugasha is
portrayed in Kiziba oral tradition as an adversary of
the earlier Bacwezi "dynasty" in Bunyoro and as an
ally of the Babito dynasty in Kiziba. Basically, the
analysis stresses that the Babito dynasty meets
fundamental opposition from Bacwezi spirit mediums, who,
along with local clan leaders and perhaps acting as
local clan leaders themselves, prevent Babito consolidation of power for at least seven reigns. During
this period of time, the Babito dynasty draws on the
assistance of Mugasha's spirit mediums to oppose the
Bacwezi spirit mediums, but Bacwezi opposition to the
throne is not neutralized until the royals establish
a rival cult.

This part of Kiziba historiography is different from
the latter part of the royal history, and it bears
great affinities to the oral tradition about Bahinda
rule in Kyamutwara. Chapter 6 explores the role of
Bacwezi spirit medium opposition to Bahinda rule in
Kyamutwara, but here the emphasis is on their continuing role of opposition to the present day.
Analysis of the oral tradition shows that the Bahinda
also draw on the assistance of the god Mugasha to
oppose the Bacwezi. In addition, the analysis
demonstrates that mythology about one of the Bahinda
kings, Rugomora Mahe, has the same structure as Kiziba
myth about Mugasha. Not until the magical aid of
Mugasha is obtained and the sacred shrines of the
indigenous clans seized is Bahinda royal power consolidated in Kyamutwara.

The repetition of the Mugasha myth as a vehicle for
Bahinda oral tradition is the result of Bahinda adoption of oral traditions once related by Bacwezi spirit
mediums. The locations of Bahinda rule on indigenous
Bacwezi shrines meant the integration of local myth
into royal genealogies. Chapter 7 emphasizes that
extensive local oral traditions are associated with
physical places once belonging to the indigenous
clans and seized by the Bahinda. Physical features at
these former shrines function as mnemonic devices to
precipitate extensive descriptions of technological
activities and explanations of natural phenomena.
Especially important is that such mnemonic devices
at the Rugomora Mahe site are associated with both
the histories of the indigenous clans and the Bahinda
royal dynasty.

Chapter 8 concentrates on the development of an excavation strategy based on the oral traditions and mnemonic
devices associated with Rugomora Mahe on the Katuruka
site. The test results, which confirmed hypotheses
about the relationship between oral tradition and
underground features on the site, are discussed.

The full ramifications of the excavation strategy
are described in Chapter 9, which also discusses the
association between specific traditions and features
of the Early Iron Age. The characteristics of the
occupation and activity history of the site are also
discussed. Dating evidence, which is the earliest
for the Early Iron Age in East or Central Africa, is
analyzed, and its relevance to African history is
assessed. Chapter 10 evaluates the iron working
evidence, which strongly suggests that technology in
the Early Iron Age in Buhaya was highly advanced and

productive.

Chapter 11 examines the fundamental hypothesis derived
from the research and test results. Also emphasized
is the value of using oral tradition evidence with
archaeology to obtain constructs for the history of
exploitation of the natural environment. Many of the
positions in this chapter are drawn from the previous
discussions about the exploitative economy, archaeological evidence for a highly productive iron
technology, the utility of explanations in oral tradition about the history of technology, agricultural
development, and settlement patterns. General hypotheses about the interrelationship of explanation in
myth, the development of an intensive multicrop
agricultural system, and a productive iron technology
are developed for future investigations.

Finally, Chapter 12 explores some of the implications
of the research methods and results for African history.
The focus here is on the development of new interpretations for the origins of iron in Africa and on the
impact of the research results on previous explanations of change and development in African cultures.

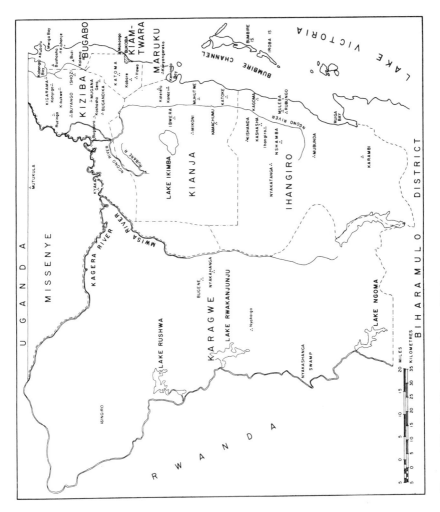

Figure 1 The Traditional Kingdoms of Buhaya

2
Environment

The physical boundaries of the culture area of Buhaya
may be defined according to diverse criteria. In the
past, it has been common to include the Banyambo
people of Karagwe as part of the culture area.
Cultural differences between the coastal Bahaya (a
term originally designating those who fished and lived
along the lakeshore; Cory, n.d.:13) and the Banyambo,
while minor, are amplified by an economy that is much
more pastoral in Karagwe and by adaptation to an
ecological niche that is very different from that of
the coastal peoples. Karagwe area, then, will not be
considered here, as it is separate from Bukoba area
in terms of geology, climate, vegetation, population
density, and economy.

Rainfall along the lake is abundant, evenly distributed,
and of low variability (McMaster, 1960:78). There
appears to be a direct relationship between distance
from the lakeshore and the annual rate of precipitation; there is a drop in precipitation of approximately
30 millimeters per mile toward the inland ridges
(Figure 1). Most of the population of coastal Buhaya
is within the 50" or 1,250 millimeters per year
perimeter. Population is most dense where rainfall is
high and most reliable. There has been a correlation
between rainfall and occupation patterns, particularly
before this century. Today there is a decreasing
correspondence between population density and rainfall
because of population pressures on the land. Increased
population pressures on coastal lands and a system of
limited partitive inheritance have led to fragmented
farmsteads (bibanja) which in many instances are incapable of supporting more population. As a consequence, many young men seek land outside the family

holding.

Several alternatives are available when seeking arable
land outside the natal village. Grassland adjacent
to a home village can be opened up to cultivation but
only after extremely difficult conversion of the poor
soil to productive land. Previous observers (Reining,
1962) have thought this procedure to be relatively
rare, for it is difficult and many Bahaya feel that it
involves an inordinate expenditure of effort. Nonetheless, this phenomenon is everpresent, and I saw it in
process in at least ten instances in Maruku, Bugabo,
and Kiziba kingdoms. The second alternative (if continued occupation in Buhaya is selected, as usually
happens) is to move to a marginal area without reliable rainfall where subsistence agriculture may be
more precarious. The banks of the Kagera River in
western Kiziba kingdom and the fringes of swamps south
of Lake Ikimba in Kianja are two examples of light-
density population areas that are quickly growing in
population because of immigration of land-deprived
Bahaya, or even people from other districts in Tanzania.

Even with these safety valves, it is not unusual to
find bibanja in northern Buhaya of two to three acres
supporting families of four to six persons. This is
a very high ratio of people to land. Many an heir,
when faced with a potential inheritance of a fraction
of an acre, will often sell or lend his inherited
share to a brother and settle in one of the more
marginal areas; or, if possible, he will open up new
land near his natal village.

Reining (1962) found that her village census (presumably of Muhutwe) indicated an approximate density of
1,250 per square mile within the village boundaries.
Nearly forty years ago, Milne (1938) found that an
entire gombolola (the smallest administrative unit
during colonial times) had the same population density
of 1,250 per square mile. My observations confirm
that in parts of Ihangiro, Maruku, Bugabo, and Kiziba
kingdoms the density per square mile on arable land is
at least 1,250 and possibly higher in some limited
areas. These localized, densely settled areas situated
on coastal hilltops are among the most highly populated
areas in Africa. Present patterns of climate and
population density in Buhaya are important environmental and demographic variables linked to exploitative
behavior during Iron Age occupation of the area. An
archaeological documentation of exploitative behavior
in the area must seek to explain how the habitat and
culture have changed through time, and how change in
one domain affects the other.

Besides Karagwe and the coastal belt, there are two
other physiographic zones: the central depression and
the Kagera basin. The central depression is a very
lightly populated valley between the coastal hills
and the Karagwe escarpment. Subject to rain-shadow
effect of the coastal hills, this area has only recently begun to support intense cultivation and settlement—most of which is located to the north and east
of Lake Ikimba. Lake Burigi, to the south of Ikimba,
is located in the midst of discontinuous hills and
thicketlike bush. The Ikimba area in the northern
part of the central depression is now a new settlement
area.

While there have been some claims (Culwick, 1939, in
Cory file, No. 239) that the central depression once
supported large settlements, before the smallpox
epidemic of the late nineteenth century, neither oral
history nor archaeological survey supports this
position. Limited archaeological survey suggests that
the central depression was not settled with agricultural
villages until recently, probably the last 100 years,
a view which may be altered after further survey. One
of the primary disadvantages for settlement in the
central depression is the low rainfall, which is not
sufficient to support a banana subsistence crop.

The Kagera basin is to the northwest of coastal
Buhaya and contains the swift-flowing lower Kagera
River. The rapid flow of the river as it passes
through Buhaya is attributed to the capture of the
headwaters by an upward-tilted lower basin. The
tilting accounts for a permanent plentiful flow and
also explains the drowned nature of the upper river,
which forms the border between Karagwe and Rwanda
(Wayland, 1934; McMaster, 1960). According to McMaster,
gallery forest at one time may have lined the Kagera,
whose shores are now choked with papyrus (McMaster,
1960:79). Whether man may have been instrumental in
altering the Kagera environment is impossible to say
at this time, but his early presence in the Kagera
Valley and his present settlement pattern along the
river, especially in Kiziba, suggest that the
attractiveness of the fertile soil in the flood
plain may have resulted in forest clearance for agriculture. The forest remnants in the lower valley,
such as Minziro Forest which is swampy and less suitable to human occupation, add credence to McMaster's
hypothesis.

The juncture of the upper Kagera to the lower Kagera
Valley (with its lake sediments) is the location of
one of the more important prehistoric sites in East

Africa. Here the Nsongezi Acheulean site is located
on a river terrace which, because of erosion, has
been stripped of much of its overburden, thus allowing
easier access to the archaeologist (Cole, 1965).
Many Acheulean sites are also scattered along the
crests and flanks of the Karagwe ridges. The quartzite
outcroppings were easily exploitable for production of
stone tools. Often, cleavers, hand-axes, cores, and
other tools may be picked up alongside the Karagwe
roads or in farmed plots, where farmers have piled
together stones while clearing their land. During
archaeological survey of Buhaya, it was also observed
that Pleistocene settlements appeared to be confined
to the Karagwe ridges, to the juncture of the upper
and lower Kagera, and to the middle course of the lower
Kagera, where the Nyabusora site is located. No
indication has yet been discovered that the lakeshore
environment in present-day Buhaya was exploited by
Paleolithic peoples. However, the type site for the
Sangoan culture period is located north of the Kagera
on the shore of Lake Victoria at Sango Bay, but the
Sango Bay habitat is flat grasslands and, therefore,
very distinct from the environment common to Buhaya.

During the periodic fluctuations of climate during
Pleistocene times, the Kagera and its tributaries
undoubtedly provided a more constant environment,
attracting game, fishermen, and hunters. The
enormous densities of tools at Nsongezi suggest that
the terrace area overlooking the river may at one time
have functioned as an important factory site as well
as a settlement of considerable importance for the
subsistence economy of its middle and late Pleistocene
dwellers.

Karagwe and the lower Kagera would not have held the
same appeal for agricultural peoples of the Iron Age
as for Pleistocene hunters and gatherers. The rocky
terraces along the river would have been difficult to
cultivate, and a low dependability of rainfall would
have made cultivation precarious. Land along the
lakeshore is a much more reliable area for cultivation.
The rainfall along the coast is plentiful and stable,
which are agriculturally conducive conditions linked
to an even, steady temperature. Milne (1938:16) observed that the monthly mean temperature lies above
or below the annual mean of 20°C by no more than 1°.

The favorable yearly rainfall and temperature conditions in coastal Buhaya are certainly adequate to
support an evergreen, high climax forest. Kendall
(1969) maintains that the rainfall regime today is not
altogether different, though perhaps slightly dryer,

than 10,000 years B.P. when evergreen forests were the
most common vegetation in the Lake Victoria area.
McMaster (1960:78) suggests that the affinities of the
forest which once occupied the coastal belt were montane
rather than equatorial. A thorough botanical study of
forest dwelling remnants in Buhaya as well as palyno-
logical studies of cores from Buhaya lakes and swamps
(a study now in progress) are needed before tendering
any hypothesis regarding vegetational patterns during
the last 5,000 years. Most remnant evergreen forests
in Buhaya are found on the flanks of hills, adjacent
to swamps, or in the swamps. Several species of the
genus Podocarpus, which usually is considered a montane
marker, are found in the alluvial flats of the mouth
of the Kagera (Kendall, 1969:157). The close proximity
of these species undoubtedly can be taken as an
indicator that they once occupied similar niches
several miles to the south in Buhaya but have since
been removed because of cultural activity. Until
recently, the few remaining forested areas have been
under the authority of the king (Mukama) of each
minor kingdom. When a Muhaya (one individual; pl.
Bahaya) wanted to cut wood within one of the forests,
he first had to obtain the Mukama's approval. Today,
the national government controls most of the forests,
and many have been closed to exploitation. On the
open country groves of Musizi trees (Maesopsis eminii)
can be seen with acanthus shrubs, which point to the
suitability of the coastal area for forest growth
(McMaster, 1960:79). More will be said about the
paleoenvironment of the coastal ridges when the nature
of exploitation of that presently denuded area is
discussed.

The most heavily settled portion of Buhaya is the 10
mile wide by 70 mile long coastal strip which runs
from 1° S to 2° S. Within this 700 square mile area
dwell 350,000 people, or 80 percent of the population.
There are three distinct subenvironmental zones here
which are differentially exploited by contemporary
Bahaya and which have been exploited in varying degrees
throughout the Iron Age: the shore of Lake Victoria,
the swampland and seasonal marshes, and the ridge tops
and flanks.

These ecological units, subenvironments, are fundamental
subdivisions of the total habitat and can be distin-
guished from one another by (1) the varying range of
fauna and flora supported in each and accessible to
human populations, and (2) the variability of exploitative systems directed at each by the Bahaya. The
latter portion of the definition, of course, is
culturally determined, for if there are distinct

subenvironmental zones today in Buhaya, which were
likely covered by evergreen forest 10,000 years ago,
then those distinctions resulted from man's cultural
interaction with and modification of the natural
environment.

Given the above assumptions and definitions, it is
clear that subenvironmental zones as they exist today
must be defined. The shore of Lake Victoria can be
delimited in Buhaya as one distinct, essential subenvironmental zone. Possibly, it has been significantly altered by the clearance of any forests that may
once have existed on its broader, now fossil, beaches.
The distinctiveness of the shoreline microenvironment
lies in its partial isolation from the hills to the
west; in most areas, the shoreline is cut off from the
hills by large, sheer sandstone cliffs (Plate 2).
Wherever the shelf between cliffs and water exceeds
100 meters, there is usually human habitation. The
other essential characteristic of the shoreline is the
food resources available.

A wide range of fish species can be obtained from the
lake, and many occupants of the lakeshore zone depend
on the lake for their subsistence. Fishes of the
genus Tilapia are particularly common and sought
after, as well as many other species, especially
catfish. Fishing is done by net either from the shore,
after the net has been dropped by boat, or from boats,
especially at night by lamplight.

Residents of the shoreline also exploit lake flies
(ishami) which they capture after huge thunderhead-like
swarms descend on the shoreline from the lake. The
lake flies are formed into hard balls, bits of which
are then added to stews as a nutritional, protein
supplement. While the shore residents grow bananas,
coffee, and sometimes other crops, they do not practice
mixed horticulture. The absence of cattlekeeping
among lakeshore peoples yet again distinguishes their
subsistence economy from the ridge-top dwellers. Some
lakeshore dwellers do not eat red meat, not because
it is taboo but because it is not a readily available
part of their diet. The food resources available to
the lakeside Bahaya are substantially different from
those in the inland regions.

The second essential subenvironmental zone is the
swampland and seasonal marshes of Buhaya. Swamplands
are found throughout the hilly coastal ridges and do
not fall into an easily definable zone. They include
large evergreen forests, such as Munene Forest in the
flooded plains of western Kiziba kingdom, and the

sedge-choked fringes of rivers, such as the Kagera,
Ngono, Bukumba, and Mwisa. The distinguishing flora
of the latter areas is papyrus (Cyperus papyrus) and
some species of bamboo.

There is limited fishing for fresh water species in
some of the rivers, and the only remaining hunting
areas in Buhaya are restricted to the swamps—particularly in the residual evergreen forests. Bushbuck,
waterbuck, dikdik, wild pigs, smaller vermin, and
monkeys were hunted in those areas in traditional
times. It is probable that much larger game, such as
is found in the wooded savannah county in Misienye
kingdom, was once available to the coastal Bahaya.
The most substantial faunal species harvested in the
papyrus swamps adjacent to the Kagera River is the
hippopatumus, a cheap source of protein. The meat
from illegally hunted hippos is commonly sold throughout the settled hills of Kiziba kingdom to the east
of the Kagera; hippo exploitation is a substantial
economic pursuit.

Papyrus is an important crop of the swamps as it is
widely harvested for its internal, white pulp (eshisha),
which is dried; it has a wide variety of household
uses—from absorbent towels to stoppers for calabashes
and bottles. Today the swamps and marshes often provide many of the resources necessary for the construction of a traditional house. House poles, usually
30 centimeters in diameter, often are acquired in the
swamp forests, and bamboo and grasses are gathered
from the seasonally marshy areas.

During the primary wet season from March to May, some
of the swamps are difficult and even dangerous to
traverse, for rivers with substantial currents flow
through them. Swampy lands also are an essential
habitat for the Anopheles mosquito and, as a consequence, malaria is endemic in parts of Buhaya where
there are permanent swamps. The presence of endemic
malaria and malarial outbreaks during wet seasons
indicates that health considerations may have dictated
the selection of settlement sites during prehistoric
times. The relationship between health considerations
and settlement area is less apparent today because
land pressures have necessitated settlement in less
healthy areas, particularly along the Kagera River.
However, there appears to be some correlation between
height of residence on the ridges and the incidence
of malaria. For instance, in Kitobo village in
western Kiziba, those who live at the base of the
ridge and closer to the swamps suffer from a
significantly higher rate of malaria than do the

ridge-top dwellers (Erika Schwartz, personal communication). Ridge tops that are now cleared of forest support densely settled agricultural land or grassland used as pasture for cattle. Most cultural activities and most settlements are confined to ridge tops. The flora and fauna of these areas are now primarily domesticated, so that ridge tops are in fact culturally modified areas amongst the other subenvironmental zones. The ridge tops can be seen as a subenvironmental zone or as an ecotone (an ecologically intermediate area or a point of tension between two environments.) As a transitional zone, an ecotone allows its human inhabitants to exploit adjacent ecologies—in this case the swamps and the lake, and in many cases swamps on both sites. While the ridge-top dwellers in Buhaya do not directly exploit the aquatic resources of Lake Victoria, they do purchase fish from fishermen who sell fish in the ridge-top villages. In precolonial times, cowrie shells were used to exchange and agricultural products were bartered for fish. Fish were sometimes also bartered for other goods, such as the materials needed for house building. Finally, the hill tops offered raw materials for iron smelting and a high climax forest which could be exploited by permanent agri-cultural settlements or through a slash-and-burn type of agriculture.

The dense population of coastal ridges seems to be a phenomenon that is not related to soil fertility. The fertility of soil along the eastern ridges is low, and Milne (1938:15) found that only one-fifth of the ridge soils were adequately and naturally fertile. However, he does not demonstrate whether so-called fertile soil is derived from sources other than Bukoba sandstone, or whether fertile areas are the result of transportation of plant nutrients—in the form of mulching—into the individual kibanja (family agricultural holding). It is clear that an abundance of rainfall alone does not explain relatively high rates of agricultural productivity in Buhaya on what are essentially poor soils. In fact. an abundance of rainfall can mean quick depletion of an already poorly based soil through leaching. The combination of high temperature, continual dampness, and the presence of bacteria, insects, and other organisms which break down organic material and aerate the soil lead to soil depletion in the Tropics. The permeation of oxygen into the soil leads to oxidation of essential pollen evidence which the archaeologist needs for reconstructing the paleoenvironment. It also produces the oxidation of iron and aluminum.

Heavy rainfall along the lake, heavy leaching of the
soil, and a steady temperature also indicate that
chemical decomposition proceeds actively the year
round. These conditions mean that prehistoric faunal
remains are extremely rare, except when carbonized,
and that bone usually deteriorates completely within
150 to 200 years. These conditions are accompanied
by a high soil acidity, which also contributes to
rapid chemical decomposition (Milne, 1938).

The soils of the ridges are derived predominantly
from Bukoba Sandstone, made up of fine to medium grade
sandstones interbedded with hard shale-like rocks
(Milne, 1938:16). The derived soil is particularly
poor because the parent materials for the sandstone
had already experienced thorough decomposition, and
as a consequence the present rocks are sometimes
little more than quartz grains with silica cement
(ibid.); the more soluble constituents of the ancient
source rocks were lost long ago. Some replenishment
probably comes from chemical decomposition of dolerite
sills, and these sources, along with the shaly fine-
grained sandstone, contribute the most useful soil-
making materials (ibid.:17).

The ridges today are capped with a mantle of soil
derived from the sandstone, and the flat-topped ridges
probably carry a mantle of detritus that belonged to
the former peneplain. Sheet laterite can be seen
near the brows of hills, and other lateritic deposits
occur as outcroppings. In many instances, these form
formidable barriers in roads, and much road repair
is devoted to transportation of soil to lateritic
outcroppings that are exposed by erosion during the
rainy season. On the exposed flanks of ridges
throughout Buhaya, grass used for pasture usually
grows in areas where there is sheet laterite, which
is sometimes so extensive that the surface is virtually
solid ironstone. Apparently, there is a strong
tendency toward laterization in Buhaya soils,
especially in those soils that are derived from the
coarser sandstones and are extremely porous. In
tropical areas where climax forest remains, laterization is held in check by protective vegetation (McNeil,
1964:4). When the vegetational cover is removed and
land is opened to intensive cultivation, leaching is
increased and the soil is robbed of its organic
materials, along with silica, potassium, calcium and
phosphorus. The end result is that the soil mantle
becomes oxides of iron and aluminum. The lateritic
ironstone sills near the brows of hills do not appear

to be the result of forest clearance.

Soil scientists have come to recognize that lush
vegetation in the Tropics is not an indication of
soil fertility. The lushness of tropical forests
is more closely related to rainfall availability and
may mask soil deficiencies (McNeil, 1964:4). What
significance does this have for the archaeological
documentation of Iron Age settlement patterns in
Buhaya? The infertile laterized pastureland appears
to be a stark remnant of overexploitation of the
former forested ridges for agricultural production.
Under a swidden system of cultivation (slash and burn),
the soil of a tropical forest usually has sufficient
cover vegetation within one or two years after a plot
is abandoned. Even though there is usually rapid
regeneration of secondary vegetation after a plot
is abandoned, once the nutrient cycle of the primary
tropical forest is interrupted by cultivation,
restoration of soil fertility is very slow in the
upper horizon (Harris, 1972:251-253). The system
can become maladaptive when the period of fallow is
shortened because of sociopolitical or demographic
considerations. Because the vegetation available
on any plot is the major source of nutrients primarily
in the form of ash, clearance of an immature secondary
forest means that fewer woody components are available for conversion into ash (ibid.:253). Progressive
downgrading of this sort may eventually lead to a
secondary cover of herbs and shrubs incapable of preventing laterization. The eseential points to
remember about exploitation of the environment in
Buhaya are: (1) that other ecological/technological
variables such as exploitation of forest for charcoal
to run smelting furnaces may affect the forest eco-
systems, and (2) that there may be a relationship
between the high productivity of a technological
system such as iron production and increased
density of population, which then might mean increasingly severe pressures on possible swidden systems
in the form of decreased fallow periods. If iron
technology is particularly productive, as appears
to be the case in Buhaya, then a permanently settled
population may result. The nature of the suggested
relationships discussed above will be explored further
in later chapters, and will be modified and employed
as tentative hypotheses about changing patterns of
Bahaya exploitation of the natural environment.

Contemporary patterns of land use and soil fertility
in Buhaya are an historiography for land use in Buhaya.
If the ridge-top area was once a forested region, then
what can the contemporary exploitative patterns

contribute to a study of change in land utilization
patterns? The sometimes large stretches of land
between villages which are today pastureland support
very poor grasses and are heavily laterized. Secondary forest regeneration in these areas is prevented
by continual grazing of cattle, which eat the young
plants and prevent forest regeneration. This was
originally the poorest soil, and widespread forest
clearance did not discriminate in selection for soil
types. Because of their very poor grass, the grasslands also have a low stock-carrying capacity. It
is not unusual for a Kiziba farmer to let out his
cattle to a remote area many miles distant during
the dry season so that sufficient grass will be available to them. The carrying capacity of the grasslands
has reached a critical level in many areas.

As previously noted, reclamation of grassland to
fertile, productive agricultural plots is strenuous
and a test of patience. However, planting grassland
with a crop such as bananas retards leaching because
of the high water absorption of the banana tree and
the protection its broad leaves provide the soil
against rain bombardment. When the Bahaya reclaim
grasslands for agricultural production, no attempt
is made to allow it to return to secondary forest;
instead, there is direct conversion of the land from
grassland to productive kibanja. The process is often
slow, and newly planted banana sprouts sometimes will
make little progress toward maturity over a one-year
period.

Once a hole is dug into the laterite mantle to
accommodate the root system of the banana, then cow
manure and compost will be added to the immediate
radius of each tree. As the kibanja owner has time,
he brings sedges and other grasses, in huge bundles,
from the swamps or marshes and deposits them on the
total plot. These grasses have a dual function: they
add their nutritive value to the soil through decomposition, and they impede leaching by holding moisutre
above ground. In some cases, a mulch of this sort is
as deep as 45 to 50 centimeters and is constantly
maintained by adding grass. This process is the
creation of a soil, and in some respects it is similar
to the wholesale transportation of foreign soil to a
barren territory. In their oral tradition, the
Bahaya claim that in several instances the Bakama
(kings) had large quantities of soil carried to
laterite mantles, so that successful agriculture
could be carried out in the vicinity of the king's

royal palace (kikale). The folklore also mentions
that these converted areas were attractive areas for
settlement, but that they lacked good soil; the kikale
of Mukama Kalemera of Kyamutwara kingdom was established in this way.

The ridge tops, then, are tension zones in that resources from both other subenvironments are essential
for maintaining life on the ridges. However, the
essential point of tension lies between the need for
more intensively cultivated land and the impoverished,
laterized grasslands which are the result of man's
overexploitation of the ridge tops. Studies by
paleoecologists help to date the period when the
first extensive forest clearance occurred in the
region.

In a study of the ecological history of Lake Victoria,
Robert Kendall (1969) has attempted to reconstruct
vegetational patterns for the last 15,000 years. He
worked from a lake core taken in Pilkington Bay, which
is located in Buvuma Island, approximately 20 kilo-
meters from Jinja, Uganda. Many of the generalizations
he formulates may be only partly applicable to the
Buhaya area, but the high similarity between the
contemporary north shore and west shore vegetational
patterns suggests that the Kendall analysis can be
extrapolated to Buhaya. Further confidence for
accepting the data is inspired by Kendall's acknowledgment that a core taken in the open lake near Entebbe
and closer to the western shore shows no significant
diversion from the Pilkington Bay pollen spectrum
during the last 7,000 years (Kendall, 1969:162).

The dynamics of pollen distribution remains insuffi-
ciently understood; hence, it is impossible to say
what the patterns of pollen rain are for the western
lake. There is no easy answer to the question of how
big a source area was sampled in the Lake Victoria
cores. However, much of Kendall's comparative
evidence was pollen types extant near the northwest
sector of the lake, and this area is very like Buhaya.
This is not to say that available comparative evidence
was biased, but that his pollen most closely matched
the contemporary taxa of that area (Kendall, 1969:159).
In his analysis, Kendall does caution that the record
is biased in favor of forest indicators and that this
phenomenon may partly be explained by the fact that
wind-pollinated species are predominantly forest
dwellers (1969:159). This latter observation tends
to affirm evidence for a later radical change from

forest-dominant vegetation to savannah grasses.

The ecological history of the lake area can be divided
into four periods for the last 15,000 years, all of
which have been dated by C14 analysis:

Period 1:   14,500-14,000 B.P. Pollen was rare and
            heavily oxidized; there is no firm evidence.

Period 2:   13,500-9,500 B.P. Initially, there were
            abundant sedge and cattails, and increasing
            grasses. Then, just before 12,000 B.P.,
            sedges and grasses decreased as swamps were
            probably inundated. Correspondingly, a
            major influx of tree pollen began, with a
            few evergreen species.

Period 3:   9,400-2,000 B.P. This was a period of
            marked forest recovery, particularly with
            the establishment of many evergreen species.
            There appeared to be a trend toward semi-
            deciduous forest between 5,000 and 6,000
            B.P., which may be an indicator for drier
            climate or more seasonal rainfall.

Period 4:   2,000 B.P. to the present. This was a
            period of major change, when forest de-
            creased and grass increased. The trend
            may have begun as early as 3,000 years B.P.
            (Kendall, 1969:159-162).

The dates from period four are essential for the study
of human exploitation of the environment in Buhaya.
The lack of significant lakeside settlement by Late
Stone Age peoples suggests that their cultural
activities were not responsible for forest clearance.
Kendall clearly argues that forest decline was not
linked to change of climate, which remained essentially
the same. He links cause of significant vegetational
change during the last 3,000 years to forest clearance
by human populations.

No significant forest clearance occurred in northern
and western Lake Victoria until agricultural activity,
approximately 1,000 B.C. to 100 B.C., removed the
forest cover. This environmental evidence is made
more significant by archaeological investigations in
Buhaya, during which I have obtained evidence for
iron production dated by C14 to about 500 B.C., and
possibly earlier (Sutton, 1972). Early Iron Age man
with iron and possibly steel tools, especially axes
and hoes, had the technological capacity to clear vast
areas of forest in a relatively short period of time

for agricultural and technological reasons. The
forest clearance activity of Early Iron Age peoples
are documented in the pollen record, which shows
widespread forest clearance during a period of
climatic stability. The Buhaya dates, which correspond with the pollen evidence, confirm that Early Iron
Age peoples in the area were producing iron while
forests were reduced. The results of forest clearance
and prevented regeneration of secondary forest have
already been discussed. These arguments will be expanded as further ethnographic and archaeological
documentation for Bahaya interaction with their natural
environment and exploitation of this habitat is discussed in conjunction with historical evidence.

If we can come to know the complexities of contemporary patterns of exploitation and the process of environmental change, then a partial history can be
developed for land usage, since the contemporary
ethnography provides a selective historiography. It
is a compilation, a selective part of a whole
diachronic range of exploitative phenomena and related
behavior throughout the Iron Age, during which adaptive mechanisms were discarded, modified, transformed,
or resurrected. If the present is the end result of
2,500 years of uninterrupted cultural history in the
Buhaya area, then its analog is the historiographic
system in the area, which is also a selective,
constantly modifying, adaptive phenomenon; it fits its
milieu, and the needs and perspective of the contemporary culture. So, too, does a contemporary ethnography
of exploitative systems and their functional relationships to social phenomena capture what has been
selected and what has been most successful in the
adaptive process.

The diachronic dimension enters when the archaeologist
provides documentation and argues logically for shifts
in the adaptive process, especially as they are manifest in changes in settlement and subsistence. Concomitant changes in other aspects of culture, such as
technology, political organization, land tenure, and
religion can be documented by the historian from
studies of historiographic systems, their structure,
and change through time. The conjunction of all these
sources then permits a more comprehensive explanation
of functional links, as well as the formulation of
testable hypotheses about how and why changing adaptations occur through time.

Figure 1: Rainfall patterns in Buhaya.

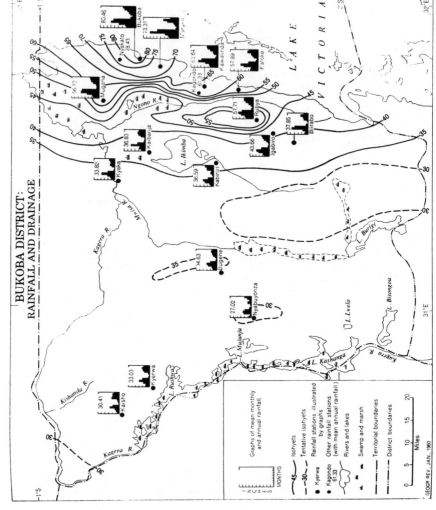

Plate I: Hill flanks in Kiziba Kingdom
(notice forest remnant in upper right-
hand side).

Plate II: Lake shore shelf with sandstone bluffs above.

3
Background: The Political System, Land Tenure, and the Exploitative Economy

The seven small kingdoms into which Buhaya was divided
before independence were each ruled by a Mukama (king),
who had a royal court attended by retainers from all
the clans in his kingdom. Before the nineteenth
century, there were only three primary kingdoms in
Buhaya: Kiziba, Kyamutwara, and Ihangiro. With the
breakup of the Bahinda dynasty in Kyamutwara during
the late eighteenth and early nineteenth centuries,
there developed the very small kingdoms of Bugabo,
Maruku (or Bukara), smaller Kyamutwara, and Kianja.
Missenyi, located on the north side of the Kagera, is
a creation of colonialism and in traditional times was
within the sphere of Buganda influence and control.

There has been some confusion among historians about
whether to refer to a minor kingdom in Buhaya as a
chiefdom or as a kingdom. Regardless of the size of
each political unit, by the nineteenth century most of
Buhaya centralized political units were states. The
state virtually controlled the religious system by
the eighteenth century, or, at least, newly developed
royal religious cults were sufficiently powerful to
eclipse the influence of Bacwezi cults led by the
indigenous priest or embandwa (spirit medium). In
addition, the state had developed sufficient control of
force to quash completely the blood feud between clans
which was widespread before the nineteenth century.
The establishment of centralized states in Buhaya also
was marked by state interference in disputes between
clans.

We cannot date the period during which state control
of lands developed, but clan ownership of land appears
to have been seriously eroded with the development of

the large estate (nyarubanja) system of land tenure,
the essential vehicle for distributing state-appointed
political offices. The interference of the Mukama
in the adjudication of clan disputes and the elimina-
tion of effective clan control of land both show that
the Mukama was the leader of a state system and not
simply a chiefdom.

Another criterion that might be used (Service, 1962)
to judge the existence of the state is the presence
of a socioeconomic class structure. This phenomenon
certainly did exist in Buhaya, for the Bahima, or the
pastoralists from the north, while they did practice
sedentary agriculture, also maintained control of
cattle as an economic resource. They had a rank
status above the Bairu (commoner) clans in a hier-
archically arranged social system. The Bairu clans are
in good part the indigenous clans in the area, although
in several cases possible indigenous clans such as the
Bayango have been raised to Bahima status as a reward
for their cooperation with the throne. The Mukama,
who controlled all force in the kingdom, could violate
this rule by taking a wife from a commoner clan. The
Bahaya openly disapprove of this kind of behavior;
thus, to avoid trouble, the king changed the status
of the woman's clan from Bairu to Bahima. These clans
are called enfuro (as are the aristocratic clans) and
form a rather ambiguous middle grade in the social
hierarchy.

The Mukama in a Buhaya state also had direct control of
all crafts. The iron workers, for instance, had to
ask his permission and provide a gift to obtain rights
to mine for iron ore and to burn charcoal in the
forests. These privileges once belonged to the clans,
such as the Bagina in Kiziba, but were usurped by the
Mukama upon the development of centralized power. Once
they had finished a smelt, iron workers had to provide
the king with some of the bloom and sometimes even
with a portion of the finished forged products.
Furthermore, in his court the king had smiths from
iron-working clans who served in the court as the
king's official iron workers. This system differed
somewhat from the labor tax, whereby each able-bodied
man had to work in the king's service at the palace
(kikale) for one month a year.

So, the state apparatus was maintained by a large
workforce drawn evenly from throughout the territory
by political officers of the king. As a consequence
of state-recruited labor, the Mukama's palace was an
elaborate structure that sometimes included thirty to
forty large houses up to 40 feet in diameter. The

periphery of the royal compound was dense with the
houses of all the court retainers (like the resident
iron workers) who came from all the clans in the kingdom. Each clan had an appointed function in the king's
court, such as custodians of the royal drum, gatekeepers, executioners, personal advisors, barkcloth
producers, or herders. It was the clan responsibility
to see that their official duties were performed in
the king's court by sending representatives on a
rotational basis. The individuals who were invested
with the care of the royal drum in fact cared for the
kingdom, as the drum was the official symbol of power
and authority. If a king lost his royal drum, as
occasionally happened, then he lost control over his
kingdom. Those invested with the care of the drum
were also schooled in oral traditions about the history
of the kingdom; these men proved to be among the most
knowledgeable informants in oral traditions.

Recruitment of labor by the Mukama was essential to his
maintenance of power. The Mukama also demanded the
labor of youth in a system of talent recruitment that
resembled the Buganda system of royal pages. Young men
at the ages of ten to twelve were asked by the local
political leader to go to the king's palace and serve
in an age-grade group called a Muteko. The young boys
were trained together in the arts of war at this time,
but they also performed much more mundane tasks such
as carrying manure to the Mukama's farms, cleaning out
the cattle enclosures, pasturing cattle, cutting grass,
and doing general maintenance work. Old men in Buhaya
today, especially in Kiziba kingdom, speak very
affectionately about the days when they served in
their Muteko. The strong sense of identity with
Muteko, especially those which were founded in the
latter part of the nineteenth century, has to do with
serving together and surviving numerous battles
against the Europeans and against political
opportunists such as Lweshabula, a contender for the
Kiziba throne during the latter part of the nineteenth
century.

Because of their small size, the Buhaya states cannot
be considered full-scale kingdoms such as Bunyoro,
although their political organization was on the same
level of complexity as Bunyoro's. Succession to the
throne in Buhaya states was not according to
primogeniture as Richards and LaFontaine (1960) claim,
but by preference to a younger son. There has been
some confusion between inheritance in the social
system and succession in the political system. Descent
among the Bahaya is patrilineally reckoned, and the
inheritance of the estate goes predominantly to the

Musika (principal heir), who is the eldest son of
the first wife or a brother of the deceased if there
are no male offspring. The second eldest son (or
the eldest son if the first wife's son is younger) is
called the Mainuka, and he also inherits part of the
estate. The main house (nyaruju) always goes to the
Musika who receives the greater portion of the estate.
The Mainuka receives approximately two-thirds as much
land as the Musika. The other male heirs (the Kyagati)
then get shares equal to half of the Mainuka's share.
(In Customary Law of the Haya Tribe, Cory indicates
that any generalizations such as these are subject to
challenge according to the different inheritance
systems of kingdoms and even chiefdoms within kingdoms;
pp. 1-3.) This system of land inheritance, even
though it has a bias toward eldest son, is partitive
and leads to serious fragmentation of land in Buhaya.

Even though a son or a grandson may receive a portion
of land which is little more than a quarter or half
acre in many cases, to be landowner is to have status
and security. Bahaya who have not inherited land and
have left Buhaya to work in Dar es Salaam will usually
return to buy a plot on which they can cultivate and
build a house. A home base in Buhaya is deemed
essential, and many emigrant Bahaya maintain residences
while absent from Buhaya. However, as population
pressure has increased on workable land during the
last several centuries, the system of partitive
inheritance has meant that in many cases there is
insufficient land to support a household. This has
inevitably led to a search for vacant land that can
be reclaimed or brought under cultivation. Oftentimes Bahaya in search of land will leave their
kingdom to travel to a neighboring kingdom where a
fee (kishembe) is paid to the local court for open
land (in precolonial days to the Mukama).

The great proliferation of clans with the same names
in Buhaya can be viewed partly as a result of this
process. The segmentation and migration of agnates
who retain their original clan name are usually the
result of land scarcity and population pressure. Many
dispersed "clans" found in several Buhaya kingdoms
have local leaders but are in fact maximal lineages
that trace their origins to a common progenitor.
Examples are the Bakuma clan of Kiziba kingdom and
the Bayango clan of Kyamutwara kingdom (both of which
will figure prominently in later discussions of oral
traditions). Population movement has been predominantly internal to Buhaya rather than to other culture
areas; this characteristic suggests that there may
have been resources, such as iron ore, which kept

lineage groups within the Buhaya region. Even so, it
appears that many areas in Buhaya reached their carrying capacity centuries ago, perhaps even millennia ago
in some limited areas. There is still much open
grassland called Rweya rwa Nanka, but it is difficult
or impossible to cultivate because of laterization of
the soil.

Land tenure before the centralization of state authority was probably controlled by a corporate group such
as the clan. Today clan lands (Rweya rwo Luganda)
still exist, but they are located in the open grasslands. Families can also own rweya land, and the
whole family inherits rights to use the land. These
lands have low fertility and support only fallow
cultivation. Within the family-held estate of kibanja,
there is usually perennial cropland (mwate) and kisi,
which is land set aside for the growing of cassava,
millet, and maize, none of which prospers under the
cover of banana trees. The clan-held rweya lands are
probably a remnant of land tenure before the development of the nyarubanja (large estate).

The origins of nyarubanja estates are not clear, but
the development of clientship, whereby a permanent
tenant incurred obligations to his landlord on
nyarubanja-held land, is linked to the growth and
development of the state. The development of
nyarubanja land tenure meant that the state was able
to recruit local labor for support of its administration system outside the royal capital. Nyarubanja
tenure supported the political structure and allowed
even closer control over clan affairs and crafts
through its supply of tribute and labor for the
landlord, often a chief or lesser official. The landlord of a nyarubanja estate was called a Mutwazi, and
the tenant a Mutwara. The Mukama had the sole right
to allocate nyarubanja land, which could be created
out of unoccupied land, clan lands, or free-held
family plots. When clan- or family-held plots were
seized by the Mukama, the former owners became tenants
and clients of the Mutwazi. Through the creation of
nyarubanja estates, the Bakama were ultimately able to
break up clan-held lands so that a fragmentary pattern
of land tenure emerged.

The development of nyarubanja was a device employed by
the Bakama to fragment clan land and to undermine the
social unity of the clans. The creation of a nyarubanja estate out of clan-held land inevitably led to
the creation of a new loyalty. No longer was a

clansman directly answerable to the elders (Bagurusi),
but his primary obligation as a tenant lay to his
immediate superior, his Mutwazi. Furthermore, the
landlord as superior and as patron had judicial rights
over disputes within his limited domain, except, of
course, when litigation developed between tenant and
landlord. If, however, it was true that the landlord
was also a subchief or village chief appointed by the
king, then legal recourse for a tenant might be limited.

By creation of a nyarubanja estate, the Mukama in
fact diverted the tribute which he normally received
to the landlord of the estate. Hence, the tenants,
instead of sending their annual tribute and giving
their labor to the Mukama, provided services to the
Mutwazi. In this way, the political officers of the
Mukama were maintained in office through the services
of tribute goods provided by tenants (Reining, 1962).
However, the estates awarded for this purpose rarely
exceeded twenty or so individual holdings. In other
words, political appointees were not provided a
resource base large enough to allow them to establish
independent authority.

A man awarded an estate by the Mukama was usually
given cattle, for cattle were essential to prosperous
maintenance of the estate. On the nyarubanja estate,
the cattle were let out to the commoner tenants. In
return for his care of cattle, the tenant would
receive use of the cattle manure. The manure was
the Mutwazi's reciprocation for his tenant's care of
the cattle. The exchange of cattle care for manure
was an important productive relationship for both
parties. It meant higher agricultural productivity
for the Bairu tenants because of manuring in the
farmed plots. In turn, this higher productivity led
to a higher tribute to the landlord, who received
bananas, millet, banana beer, and barkcloth. Through
the development of this system, it was possible to
create and maintain soil fertility in naturally
infertile areas. The ramifications were probably
multitudinous, but most important to recognize perhaps is that dense concentrations of population might
have led to overexploitation of the natural environment.
An extremely productive iron technology probably
encouraged adaptations that allowed people to continue
occupying the area. Soil conservation techniques when
combined with regular manuring undoubtedly led to
maintenance of an already dense population.
Archaeological evidence also confirms these ecological
observations.

The contemporary Bahaya subsistence economy is a mixed

husbandry system wherein cattlekeeping is mixed with
a banana-based sedentary agriculture. The advantages
of this system on a low fertility soil are obvious.
Bahaya cattle enclosures are used in three basic ways
in agricultural production. In one arrangement, the
cattle are kept within the kibanja among the banana
trees but away from the coffee trees. There is a
permanent structure which is never moved but from
which manure is removed and distributed on the kibanja
on a regular basis—section by section. Grass is cut
in the rweya or in the swamps, brought to the enclosure
and mixed with manure, and then removed to the kibanja
after several weeks. Another type of enclosure in
the kibanja is one that is moved periodically from
area to area, so that the residue at the enclosure
which is impossible to capture can be evenly
distributed throughout the farmed plot. The third
type is a temporary pen in front of the compound or
house where the manure can be scooped from the packed
clay daily and distributed without accompanying mulch
to the kibanja.

The above manuring methods, which are practiced on
many plots, allow for high productivity. But an
integral part of the agricultural system is the
transportation of mulch from the swamps and rweya. All
plant remains are returned to the soil—from finely
chopped banana tree stems carefully arranged to
prevent water runoff to banana peelings. These
manuring, mulching, and conservation practices have
allowed long-term occupation of the Buhaya area under
sometimes adverse conditions. They have also led to
the development of an intense, multicrop agriculture.

In many respects, the agricultural adaptations of the
Bahaya resemble those of the Kara on Ukara Island in
Lake Victoria. Rounce (1956) observed that the Kara
population density is over 1,220 per square mile of
arable land, a density similar to the most densely
settled areas in Buhaya. The Kara use of land has
also developed as a consequence of poor, acidic soil
with little organic material. The Kara have a
favorable rainfall as do the Bahaya, and they have
developed a system of mixed farming integrating crop
husbandry and livestock.

The system of manuring and compost on Ukara Island has
some similarities to Bahaya practices. The Kara keep
livestock in their houses, which have 4 foot deep pits;
the pits are gradually filled with manure, fodder,
and bedding, which are brought in twice a day. This
compost is then removed and allowed to decompose, and
is placed on the farmland at an estimated rate of 4

tons per year. For the Kara this practice maintains
the status quo in soil fertility. The Ukara parallel
is a good example of how extreme pressure on land can
cause an evolution of better agricultural methods
under conditions of intensive use. The Kara use of
"green manure," leguminous crops, also resembles the
Bahaya use of several varieties of beans. However,
the Bahaya plant their beans under the banana trees
every year, the Kara plant theirs once in a three-
year cycle of crop rotation.

The Bahaya provide ground cover and protection from
erosion and leaching by planting coffee trees, the
cash crop, under their banana trees. The ecological
reasons for coffee plantings in the kibanja rather
than on open land are apparent. With a bean and
pumpkin crop on the ground, coffee tree crop in the
middle level, and banana tree crop at the highest
level, the multicrop intensive agriculture—which
uses manure compost, anti-erosion conservation
measures, green manure, and triple canopy protection
for the soil—maintains a high rate of productivity
on a relatively poor soil.

This background provides a basis for further discussion
of the history of Bahaya exploitation of the natural
environment. It has been stressed that a key factor
to understand is the interplay of different parts of
the exploitative technology, particularly intensive
agriculture and iron production. Study of iron
technology in Buhaya is difficult, as smelting has
not occurred during the last forty years. Consequently,
to obtain information about iron production I have
had to depend on ethnohistorical research among old
men familiar with iron technology.

The use of ethnohistorical descriptions of pre-colonial
and early colonial iron technology and its associated
behaviors provided a highly variable range of description. Memory distortion was significant, particularly
in descriptions of social matters, and to a lesser
degree in descriptions of temporal matters. Most of
the old men who provided oral histories had ceased
smelting iron or assisting in smelts during the 1920s.
Most often, they provided generalized accounts of
smelting if an interview was not structured to elicit
specific data.

Structured interviews, then, were necessary to obtain
specific technological information such as the size
and shape of the furnace, the phases of construction

and their sequence, and ritual practices. Even when
specific questions were asked, very often the testimony
given generalized or idealized technological procedures.
For example, in Kianja kingdom, former smelters
claimed that the furnace bowl was excavated in the
ground to a diameter of 2, 4, and even 12 feet. This
was either extreme variability, or the passage of
five decades had left many men with unclear notions
of a process that they once executed in a highly
routinized way. Special data such as furnace
diameter, depth of furnace bowl, and height of
furnace wall were subject to considerable variability.
Spatial distortions influenced by passage of time and
removal of the technological process from everyday
life led to highly divergent descriptions of iron
smelting in the same village.

Evidence about iron smelting and forging obtained
in Kiziba kingdom was much less variable, and
descriptions often agreed. When possible, the
informant would be taken to the traditional smelting
or mining site where he had worked; it was hoped that
the physical presence of the site would help freshen
his memory of activities performed on the site. In
several cases, particularly in regards to mining
behavior, this procedure proved to be a fruitful one,
but in most cases it succeeded at best in eliciting
interesting personal anecdotes with little value in
delimiting the technological aspects of iron smelting.

Research focused on two general areas where iron
production is known to have been conducted in the
past. One area was northwestern Kianja and Kyamutwara
kingdoms, and the other was Kikukwe village in northern
Kiziba. Most of the old men interviewed in Kyamutwara-
Kainja were former smiths and consequently did not
have detailed knowledge about smelting. The apparent
bias of the Kianja research was corrected in Kiziba
kingdom, where many interviews were held with people
who had observed or who had participated in the
smelting process.

In full-time smelting operations, there was usually
a head smith who recruited other men to help him.
The Barwani clan had most of the iron workers of the
Kyamutwara-Kianja area in its ranks. However, since
a Murwani smith could hire helpers from other clans,
there were no closely guarded secrets associated with
any aspect of the technology. Because the Barwani
tended to be primarily smiths rather than smelters,
there were gross divisions between clans for different
phases of iron production. The most commonly produced
items made of iron were spears, hoes, knives, and axes.

The smith, when he was not serving in the court of
the king, had to give a percentage of his final
product to the king as a gift. The Mukama in turn
would take the iron goods and give them to his people.
Iron, then, was a major part of the redistribution
system in the centralized state.

Iron goods were the only basic nonagricultural
commodity regularly or widely redistributed to the
people. Hence, the Mukama was dependent upon a
successful and continuing technological system, the
products of which maintained the redistribution system.
The utilization of the productive economy by the state
may in part explain why such large quantities of
iron produced, especially in the several centuries
preceding colonial rule. That the production of iron
was on a very large scale is unquestionable. Mr. R.
Baguma, a University of Dar es Salaam student who
assisted in a survey of iron-working sites, knew of
a large slag heap in his natal village, Kangantebbe,
Kianja.

We were able to define one 120-meter long slag heap
that was 2 to 3 meters wide and approximately 2
meters high (Plate 1). The slag had been picked up
from smelting sites and carried to a border area to
construct a fence, which is where most of the slag
is today. The remainder has been used to build
houses; this practice is common throughout Buhaya.
As can be seen in Plate 1, the slag is consolidated
into large blocks approximately 25 to 45 centimeters
in diameter. Donald Avery, a metallurgist at Brown
University who has studied and experimented with
early iron-smelting techniques, feels that the sizes
of the slag blocks illustrated indicate a bloom
process whereby the slag is almost completely
separated from the bloom. Slag and bloom are usually
mixed together so that the slag has to be hammered
away and shattered to extract the workable bloom.
This apparently is not the case in some areas of
Buhaya, where large blocks of slag may either be
testimony to smelting with efficient separation
of slag and bloom, or to the willingness of
smelters to accept some loss of bloom to the slag.

Also at Kangantebbe were several large (4 to 6 meters)
circles of slag about 0.5 to 1 meter high. These
appeared to mark specific smelting sites. From this
village north to Kimuli village along the Kanazi-
Ibwera road, there are numerous smelting, forging,
and mining sites; Kyema is one of the largest of the
mining sites. The mining sites, which were controlled
by the Mukama, show extensive exploitation. For

example, a mining site to the east in Kikukwe village
in Kiziba showed extensive evidence of iron ore extraction. Half way down the hillside to the east of
Kikukwe, which was a major iron production center,
there was an outcropping of ironstone on a 100-meter
wide ledge. In an area approximately 150 x 100 meters,
there were scores of mine pits.

Walking through the area was treacherous, for the pits,
covered with grass and brush, were located every
several meters. It was clear from the site characteristics that most of the high quality ore, which was
haematite, had been exhausted at the Kikukwe site.

There were five different types of mines, some of
which may have been tests. Figure 1 shows that the
deepest mine was a narrow cylinder that reached a
depth of 5 to 8 meters. Any attempt to excavate this
type of mine would be extremely difficult. The
largest mine was a bell-shaped pit with a narrow
opening; the highest volume of ore would have been
extracted from this type of pit. There was also a
mine that went into the side of the hill, sometimes
up to 2 meters deep. Finally, there were dish- and
bowl-shaped pits that were probably the result of
testing attempts to find rich iron ore.

The Kikukwe and Kyema sites as well as scores of other
smaller mining sites, such as in northeastern Buyango
village, Kiziba, all testify to the extensive exploitation of iron ore in the past. A partial survey of
mining sites shows that they often tend to be located
on the open rweya land, but that the adjacent
villages support very dense populations. It is within
the adjacent villages that piles of slag can be
found today. Slag heaps of a lesser scale were also
observed in Kikukwe, Ibwera, and Bwanjai villages.

Iron was smelted and forged in many villages such as
Kansenene, Itongo, and Ibwera in Kianja and Kyamutwara
where iron-working clans resided. The clans involved
in iron production commanded respect among other
Bahaya who looked on iron workers as second only to
chiefs as influential and powerful men in their
villages. Influence derived from their production of
essential goods for the community. The production
of hoes, knives, and sickles was essential for
agricultural life, and the production of knives,
arrows, and spears was essential for the maintenance
of political authority. However, a smith was forbidden
to sell or trade weapons outside the kingdom during
time of war; if he did so, he faced execution. Weapons
could be traded elsewhere during times of peace if

the Mukama's approval had been obtained.

Smelting took place under the direction of a head
smelter who recruited and organized a workforce of
up to thirty men to mine iron ore, transport it to
the smelting site, construct the furnace, and then
conduct the smelts. The iron ore was pulverized into
small pieces, and charcoal was made for the smelt.
Charcoal was produced from michwezi, migege, and
mishasha trees. In Kianja, one less common way of
building a furnace was to dig a 30 centimeter deep
hole approximately 2 meters in diameter, so that a
shallow bowl was obtained (Juma Nishangeki, 5/16/69,
in Kansenene, Kianja). Grass was put in the bottom
and fired. Then ironstone and charcoal were piled
to a height of 5 feet. This pile of charcoal and
ironstone was enclosed by rocks and mud mortar into
which tuyères (blow pipes) were placed. The grass
was then fired, and up to a dozen bellows operators
backed up by relief operators would force a draught
into the furnace, while charcoal and ironstone were
added through the top for approximately eight to ten
hours. A more common means of construction was the
erection of a 2 meter high wall of mud and slag with
a hole in the top. Grass was then fired in the
bottom, and alternate layers of charcoal and iron ore
were added until the furnace was full.

The furnace was broken into after the slag and bloom
had cooled by using green wood poles. The slag and
bloom were then pried from the bottom of the furnace
and the bloom removed for forging. Other descriptions
from the same area show a somewhat different procedure
and furnace form. Joseph Lukwe of Kangantebbe said
that first a hole 3 feet in diameter was excavated
and grasses were placed in the hole. The grass was
burned to make a bed or ash and the ironstone placed
on the ash bed; charcoal was then interlayered with
ironstone to a height of 2 meters and enclosed with
a circular wall. At ground level tuyères would be
stuck into the furnace. The bloom would settle into
the hole excavated below the ground surface. Those
who assisted the head smelter would be paid a portion
of the bloom. This suggests that the bloom must have
been plentiful enough to provide each man with a share
and the king with his share as well.

The smelting process appears to have had a fairly
large repertoire of furnace forms—from shallow dish-
shaped furnaces to deeper bowl furnaces. In all the
descriptions of the process, grass is said to be placed

in the bottom of the pit; ash is used as a bed for
the ironstone; charcoal is interlayered with ironstone,
and a wall (usually including slag) is constructed of
mud with an open top. There could be up to thirty
men present to relieve the eight to twelve men working
the goat-skin double bellows leading into 1 meter long
tuyères.

There were taboos surrounding smelting. While the
furnace was being prepared, the smelters had to ab-
stain from sexual intercourse, and during the smelt
women were not allowed to observe the smelting process.
If a menstruating woman came into physical contact with
the furnace, the smelt would be stopped and a new
furnace constructed.

The production of iron goods deeply involved the Buhaya
kingdoms in trade with neighboring peoples. During
the nineteenth century, iron products were traded to
the north in Bunyoro, Buganda, and Ankole for goods
such as ivory, and during earlier times, commodities
such as salt and cattle were traded. Trade also extended into the south as far as Lake Tanganyika and
the Uvinza area where salt was obtained in return for
iron products.

One type of salt obtained was called kabumba (a fine
salt dark gray in color); a second variety was called
rwabarara (a dark gray rock salt); and a third type
was maehule (a large grained, light brown rock salt).
Rwabarara was the most favored trade item, but it was
also the most expensive. A salt called mukuyege came
from the Ivinza salt workings near Lake Tanganyika.
This salt was preferred over the salt from Lake Katwe
in Ankole because it was more suited for cooking.
Most of the iron trade in Buhaya was for perishable
goods such as cattle, barkcloth, and salt, or for
cowrie shells, used as a currency. In the nineteenth
century, the trade was expanded to include ivory from
the north.

The high productivity of iron technology in Buhaya
meant extensive trade contacts in East Africa. It
also meant that the Bahaya supplied iron to Rwanda,
Ankole, Bunyoro, Buganda, Buzinza, and other areas to
the south. There is no record of iron goods passing
through Buhaya in a more extensive trade network.
Nor is there presently any evidence that Buhaya was
involved in the Central African trade network which
carried copper and gold to the coast and in the
interior. Buhaya appears to have been the center of a

regional trade in iron goods which radiated from
Buhaya to the north, west, and south in exchange for
goods used by the Bahaya rather than as further exchange in another trade network; the exception was
the use of cowries to purchase ivory from the north.

The huge slag heaps and dense population concentrations
near smelting sites show that Bahaya culture had had
a strong orientation toward iron production. The
extensive mines and relatively rich iron ore also
point to a prosperous iron technology. Through trade,
the Bahaya were also iron producers for a large
population on the western, northern, and southern
sides of Lake Victoria. Iron production was also the
means by which the state maintained a system of
redistribution. Through close state control of iron
production, shares of the product went to the Mukama
during smelting and forging. Royal control of clans
that worked iron must have been an important development for the evolution of state systems in Buhaya. As
we shall see in the following two chapters, some oral
traditions stress that in ancient times local rulers
were the heads of iron-working clans. The leaders of
indigenous iron-working clans and Bacwezi spirit
mediums (embandwa), many of whom appear to have had
political leadership as clan or lineage heads, were
the source of primary opposition to the Babito and
Bahinda dynasties and their Bahima followers. The
alien dynasties from Bunyoro were not able to consolidate their power until they established control over
the clans that managed the productive economy and
over the spirit mediums.

Plate I: Slag heaps in Kangantebbe Village, Kianja kingdom.

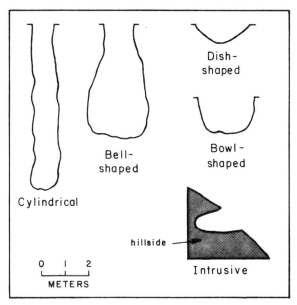

Figure 1: Variety of iron ore mines in
Kikukwe Village, Kiziba kingdom.

4
Aspects of Oral Tradition

Historians of African and other non-Western cultures
have long recognized the bias of royal genealogical
histories. Even so, most historians have relied on
them to construct histories of kingdoms, inasmuch as
royal genealogies are often the most common and widely
recognized form of oral tradition in centralized state
systems. In many cases, internal criticism and careful
cross-text analysis have been employed with success,
but the overwhelming presence and availability of
royal-influenced sources have more often resulted in
a history with a political flavor and a predominant
emphasis on affairs of state. In short, culture
history is difficult to distill from royal political
history.

In some instances, royal sanctions against versions
departing from the officially accepted interpretation
have been very strong. Such pressures were evidently
at work in Kiziba kingdom and perhaps elsewhere in
Buhaya. A number of Bahaya insisted that as long as
they had been subjected to the traditional authority
of the Mukama, then versions of oral tradition that
departed from or challenged the officially sanctioned
version could not be circulated. Many Bahaya felt
strongly that F. X. Lwamgira, who edited a history
of Kiziba, Amakuru ga Kiziba (1949), had represented
a distinctly royal point of view. In fact, Lwamgira
did not research, nor did he write, the basic work.
King Mutahangarwa (1903-1916) had been responsible
for the research and had directed the writing.
Between 1904 and 1909, Mutahangarwa gathered together
old men who were trained in the oral tradition, mostly
men from his own Babito clan. He directed them to
relate their tradition to him, and while he listened,

his court scribes wrote down their testimony.

After Mutahangarwa's death, this very long history of
Kiziba sat dormant under Lwamgira's care. Lwamgira
edited the manuscript substantially and had it published by the Catholic Mission Press in 1949. It is indeed
a royal history, and its circulation in Kiziba is
widespread. Virtually every man of means has a copy
in his household, and most of the inhabitants now
refer to it as the history of Kiziba. Functionally,
it has replaced the zither (enanga) players and others
who in traditional times were responsible for training
young men in the oral traditions of the kings. I
arranged for a translation as soon as possible so
that I could compare testimonies to the written
version and thereby judge how much influence the work
had on testimony.

While the Baziba may tend to accept a royal history
as their own historical identity, they acknowledge
that the tendency is directly related to strong
official sanctions that demanded uniformity in
political tradition. The royal sanctions did not
sit well with many and, certainly, the Mukama could
do little to control the oral traditions of the clans.
Consequently, clan histories that differ from the
official version can be obtained. However, in cases
where a clan was in a state of tension with the
political leadership, the contrary histories remained
underground for so long that even today there is
still some reluctance to relate them in their entirety.[1]

The Baziba have chafed under this yoke of official
claims to correct political history. With the
publication of Amakuru ga Kiziba, the oral version
was transformed into a concrete, common, attackable
document. The publication date corresponds to the
significantly decreased power and authority of the
Bakama under colonial rule. Many Baziba seized the
opportunity to meet informally in beer (pombe) shops
and to argue the merits of the book. It was not long
before a number of clan groups were meeting officially
to dispute Lwamgira's edited version of Kiziba history.
Notebooks were often kept to record the differing
versions offered in these meetings, and it has been
possible to make several copies of these histories
(see Bibliography). Written accounts of Kiziba
history and other kingdoms in Buhaya are plentiful.
They seem to have been motivated in part by Lwamgira's
edition of Kiziba royal history, as well as by his
pamphlets on the histories of the other Buhaya kingdoms. Whenever possible, I made an attempt to make
copies of written documents, especially if they were

written expressly to represent a different perspective
in oral tradition.

The aura of challenge to royal tradition grew during
the late 1940s and early 1950s, and persists to this
day in the pombe shops of Buhaya. This atmosphere
has also touched those descended from royal lineages.
One informant, a member of the Bakuma clan (the pre-
Babito ruling clan in Kiziba) and thus not an altogether disinterested observer, related that sometime
after the publication of Amakuru ga Kiziba, the
princes (Balangira) met in the kikale during the
absence of Mukama Lutinwa. One Mulangira insisted
that the royals were descended from Ishamula Makambala,
and not from Kibi, the first ruler in the Babito
dynasty. Others present in the kikale vehemently
protested, accused the speaker of ill will, and
pointed out to him that he would cause trouble with
such inflammatory talk. He was then fined a cow for
his behavior, following which Lwamgira publicly
condemned the man. After the event, all such contra-
dictory talk was officially discouraged and even
suppressed. The same informant pointed out that this
development was remininscent of precolonial days when
people had to accept the version of stories endorsed
by the royals; anyone who related a differing version
of an oral tradition did so at the risk of execution
by the Mukama.[2]

Because of the strong traditional sanctions that
encouraged propagation of the official royal history,
because of the widespread reactions to Lwamgira's
edition and the documentation associated with this
response, because of easy access to royal histories,
and because of the influence of Lwamgira's book on
contemporary oral accounts, research methods were
adapted to account for these phenomena. As a consequence, I spent most of my seven months in two Kiziba
villages collecting texts from commoner clan informants.

A review of the literature on Buhaya before I
established residence there indicated that its
political life and demographic patterns were so complex
that I would need a special introduction to areas in
each kingdom. Accordingly, I welcomed the offer of
help from three research assistants from Makerere
University in Kampala, Uganda.

The Makerere students and two students from the
University of Dar es Salaam, Tanzania, provided me
entree to villages in which I did not reside. I was

able to draw on these initial contacts for the
remainder of my stay. The observations of these
assistants were essential in developing my later research plans, especially for Kyamutwara kingdom and
its oral tradition.

Because of my previous training in Swahili, it rather
than Luhaya was used as a field language. However,
translation from Luhaya into English was much more
accurate than working with Swahili, for many older
Bahaya did not have a sufficient Swahili vocabulary,
and as a consequence were frequently unable to capture
the concepts they expressed in Luhaya. Hence, a
rendering from Swahili to English was yet another
step removed from the original concept. All social
discourse was conducted in Swahili, and questions
were often asked of informants in Swahili. During
all of 1970, my research was carried on in Swahili
while my Luhaya interpreter was transferred to the
archaeological laboratory.

Interviews usually lasted from two to four hours;
often an entire day was spent with one informant.
I tried to avoid interviewing the same man on succeed-
ing days. If one informant had extensive knowledge
of oral tradition, then he would be visited several
times a week. Contacts were first established by
asking several old men whom they knew to be the oral
tradition experts in the village and in their clan.
Their recommendations were followed systematically
by visits to all those suggested.

The old men would usually suggest that I contact
the leader in his clan or subclan. After several
months it became apparent that clan heads tended to
possess limited knowledge of oral tradition. This
appeared to be the result of change in the jurisdiction
of clan officials in the litigation of disputes.
Currently, most litigants, even in intraclan disputes,
take their disputes to the gombolola court. The clan
head, then, no longer needs to have a command of the
traditional clan history which holds many discussions
of case precedents. Even though the clan heads
were of little direct help, they were keenly aware
of those in their clans who did possess significant
knowledge of oral tradition. I was always careful to
pay official visits and to return repeatedly if I
had heard from another source that someone from his
clan was a good oral historian. This procedure proved
to be useful, for in several cases official encouragement from a clan or lineage head opened up hesitant
informants. I never concluded on the basis of one
interview that a man was not a good informant, for

while the Bahaya are usually hospitable to strangers,
occasionally some are less willing than others to
share their knowledge. In only one case did an oral
historian refuse his cooperation, although a number
of other individuals were not very voluble. If I
had interpreted cautiousness as incompetence, I would
have missed many valuable texts.

After several months of work, I realized that most
of the excellent informants had reputations that cut
across clan boundaries and even across geographical
areas. If a man knew of someone who was familiar
with oral traditions from another clan, that lead was
followed up immediately and usually successfully.
During this time, work was conducted with men from
Bairu (commoner) clans. It was usually obvious if a
potential informant considered me a welcomed guest;
such a one would offer me the traditional dried coffee
beans or a substitute, such as konyagi, which is
distilled from banana and millet beer. At the outset,
I refused to pay money for information, but I was
always prepared to offer staples or other goods in
return for a man's time and hospitality. When I
learned that the Bahaya often pay enanga (zither)
players in cash, I changed my policy to accommodate
this custom. Spirit mediums were usually given several
shillings as an offering to their possession spirit
in the little grass house reserved to receive offerings.
This procedure was expected and proper, for in drawing
on the services of the spirit medium, any Muhaya who
asked for services would also offer a contribution to
the ancestral spirit.

Interviews were recorded by extensive notetaking. The
tape recorder was not used except to record fixed
texts and long, detailed narrative free texts. Based
on a number of controlled experiments I conducted to
test the efficacy of notetaking and interpretation,
notetaking was found to be an efficient and reasonably
accurate procedure.

Many Bahaya refused to consider multiple interviewing
on the same oral tradition, which is a method suggested
by Vansina (1965). They reasoned that we had covered
the subject already and that another discussion was an
obvious waste of time. Since I respected and
sympathized with this firmly expressed point of view,
I had to rely on multiple accounts from the same
clan or lineage on a similar subject in order to
create a context for checks on variability, omissions,
and imaginative elaborations.

A man's home was often visited several times before

matters relating to oral tradition were discussed.
My major concern was to be accepted as a member,
though a very temporary one, of the community. In
other cases, an explicit invitation would be offered
to come to a home, and an interview would commence
immediately.

An interview usually started in very general terms—
for instance, by asking a man to relate the history
of his clan or the royal dynasty. In this way, most
men proceeded to speak and were interrupted only
when their narrative sequence was not comprehended
or when place names were not recognized. Once the
narrative was completed, questions were asked to
clarify and expand points mentioned in the narrative.
(These final clarifications are not included as part
of the final narrative.) In cases where very
knowledgeable informants provided long texts, the
narrative continued uninterrupted, perhaps for days,
until it was completed. In rare situations, an
informant insisted on being asked specific questions,
usually in instances where he felt his general
knowledge was insufficient. These requests were
honored.

A group interview was conducted only once, during
the first month of research. An interview had been
arranged with Mzee Gaulwa, a former chief minister
(Katikiro) of Mukama Mutahangarwa of Kiziba. When I
arrived, his main or big house (nyaruju) was filled
with his advisors and neighbors, several of whom
acted as spokesmen for the infirm Katikiro. The
recording of this session was so complex and confusing
that I avoided all subsequent suggestions for group
sessions. However, out of the experience came an
introduction to Mzee Kamurasi, a man with a prodigious
memory and astoundingly full knowledge of the oral
tradition of Kiziba kingdom.

The Bahaya have a large repertoire of oral traditions,
some of which fit into tightly defined categories.
Explicit categories do not exist for most oral traditions which discuss political affairs, such as the
history of the Bahinda, Bankango, and Babito dynasties.
The use of indigenous categories of oral tradition
has been well demonstrated by Malinowski (1948) in his
study of myth and legends among the Trobriand
Islanders. He stresses that an emphasis on functional
aspects of oral tradition will allow a comprehension
of context, or, how, where, and why a type of oral
tradition is related. If an oral tradition is not

clearly assigned by a people to a category, then a
contextual study of its form will lead to an understanding of its role in the culture. A contextual
study also has good possibilities for defining change
in form, which may accompany change in other aspects
of the culture. (This particular question will be
addressed in the discussion of enanga song players.)
Variability of function according to context may not
only help define recent culture change, but also help
to discover where oral traditions have traditionally
variable functions. These distinctions can be
determined through in-depth interviewing over extended
periods of time and by observation of context.

Malinowski's functional emphasis of oral traditions
concentrates on what myth and other oral traditions
mean to the people relating them. The contextual
aspect of his study was not revived until recently
by folklorists. African historians might profit from
these studies, for some of these historians apparently
assume that survey interviewing or interviewing an
informant outside his cultural milieu can produce
the essential oral evidence. Given the nature of
much of the historical evidence being sought, this
method can certainly elicit relevant data in many
instances. However, when the African historian must
of necessity work with mythology and mythologically
related forms, a sensitivity to context becomes more
important for recognizing significant shifts in content
and structure.

Not all forms of oral tradition in Buhaya were studied
in context. In some cases, they did not impinge upon
my research, and in others, the traditional context
no longer exists. A categorization of types of oral
tradition among the Bahaya is appropriate for setting
the scene for the following discussions.

Oral tradition with fixed texts falls into the following categories: enanga songs or panegyric epics,
okwebuga or praise songs, and emigani, tales or proverbs. The enanga is the most complex form. Enanga
songs are sung to the accompaniment of a trough zither
with six to eight strings, which in fact are one
continuous string tuned by pulling on the one string.
The enanga (which is both the instrument and the
song) is placed against a large calabash which acts
as a resonating chamber. In pre-independence times,
enanga players served at the court of the Mukama.
Their function was to sing epic songs praising the
exploits of the dynastic kings. At times, there may
have been several enanga players in the king's court,
which created a competition among them to sing the

most praiseworthy songs. According to enanga
players in Kiziba, an enanga player could spend up to
six months a year in the court if the king particularly favored him. The rewards in precolonial days were
often handsome—perhaps several cows or even a
nyarubanja estate if the enanga player particularly
pleased a Mukama. During the first half of this
century, a dress suit or some comparable gift followed
an enanga player's court residence.

In earlier times, the enanga player's court duties
resembled the one-month period of labor each man had
to give the Mukama. Rather than care for the fields
of the Mukama, an enanga player would sing epic
praise songs. His service could be extended if the
prospect for a large reward appeared probable or if
the king found his songs particularly good. Sanctions
for the performance of what a Mukama considered a
good or "accurate" enanga song may have been considerable; undoubtedly, if the king did not find the text
satisfactory, it would be altered immediately.

These days when the Mukama is pleased by an enanga
song, he interrupts with exclamations of pleasure and
then rewards the enanga player by tossing money into
the calabash-resonator. Displeasure is expressed by
bored silence, by talking to guests while the enanga
song is performed, and by asking pointed questions,
after a song, about why the player has chosen a
particular interpretation. The king's retainers
follow these signs of approval and disapproval and
amplify them. The amount of immediate reward also
varies according to the king's judgment of the
enanga song. These sanctions, together with the fact
that the enanga player's repertoire is predominantly
oriented to the dynastic rulers, indicate that enanga
songs have an inherently royal bias. Until recently,
this bias was continually reinforced by strong
sanctions personally enforced by the Bakama themselves.

Today only a few enanga players can be characterized
as excellent. Most of the men who, as young boys,
received training at the king's court, usually by
their fathers, have died. One of Kiziba's best
enanga players, Philipo Rutalembwa of Buyango village,
died shortly after my departure, thus leaving a group
of enanga players with a smaller repertoire and less
talent to represent Kiziba epic poetry. I have also
worked with a man in northern Kiziba whose father
had traditional clan duties to perform in the Mukama's
court. While there with his father, he learned the
enanga songs but without musical accompaniment. He
chants each enanga song at a rapid pace, even

integrating nonsense phraseology where he learned
it. His feats of memory are considerable, and
comparison shows that his texts have as high a
regularity as do enanga-accompanied texts. He explains that he spent much of his time learning the
songs of enanga players but that he was never chosen
to be trained as a player-singer.

The social context of enanga playing has changed considerably during the last several decades. Once the
clients of kings and dependent on the king's patron-
age, the enanga players today are independent and
maintain other forms of livelihood. They may, of
course, still be summoned to the royal court to
perform, but if they are, it is for a short stay and
for immediate compensation. Today, only one enanga
player in Buhaya earns his living as a full-time
performer. He plays and sings for fees to private
audiences and accepts requests by patrons in bars.
This is an altogether different social milieu from
the royal court; consequently, the enanga songs have
been transformed in response to popular demands from
the audience. The context for enanga songs is
enormously important, for the text will be arranged
to respond to a king's need, the desires of a
serious private audience, or the demands of a bawdy
bar crowd. Conlusions about the nature of a "fixed"
text cannot be developed until all contexts have been
thoroughly explored and compared.

The okwebuga is a praise song usually sung before
the Mukama or a lesser official in praise of the
superior authority through praise of oneself. It
is rarely performed today as a greeting ritual. In
the days when it was used as such, the text was
accompanied by the pumping of a spear at shoulder
height. An okwebuga often mentions the origins
of the praise singer, his exploits and travels,
perhaps something about his personal family history,
and then finally praises the one addressed. As
praise songs are passed on from generation to
generation, they record family histories and oftentimes the geographical movements of a lineage, for
place names are often included. This form is
virtually a lost art today, and when it is used, it
is in modified form. For example, an okwebuga is
modified to include the praises of President Nyerere,
who on several occasions has been greeted with this
traditional form of respect.

There are other categories of oral traditions but they
do not directly concern this study. Emigani are
stories, or what we might call folk tales, which are

used for entertainment but primarily for the didactic
purpose of socializing children. They have themes
in which animals, such as hares, lions, and snakes,
play personified roles. Some emigani formats use
both humans and animals, and in these the meanings are
less allegorical and more forthright. These are
commonly told to children.

Emiizo, or proverbs (belonging to the above category)
are highly valued by the Bahaya as a metaphoric form
of speech. The Bahaya use these proverbs to assure
peaceful behavior and to demonstrate violation of
social mores[3]; therefore, they are not texts per se.
They liken the use of emiizo to the use of medicine
to prevent rather than cure disease. Accordingly,
proverbs are intended as warnings against bad or
disruptive behavior. It is a virtue to display the
values propounded in an emiizo. But if one has been
exposed to an emiizo and has not responded, then
Embelu k'esara etakuba eti n'chwekire, or he who does
not remember proverbs does not have the virtues they
express.

There are many instances of historical emiizo which
usually refer to virtues or vices displayed by someone in the traditional history. When someone exhibits
similar behavior, the historically based proverb
will be employed to comment metaphorically on his
behavior. In this way, the Bahaya avoid direct,
critical confrontation, which is especially important
among close kin and social equals.

The remaining oral traditions in Buhaya are found
outside most of the above categories and are generally
known as amakuru, or history of a kingdom, kings,
clans, lineages, or families. An amakuru includes
historical legend and myth, both of which are taken
to be historically true.

The Bahaya recognize several types of amakuru. One
type is Amakuru ga Bacwezi, which is the ancient
mythology about the Bacwezi dynasty.[4] This is
didactic myth in that it is a functional model or
charter for the structure of the social and political
system. It is also sacred myth in that it is the
buttressing force behind Bacwezi spirit mediumship.
In former times, the telling of Bacwezi myth was the
primary responsibility of Bacwezi spirit mediums, or
embandwa, who related the mythology in their official
capacities as diviners.

Clan histories, Amakuru go Luganda, usually include
predynastic myths that are often integrated into

later clan histories. Each _ihiga_, or subclan, also
has its own history, which usually begins at the time
of lineage segmentation within the clan. Clan and
subclan histories are particularly detailed about
migrations to and within Buhaya, so that a geographical
history of clan distribution in Buhaya can theoret-
ically be constructed on the basis of geographically
dispersed groups claiming membership of the same clan
and acknowledging the same progenitor. There are no
prescribed oral historians for clan history, although
it seems that elders who once served as judges in
clan disputes and those who were official clan
representatives in the kings' courts are the best
clan historians. Family histories are usually added
to the end of clan histories and attempt to
genealogically relate an informant's lineage to the
clan progenitor.

The most widespread history in each kingdom is the
Amakuru ga Bakama, or history of the kings. In one
sense, the primary conveyors of kingly tradition are
the _enanga_ players, so that people who are familiar
with the _enanga_ renditions of Bakama history can
relate more complete histories of kingdoms. Limited
popular knowledge of Bacwezi myth has also developed
from _enanga_ playing, but the Bacwezi repertoire of
enanga players is today very restricted. Most men
and many women who belong to the royal clans have
intimate familiarity with the royal histories, for
their genealogical distance from the throne is
important in terms of the social status and political
power they command. Clans that had functionaries in
the royal courts, such as gatekeepers and drumkeepers,
are more familiar with royal histories. The keepers
of drums and their descendants, always men, are excellent sources for kingdom histories, for as part of
their duties they also kept the history of the kingdom, which is the history of the royal drum. This
historical function was not as highly regularized
as that of the _enanga_ players, who became the
institutional oral historians for Buhaya kingdoms.
The texts of _enanga_ players, however, are difficult
to use, since the form is essentially poetic and
rhetorical. Hence, the vocabulary used is often
employed for its poetic value rather than for its
historical clarity. Much of this vocabulary is
archaic and has undoubtedly been retained in _enanga_
playing for centuries.

As a prelude to the study of themes in Kiziba and
Kyamutwara oral tradition, it will be helpful if the
structure of king lists in both kingdoms is outlined.
This discussion of the lists will provide a basic

background for subsequent analyses. The Kiziba
history is the most regular of the two. There is
little departure from the sequence of Bakama listed
in the Lwamgira-Mutahangarwa version. The great
regularity in Kiziba traditions suggests that Kiziba
had stronger sanctions against oral traditions
diverging from the royal point of view. On the other
hand, the wider variability of oral traditions in
Kyamutwara results from a long tradition of variation
that has been actively promulgated by Bacwezi spirit
medium opposition and Bankango clan opposition to the
Bahinda dynasty.

In column one below is the Lwamgira version of the
Kiziba royal genealogy, and in columns two and three
are versions provided by nonroyals:

Lwamgira-Mutahangarwa	Amdeni Kalembo	Bernardo Muhambo
Kibi	Kibi	
Ishamura	Ishamura	Ishamura Nyakabingo
Wanumi	Wanumi	Wanumi
Matwi	Matwi	Matwi
Magembe	Magembe	Magembe
Muzinga	Muzinga	Muzinga
Mwigara	Mwigara	Mwigara
Burungu I	Burungu I	Burungu I
Magembe II	Magembe II	Magembe II
Mboneko I	Mboneko I	Mboneko I
Nyarwangu	Nyarwangu	Nyarwangu
		[Ikanga]
Ruhangarazi I	Ruhangarazi I	Ruhangarazi
Rutajwa	Rutajwa	Rutajwa
Burungu II	Burungu II	Burungu II
Ruhangarazi II	Ruhangarazi II	Ruhangarazi II
Mutatembwa	Mutatembwa	Mutatembwa
Mutahangarwa	Mutahangarwa	Mutahangarwa

The Kiziba oral traditions obviously demonstrate
great consistency. Such is not the case in Kyamutwara,
where variability is more the rule than the exception.
As the following genealogies indicate, there is some
variability in the very early period from Bwogi (son
of Ruhinda) to Rugomora Mahe. All oral traditions in
Kyamutwara make clear that Ruhinda never attempted to
directly establish his authority in Kyamutwara. Of
particular interest in Kyamutwara genealogies of the
Bahinda is the great variability of testimony about
the reigns between Kahigi I and Kinyonyi. While
there is thorough agreement about the reign of Kahigi—
that he was a strong king and warrior who brought the
kingdom to full flower—the traditions about the
kings following Kahigi are vague, abbreviated, and

highly variable. Apparently during this period, local
clans once again assumed influence and the Bankango
increasingly gained power in what is today smaller
Kyamutwara and Bugabo.

BAHINDA KINGS OF KYAMUTWARA

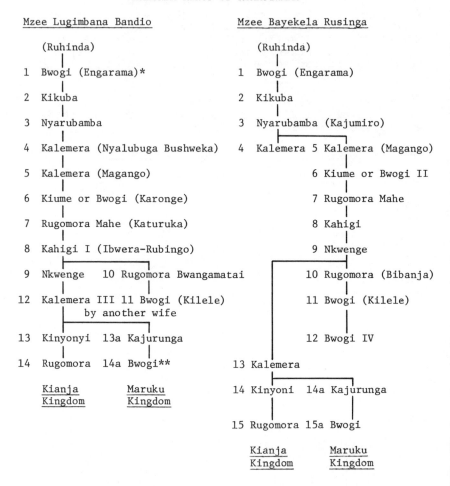

*Names in parentheses indicate places of residence.
**The reign during which Europeans arrived in Buhaya.

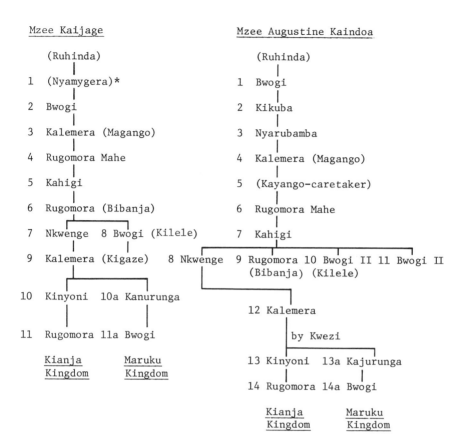

*In most versions she is mentioned as the mother of Kikuba;
 she succeeds Bwogi I in Rehse's account (p. 290).

Bankango power finally became so strong that the kingdom was controlled by two Bankango kingmakers, Ketekere
and his son Kaitaba. Both Kinyonyi and Kajurunga
(born of a different mother, Kwezi) were put on the
throne simultaneously and were subsequently harassed
by the Bankango. It was this period that witnessed
the development of two separate ruling Bahinda
lineages in Kianja and Maruku.

It is important to subsequent discussions that other
conditions of Bahinda weakness be understood. Prior
to the Kinyonyi period, which signals control by
nonroyals, there was a long period during which the
indigenous people were in control. This was Kiume's
reign, which is rarely acknowledged as legitimate;
most Bahaya stress that Kiume was not really

legitimate (because he was blind) and that Kayango
ruled during his absence. In some accounts—as the
charts indicate—Kayango is explicitly mentioned as
a caretaker Mukama. The sketchiness of oral traditions about the early Bahinda and the open discussions
by the Bahaya about limited Bahinda power in the
period before Rugomora Mahe further suggest that the
Bahinda state did not take form until approximately
generation number seven (if Ruhinda is counted).

The Bahinda consolidated their power and authority
in Kyamutwara during the same generations (Rugomora
Mahe, #7, and Kahigi, #8) as the Babito acquired full
power and authority in Kiziba (during the reigns of
Mwigara, #7, and Burungu I, #8). In the subsequent
analysis of oral traditions, it will be shown that
the royal line in both kingdoms acquired legitimacy
through royal alliances with local rainmakers, the
spirit mediums of Mugasha (a Mucwezi). These
alliances alone were not sufficient, for in Kiziba
a royal cult had to be created in order to neutralize
the opposition of Bacwezi spirit mediums, and in
Kyamutwara one of the most important indigenous
shrines (also associated with the Bacwezi) had to be
seized and occupied in order to gain control of the
productive economy and to offset the influence of the
Bacwezi authorities by seizing one of their most
important ritual centers.

The following chapter will begin with references to
selected examples and texts to demonstrate the relationships between the Bacwezi myths of Kiziba and
Bunyoro. There is great affinity between the mythemes,
and a comparative examination will lead to a better
understanding of the possible historical relationships
between the two kingdoms. More important, however,
is an examination of the genealogical structures in
the Bacwezi myth in Bunyoro and in Kiziba to determine
whether Bacwezi genealogies provide structural models
for other Bahaya genealogical histories.

The second major analytical approach to Kiziba oral
tradition will be an examination of themes about the
opposition of spirit mediums (embandwa) to the throne.
The place of spirit mediumship in political life
causes us to examine the role of religious groups in
political history, a topic only recently approached
analytically by African historians (Ranger and
Kimambo, 1972). The essential point is that the
royal genealogical history in Kiziba, regardless of
suppression of divergent views, holds the basic
evidence for studying characteristics of the
historiography. Once these phenomena are recognized,

it becomes possible to construct a tentative historical
outline for the early pre-Babito dynastic period in
Kiziba.

The historical perceptions developed from an analysis
of the relationship of Bacwezi spirit mediums to the
throne are distinctly different from the royal view.
The experiences of Bacwezi spirit mediums with the
royals in Kiziba and in Kyamutwara appear to have
influenced how they relate and manipulate didactic
myth. It is important to understand these patterns
in Kiziba, for they set the scene for understanding the
integration of Bacwezi mythological themes into
Kyamutwara royal genealogical histories by the royals
and by Bacwezi spirit mediums. In other words, some
patterns in the oral tradition of Kyamutwara have a
historical explanation and can be elucidated by a
study of similar patterns in Kiziba genealogical
histories.

Notes

1. The Bakuma clan in Kiziba is an example of this
    phenomenon. While some clan members openly voice
    oral traditions which stress that clan's political
    power and authority both before and after Babito
    rule, there are many who prefer to emphasize the
    Bakuma role as chief assistants to the royal
    Babito.

2. Petro Nshekela, 9/7/69, in Kigarama, Kiziba.

3. In an excellent study of emic proverb categories
    among the Haya, Peter Seitel has demonstrated
    that among all proverbial forms only one, the
    omugani ("tale or proverb") can be said to refer
    to a text per se. See Peter I. Seitel, "Proverbs
    and the Structure of Metaphor Among the Haya of
    Tanzania", Ph.D. dissertation, University of
    Pennsylvania, 1972, University Microfilms, 1974.

4. These are etic categories created by the author
    and have yet to be confirmed as emic categories
    of the Bahaya.

5
Political-Religious History in Kiziba Kingdom from Oral Traditions

The similarities between Kiziba and Bunyoro myth are considerable. A brief comparison of the two will illustrate some of the basic similarities and differences. Since the full texts are extremely detailed and long, the basic structures have been abstracted and the first part of the discussion has been built around (1) a structural comparison of genealogies and (2) themes centered on Mugasha, the god of the waters and storms in Buhaya. The discussion of genealogies will focus on the origins of the Bacwezi and their opposition to the Babito, and the place of Mugasha in mythology about the Bacwezi gods. As we shall see, an understanding of Mugasha's place in Bahaya historiography is of central importance in the archaeological investigation of the Early Iron Age.

The political-religious opposition to the Babito dynasty in Kiziba will also be discussed. This discussion does not assume any specific historical chronology, but it will dwell on the theme, as the Baziba do themselves, that early and alleged kings of the Babito dynasty met significant political opposition from Bacwezi embandwa. A comparison of royal and nonroyal texts is essential. The embandwa opposition was so prevalent and strong in early Babito times that it figures prominently in this recounting of Kiziba royal history. Finally, the themes developed here, especially the alliance between the royals and Mugasha, are essential for understanding the history of Kyamutwara kingdom and the history of King Rugomora Mahe.

The Bahaya relate Bacwezi myth in great detail, and a comparison of Bunyoro and Kiziba texts demonstrates

much greater detail in the Bahaya oral traditions
about some of the Bacwezi. Distinctly different
perspectives are expressed in both areas about what
the Bacwezi are. The Bunyoro version provided by
Nyakatura, for instance, states that the Bacwezi are
"a race of white people"; Fisher refers to the Bacwezi
as gods.[1] The Bahaya who relate Bacwezi myth, however,
usually are very explicit in how they conceptualize
Bacwezi. Bacwezi are spirits, they claim, who came
into existence only upon the demise of Chief Wamara
and his followers. The death of Wamara is the beginning of the Bacwezi:

> Wamara threw himself into the water; medicine was
> made from Mshambya tree in order to dry up the
> water. When the water had evaporated, Muzora
> [Kagondo] fetched only the Kisingo [the diviner's
> hat] of Wamara. When he took out the Kisingo,
> his (Wamara's) spirit took one of the people,
> who then became one of Wamara's Mucwezi. This is
> the beginning of the Bacwezi.[2]

This perspective is widely expressed by the Bahaya,
who are disinclined to see Wamara and his predecessors
as Bacwezi. They become Bacwezi—a term which the
Bahaya often use interchangeably with "spirit" when
discussing these matters—only when the spirits of
Wamara and his kin are released to possess people
upon their death. The Bacwezi mean the same thing
functionally to the Bahaya today, who may communicate
with a Mucwezi when the embandwa is possessed.

This distinction is an important one, for it clears
up a lot of confusion about the Bacwezi. Those working from texts collected by early investigators such
as Fisher and Roscoe have always assumed that the
Bacwezi are a dynasty. According to the Bahaya
versions, this is a retrospective view, for the
Bacwezi did not develop until the spirits of a group
of men—known as Bacwezi in myth and now spirits who
possess spirit mediums—were released upon the death
of Wamara to possess people. Part of the previous
tendency to attribute political attributes to the
Bacwezi may also be explained by the fact that in
predynastic times Bacwezi spirit mediums were also
local political leaders, such as clan headmen.

The Bahaya versions emphasize that the Bacwezi were
a religious phenomenon rather than an identifiable
political dynasty. The ambiguity in the Bunyoro
versions of Bacwezi origins is perhaps a result of a
similar emphasis which heretofore has been misinter-
preted by historians using the mythology to construct

political-dynastic histories. The disparities among
different Bunyoro versions about Mugasha and his
relationship with the Bacwezi also affirm that the
mythology is about different religious cults more than
about political entities. For instance, Fisher's
version refers to Mugasha as a Mucwezi, but at the
same time he does not die nor is his spirit released
after the death of the "Bacwezi." In Buhaya, Mugasha
is associated with rainmaking and agricultural
prosperity—a responsibility not associated with
Bacwezi spirits. The following discussion will help
elucidate the role of Mugasha in Bacwezi myth and in
the political oral traditions of Kiziba and Kyamutwara
kingdoms in Buhaya.

A genealogical abstraction of Nyakatura's version of
Bunyoro oral tradition is provided in the following
diagram. In the Nyakatura version, Ndahura is the
first of the Bacwezi. Nyakatura initially fails to
place Kagoro genealogically, but he eventually
mentions him as a favorite nephew of Ndahura. As
such, Kagoro is also a brother to the eventual Babito
rulers of Bunyoro. It must be noted that Kyomya is
also considered a Mucwezi, and it is only those progeny
who are the issue of Nyatworo (another wife), daughter
of Lango Omukidi from the north, who are considered
Babito.

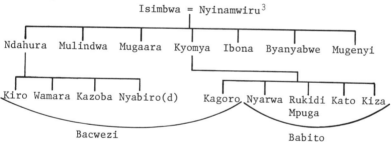

The conventions used in naming the Babito are universal, and Fisher's version credits their naming to
their presence beneath the Bito tree where they are
greeted as Babito when the Bacwezi pass from the
"kingdom." Mugasha does not have a place in the
version provided by Nyakatura. However, in Fisher's
version, the place of Mugasha as a brother of Kyomya,
half brother of Ndahura and uncle of Wamara, is clear:

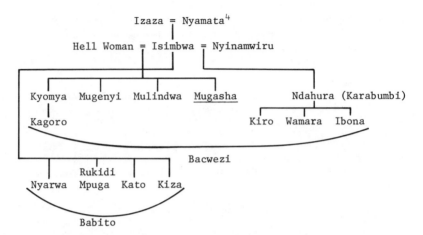

The differences between the two Bunyoro genealogical
structures are apparently negligible but, on further
consideration, important. The Nyakatura version,
besides omitting Mugasha from the Bacwezi genealogy,
also provides very little myth about Mugasha other
than his characterization as a "White Mucwezi." While
the Fisher version integrates Mugasha into the Bacwezi
genealogy, it fails to develop mythological episodes
that portray Mugasha kindly, as is the case with all
the Bacwezi. Significantly, Mugasha is painted as
one in opposition to the throne:

> Very soon the Bacwezi began to quarrel among
> themselves, and Mugasha, the uncle of Wamara,
> rebelled against him and sought to wrest the
> kingdom from him. But Wamara successfully
> quashed the rising and took the six children
> of Mugasha prisoners. After many futile attempts
> their father, however, managed to reclaim them,
> and took them away to Heaven with him, so as to
> remove them from any further danger.[5]

Mugasha is acknowledged in Buhaya as god not only of
the waters and all animal life of the waters, but also
of lightning and thunder. Relatively few embandwa
are possessed by the spirit of Mugasha. However,
spirit mediums possessed by the spirit of Wamara (the
most important Mucwezi) are found in all parts of
Buhaya. Mugasha's place of abode is Isheshe, or the
Sesse Islands in Lake Victoria, while Wamara is
associated with no consistent place in Bahaya
cosmology. Fisher's text develops the theme of conflict between Mugasha and the Bacwezi but in a way
that does not emphasize the dominance of Mugasha
over Wamara and Kagoro:

> Now, Mugasa had made himself king of Heaven,
> and one day when he was out hunting with his
> servants, they found Kagoro sitting alone in a
> field, on the spot where the fowl had dropped
> him. So Mugasa took him back to his home, and
> gave him to his daughter as a slave. . . . On one
> occasion they took him with them as they visited
> the capital of Heaven, and as they went along the
> road everybody did obeisance to Kagoro. So they
> turned and asked him of his parentage, and when he
> said he was the son of Mugenyi, [sic], they
> embraced him and wept for joy. . . . The king one
> day went out to hunt, and ordered Kagoro to attend
> him, but they tramped about all day, and met with
> no success, so Mugasa was weary, and rested
> under the shade of a tree. While he slumbered,
> Kagoro cautiously came toward him with his spear
> quivering, and thrust it at his knee. The king
> immediately woke up with a start, and cried out,
> "Do not kill me; do I not know who you are; ask
> what you will, and I will give it to you."
> Kagoro then demanded that he should give him all
> of his children that he had taken out of the
> world. So Kagoro saved them from Heaven, and
> brought them down again to earth, and left
> Mugasa ruling there.[6]

The Bahaya perceive an altogether different role for
Mugasha in Bacwezi mythology and in their culture.
The royal Bahinda and Babito dynasties draw extensively
on the divining and magic of Mugasha. Rehse (1910)
observed that in the courtyard of the Mukama of Kiziba
there was a shrine dedicated to Mugasha, who appeared
to have a special relationship to the Mukama. While
Irungu, a Mucwezi, had two small spirit houses
dedicated to him, Mugasha's shrine was the predominant
central shrine in the kikale, and it is testimony to
the special relationship between the king and Mugasha.
Rehse commented:

> For this reason the kingly family is placed in a
> very special relation to this spirit, and that is
> the reason why the arch of Mugasha is only to be
> found in the kings' court. Two bundles are made
> out of brushwood and bamboos (also banana leaves),
> about 1 1/2 metres long, which are put into the
> ground about a metre apart. The two loose ends
> are joined together and pressed somewhat downwards
> and backwards. From the centre usually hangs a
> strip of bamboo to which are tied some cowries
> or banana seeds. They spread the same kind of
> soft grass which they use for the floor of the
> dwelling house, and they place a miniature boat

with an oar in it or with some other symbol of
the water (it may be a rotten fish) under the arch.
The ordinary man may not come into contact with
Mugasha, as he is also supposed to be the spirit
of the banana groves. Only the fishermen of Lake
Victoria are not bound by this restriction.[7]

The close relationship of the Bahinda and Babito
dynasties with Mugasha may have had a prejudicial
effect on how Mugasha is represented in oral tradition
in Buhaya. It may tentatively be posited that the
emphasis on Mugasha in Buhaya myth is related to
this relationship and that the relationship itself
is one of alliance against the Bacwezi, who are manifest through spirit mediums. In this sense, the early
histories of the Babito and Bahinda dynasties have
the same structural opposition to the Bacwezi, as
do the myths previously related about Mugasha's opposition to the Bacwezi, namely Wamara and Kagoro.

Many Bahaya myths begin with a discussion of "god"
Rugaba and then of Kintu and his three sons. This
discussion is followed by an episode in which the
three sons go to sleep with their milk pots full and
in the morning find varying amounts of milk in the
pots. They then pick different objects from the road
and thereby choose their social-political roles as
Mukama, Bahima, and Bairu. The narratives that concern
us here are the Bacwezi and immediate pre- and post-
"Bacwezi" periods. The following mythological outlines provide important comparative material for a
discussion in Chapter 6. This discussion shows that
Bacwezi myth, starting with episodes about Nyinamwiru,
provides the basic structure (along with the myth
about Mugasha) for the oral tradition about Rugomora
Mahe, a Mukama of the Bahinda dynasty in Kyamutwara
kingdom.

One Kiziba narrative can be reduced to the genealogical
relationships shown in Case 1. (Territories awarded
to the sons of Wamara are noted when mentioned.)

Nyinamwiru, the daughter of Bukuru (also spelled as
Bukuku), is built a separate residence and is isolated
because she has one breast; in the Bunyoro versions,
she tends to have one eye and one ear. She successfully avoids her father's protective care, sleeps with
the stranger Isimbwa, and gives birth to a boy. The
grandfather, Bukuru, orders that the boy be thrown
into the lake, but the child is snagged on a tree and
is saved by Kibumbi. Eventually, Nyinamwira plots
with her son, who then kills Bukuru and acquires the
throne, taking the name Ndaura. According to Bahaya

CASE 1

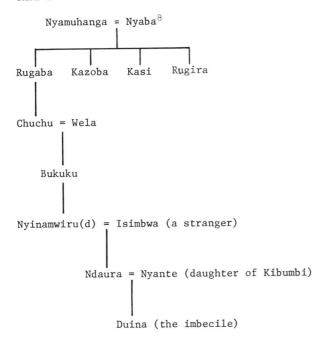

Nyamuhanga = Nyaba[8]

Rugaba   Kazoba   Kasi   Rugira

Chuchu = Wela

Bukuku

Nyinamwiru(d) = Isimbwa (a stranger)

Ndaura = Nyante (daughter of Kibumbi)

Duina (the imbecile)

Discontinuity

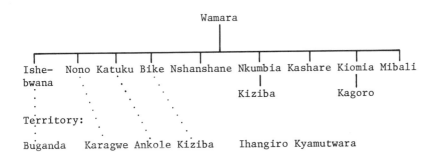

Wamara

Ishe-   Nono Katuku Bike Nshanshane Nkumbia Kashare Kiomia Mibali
bwana

Kiziba   Kagoro

Territory:

Buganda   Karagwe Ankole Kiziba   Ihangiro Kyamutwara

values, this is an inversion, for the greatest affec-
tion is expressed between grandfather and grandson.
Conflict occurs and can be expected to occur between
father and son. This myth in functional terms is
certainly didactic in that it demonstrates the result

of bad social values. While the reign of Ndaura is
propserous, the Bacwezi dynasty soon falls on hard
times and is eventually overcome through the forces
of a foreign diviner (according to the Fisher version).

It appears that Ndaura does in fact encounter difficulty with spirits, although it is not clear that
he is possessed. The Fisher version has Ndaura going
to and returning from Hell and thereafter being
illegitimate; he gives up the throne to his son
Wamara. In the Kiziba variant cited, there is a
discontinuity after the reign of Ndaura, and Wamara,
a neighboring chief, assumes the throne. This
variation appears to be exceptional, for other versions maintain that Wamara was descended from Ndaura.
The version shown in Case 2, which was also collected
in Kiziba, makes clear the tie between Wamara and
Ndaura, who is definitely Wamara's father.

CASE 2

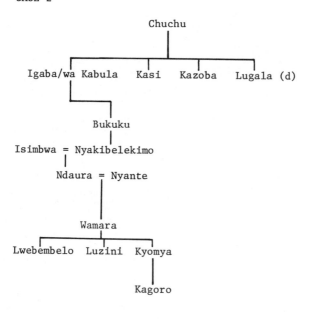

Case 2 also differs from Case 1 in that Kagoro is a
grandson rather than a nephew of Wamara, and, in that
Kyomya is a grandson rather than a brother of Ndaura.
In addition, there are two Igabas, but the origins
of the earlier are made explicit. This variant, with
its repetition of names, suggests that the second
Igaba, who is the stranger and diviner who foretells
disaster for the Bacwezi and then assumes power, is
conferred legitimacy by being given the name of a
previous ruler. This variant is divergent but instructive; there is a clear discontinuity between the
Bacwezi and the Babito. The mythological convention
is a magical one, and Igaba gains power through
magical devices, and not by sexual access and
paternity as Isimbwa does. The distinction is an
important one, for an opposition is set up at this
point which is also found in Kiziba and other
histories of Buhaya; the Babito newcomers are in
magical opposition to the Bacwezi. This is an oft-
repeated theme in other contexts. The chief ally in
the Babito and Bahinda opposition to the Bacwezi
spirits is Mugasha.

Some texts are even more explicit about Igaba's use
of medicine against Wamara: "Igaba killed Wamara by
magic, and then was tempted by the spirit of Wamara.
And when his wife Njunaki bore a child, it was called
Ruhinda (which means—I've taken him from the ruling
throne)."[10] The essential point in this variant is
that Igaba is possessed or at least troubled by the
Mucwezi or spirit of Wamaru. The same basic theme is
repeated in Babito oral traditions when the Babito
are opposed by Bacwezi spirit mediums, especially
when the Babito are possessed by Bacwezi spirits.

The version (Case 2) which has Bukuku (or Bukuru in
some versions) as a son of Igaba is not an isolated
example. The Lwamgira-Mutahangarwa version also
claims that Igaba precedes Bukuku, but as his
grandfather, viz:

Igaba
|
Chuchu
|
Bukuku [11]

Most Kiziba mythological texts cite Bukuku as a
predecessor to Ndaura, who kills his grandfather. In
his analysis of the oral traditions of Buganda,
Kiwanuka mentions that the tradition surrounding
Bukuku, or Bakuru in Buganda, is particularly
mysterious and problematical.[12] Part of the problem

from a Buganda perspective is that there is relatively
little tradition about Bukuru, except that he is the
chief of the Sesse Islands. Most of the data Kiwanuka
uses are in fact Bunyoro myth about Bukuru. We must
keep in mind that Mugasha also stays in the Sesse
Islands and that Ndaura, as the first of the Bacwezi
line (which many Bahaya specifically refer to as the
Baranzi clan), kills Bukuku.[13] Kiwanuka also claims,
without naming his source, that both a Bunyoro and
Buganda version say that Mugasha was the grandson
of Bukuku; thus, Mugasha would be structurally parallel
to Ndaura and a potential political competitor. If
this is so, the evidence tends to affirm the deduc-
tions already arrived at—that Mugasha is symbolic
of political opposition to the line of rulers starting
with Ndaura. Significantly, Kiwanuka also points out
that the alleged Bunyoro version claims that Bukuku
belongs to the Baranzi clan, which is the equivalent
to the Otter clan in Buganda.[14]

Mugasha's affilitations in Buhaya, of course, are with
the water animals—otters, hippos, crocodiles, fishes,
and all other species of the water. It would appear
that Mugasha may occasionally appear in Bunyoro
versions as a Mucwezi because he and Ndaura have
their origins in the same lineage or are in fact
brothers. The Bahaya, however, perceive the matter
in terms of segmentation and separate identity, or
opposition. If the Bunyoro variants omit or deempha-
size Mugasha and his opposition to the Bacwezi-to-be,
the Bahaya versions develop the opposition of Mugasha
in great detail, a phenomenon that may be functionally
related to Mugasha's place in Bahaya political life as
an ally of the throne:

> Wamara's daughter, Nyabibungo, on the morning
> of [Kagoro's] departure [for Buganda] went to
> cut grass with other girls. Nyabibungo met
> Mugasha who was going to the river to fish.
> Mugasha put down his paddle and stood to greet
> Nyabibungo. She was disgusted when he greeted
> her, and she spit on the ground as a sign that
> she despised being greeted by fishermen. Mugasha
> was unhappy, and called his people to tell them
> he would marry the girl, so she would stop
> despising fishermen, because he, Mugasha ruled
> everything which lives in the water. He called
> all of these animals for the marriage feast.
> Nkolongo Munywataba (a small fish with a beard)
> was called to go to Wamara and tell him that
> Mugasha wanted to marry Nyabibungo. Mugasha
> told Nkolongo that if they beat him, then to
> beat them back, and if they killed him, then

Mugasha would come to fight them.

Nkolongo went with a spear and delivered his
message. Everyone around Wamara became angry and
they beat Nkolongo; and the spear with which he
went was pushed into his backbone. Mugasha waited
for sometime for Nkolongo, but he did not fear
that his emissary had died. Mugasha told Nkuba
Kanyarumanzi (thunderstorm) to start fighting
with Wamara. Nkuba broke a stone the size of a
hill and threw it at Wamara's home, so that it
would land at a place where Wamara would escape
to when it started raining. It rained for two
days and all of Wamara's kikale was covered with
water, so that a hippo and a crocodile were playing there. The people became frightened and took
Nyabibungo to Mugasha to be married. The hippo,
crocodile and fishes took her to Mugasha, who was
very happy. He made a cloth from the scales of
fish for her. Nkuba was sent to remove the stone
blocking the way to Wamara's home, and then all
the water dried up.

When Lukungu saw that the water had disappeared,
he went to find Kagoro in Buganda, where he met
him and explained matters. He explained that
Nyabibungo had married a fisherman. Kagoro
returned the same way as he had when returning
from Rwanda. Lukungu reported to Wamara that
Kagoro was going to fight Mugasha. When Kagoro
reached a rock called Rwazi rwa Janja, he cried
so loudly that the cry was heard by Wamara's
people and by Mugasha's people. Mugasha returned
in his boat to see what was happening. When he
reached the bank Kagoro saw him, as Mugasha
was very fat. Kagoro fired at Mugasha with an
arrow, but it hit him in the thigh, and Mugasha
thought it was a mosquito. Kagoro sent another
arrow which struck Mugasha's knee, and this one
stiffened his knee.

Mugasha had by this time become furious and
attacked Kagoro with a paddle. Kagoro fell down
and hit his head on a rock, which split in two.
Kagoro's tongue was cut and Mugasha was standing
on one leg. Kagoro departed and went to his
home; he took Nyabibungo to Wamara. Nyabibungo
when taken to Wamara was prevented from entering
Wamara's house. She was built a separate house
outside the kikale. In the morning Mugasha
visited to ask forgiveness. Wamara listened and
said that if Mugasha would come from the water
Wamara would build him a house near his kikale.

> When Mugasha came from the river with all his
> possessions, the entrance that Nyabibungo used
> was too small, so that a new entrance had to be
> constructed. To this day if you look at the house
> of Mugasha near the kikale, one will see that it
> has two entrances.[15]

Other versions do not maintain that Mugasha and Wamara
reconciled but rather that Mugasha became a servant
in Wamara's household.[16] The official royal history
of Kiziba agrees with this detail and in fact claims
that "Mugasha used to shoo away flies from the king."[17]
Most Kiziba variants, both royal and nonroyal, include
the detailed Mugasha myth. One version, collected by
a White Father about four decades ago, forcefully
stresses the opposition between Mugasha and Wamara.
At the time of Wamara's death by drowning—after he
pursued his favorite white cow into the water:

> Chief Wamara wanted to kill himself; he turned
> this way and that way, but he could not drown.
> As Mugasha was trying to keep afloat, he turned
> around and happened to catch Garushansha (the white
> cow) and pulled it to shore. He made two pointed
> sticks and stuck one on each side of the cow, and
> then started to roast it. When it had cooked a
> bit, he ate all of it in one bite and set off for
> Isheshe Bubembe which is his village.[18]

The role of Mugasha in the affairs of state in the
Babito and Bahinda dynasties of Kiziba and Kyamutwara
kingdoms will be discussed further, but first an
explication of the origins of the dynasties is
necessary. Igaba, the magician/diviner/usurper, had
many sons, some of whom were given kingdoms to rule
to the south of Bunyoro. A typical genealogy for
this period also assigns kingdoms to each son of Igaba;
there is a relatively high degree of regularity in
Bahaya claims about the progenitor of the Bahinda
and Babito dynasties. The variant given in Case 3
is the same as the official version and can be
related as:

CASE 3

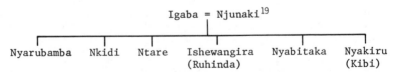

Igaba = Njunaki[19]

Nyarubamba	Nkidi	Ntare	Ishewangira (Ruhinda)	Nyabitaka	Nyakiru (Kibi)

TERRITORY:	Buganda	Ankole	Karagwe		Bunjalwe or Kiziba

If we compare genealogical Case 3 from the Babito
genealogy to Case 1, we can see which Bacwezi had
power in areas to which the Babito-Bahinda were
appointed. The Baziba claim that Nono of Karagwe
was killed by Ruhinda, and that Katuku of Ankole
was ousted by Ntare. Bike of Bunjalwe or Kiziba was
eventually killed by Kiziba, the son of Nkombya of
Ihangiro before the arrival of Kibi, the Babito ruler.
This last twist, an alleged descendant of Wamara who
kills his uncle, is particularly important in
following out the structure of myth in Buhaya.

The royal version as compiled by F. X. Lwamgira also
relates how Wamara distributes his kingdom to his
sons. Lwamgira mentions that Ishebwana obtained
Buganda, Nono lost Karagwe to Ishewagira, Katuku lost
Ankole to Ntare, and Bike failed to hold Bunjalwe
or Kiziba.[20] There is also the claim that Kiziba, the
son of Nkombya of Ihangiro (Bike's brother), kills his
uncle, Bike, with bad medicine and then sits on the
throne. This is the same structure and sequence as
shown in Case 3. According to the genealogy related
by royals and nonroyals in Kiziba, Bike and Nkombya
belong to the Bacwezi line. Chief Mutaihwa Lubelwa,
Bakuma clan head and descendant of Ntumwa, made this
tie most explicit in one of his texts:

> My clan is from Ihangiro. Kizindo originally
> came from Bunyoro, where there are two kinds of
> chiefs: one type belonged to Wamara and the others
> were Babito. Kizindo comes from the Wamara type.
> Kizindo summoned his brother and a witchdoctor
> to cure the infertility of women. Mugunda's bag
> was called Kiziba. He came with medicines and
> removed Bike, and Kizindo became chief.[21]

An abstraction of the genealogical relationships reads:

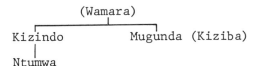

After Kizindo died, the throne was inherited by Ntumwa.
This elaboration is the only case in which Kizindo is
mentioned as a separate personality, for the Baziba
usually refer to Kizindo as Kiziba and maintain that
they are the same.[22] A fellow clansman clarified the
confusion when he said: "Bike suffered during his
reign, so he sent a messenger to his brother, Nkombya
in Ihangiro. Nkombya sent his son Kiziba-Kizindo with
a helper called Mugunda."[23] This, then, is the

convention among most Baziba:

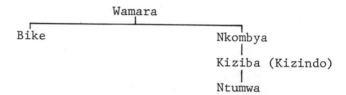

It should be noted that this is the royal version as
well.[24] Ntumwa is from the same line as Nkombya,
the descendant of Wamara, and is variously represented
as a nephew, grandson, or brother of Nkombya. In any
case, Ntumwa's affiliations are Bacwezi.

The present-day descendants of Ntumwa, the Bakuma
clan, maintain that in fact they are Bayango/Bahinda,
which is essentially a claim linked to descent from
Kayango and Ruhinda. This is strongly stated by the
Bakuma but is widely contradicted by other clans who
maintain that the Bakuma cannot be Bahinda because
they have a different totem from the Bahinda. The
clan name Bakuma is taken from an early clanswoman,
a detail other clans point to as evidence that the
Bakuma clan is simply trying to gain legitimacy by
claiming descent from the Bahinda. The Bakuma
themselves, of course, deny their own claim by their
explicit, direct ties to Wamara.

Ntumwa, descendant of Wamara, is on the throne when
Nyakiru, the Mubito, arrives from the north to claim
Kiziba for the Babito dynasty. Nyakiru obtains magical
devices belonging to his father, Igaba, who uses
them against the Bacwezi, when his mother Njunaki
steals them for him.[25] According to two other
variants, Nyakiru also visits Mugasha on the Sesse
Islands to obtain more magical devices:

> He left his people and his mother Njunaki at
> the waterpond and he went to Isheshe-Bubembe
> to visit the home of Mugasha for divinations.
> When he got there Mugasha gave him fire which
> was a symbol of authority in Kiziba, and Mugasha
> warned, "Do not blow it out." He gave Nyakiru
> horns which could be used for divining.[26]

Mugasha is recruited as an ally against the descendants
of the Bacwezi. This is an affirmation of Mugasha's
magical opposition to the Bacwezi, and we will see
that it is the beginning of significant Babito-Bacwezi
opposition in Kiziba kingdom.

Eventually, Nyakiru gains the throne by magic, which

he uses to create a storm of grasshoppers, insects
traditionally considered a delicacy. Nyakiru kills
Ntumwa while his people are off hunting grasshoppers.
Furthermore, Nyakiru, who becomes Kibi (the evil one),
is assisted by Kanyamaishwa who is unfit for the
throne because as a child he sprouted his upper in-
cisors first. Kibi rules with Kanyamaishwa as his
chief advisor and as his puppet. Of the several
dozen versions of this myth collected, there is
virtually an even division on the last point.

Once Kibi acquires power, though perhaps not legitimate
authority, he experiences difficulty with Ntumwa's
Mucwezi and later with Kanyamaishwa's spirit:
"Kanyamaishwa died before Kibi I. Kibi did not
appoint anyone else to succeed Kanyamaishwa. After
a few days he began to suffer from Kanyamaishwa's
spirit, so he gave his son Ishamura Njobe to the
spirit of Kanyamaishwa in the house where the spirit
stayed."[27] The same informant had provided a similar
text a week before, but one that stressed the role
of spirit mediums in stopping the troublesome spirit
of Ntumwa. The Lwamgira-Mutahangarwa version maintains
that Kibi did not give up his own son but that
another man was called his son as a means of appeasing
Ntumwa's spirit.

This period, probably the most controversial in
Kiziba history, has been subjected to close review
by special clan meetings convened to reexamine royal
history. There are two Ishamuras, Njobe and Nyakabingo
(who is summoned by Kibi from Buganda where he has
been staying with his uncle, Nkidi or Kimera).
Eventually Ishamura Nyakabingo, a Mubito from Buganda,
obtains the throne after kissing his father's boat,
which is used for burial. There is a great proliferation of claims about whether or not Ishamura Njobe
was in fact killed to appease Ntumwa's spirit. These
claims and counterclaims are not of immediate concern
in the present analysis. The essential point is that
Kibi, a Mubito and founder of the dynasty in Kiziba,
is challenged by the spirits of Ntumwa and Kanyamaishwa,
or, Bacwezi.

A good portion of the oral tradition about Kibi once
he attained power addresses Kibi's attempts to acquire
medicine to protect himself from the magical devices
of his opponents. He summons Lule (who is sometimes
referred to as a brother) from Ihangiro. Most texts,
and particularly the versions sympathetic to the royal
perspective, stress conflict between Lule and Kibi.
Kibi uses Lule's son to lead his warriors in order to
have Lule's son killed. However, Kibi is able to

appease Lule's wrath by awarding him a subchieftain-
ship in Bugandika. None of the many texts about this
phase makes clear why the state of antagonism between
the two is so vividly represented in the oral tradition.
The following text portrays Lule in a derogatory light
(as the man who carries around a calabash to urinate
in, so that people will not make magic against him):

> Lule was the brother of Kibi. Lule was a
> magician [diviner is probably more accurate] for
> the chiefs with the Barenga clan to help the
> chiefs facilitate their rule. Abagaha, Lule,
> and the Barenga were all responsible for making
> divinations for the Mukama to see if invaders
> might be coming. They also made magic to protect
> the Mukama against the spirits of people who may
> be killed for spoil, gain, and crimes. Lule was a
> magician for Kibi, Ishamura, and Wanumi, during
> whose reign he died.[28]

This is a key text for understanding the dynamics of
Bacwezi spirit medium opposition to the throne. After
the passing of Lule, the Bakama of Kiziba experience
strong and sometimes crippling opposition from the
Bacwezi via the spirit mediums. The embandwa appear
to be from the indigenous clans that had turned to
religious means to oppose those attempting to
establish centralized political power. The oral
tradition of Kiziba, though governed by strong royal
sanctions, includes these discussions about Bacwezi
opposition, but it also maintains that there is an
uninterrupted sequence of Bakama.

When Wanumi succeeds his father, Ishamura, matters
begin to worsen for the Babito. Historians of East
Africa have usually assumed that the Bahinda and
Babito dynasties were imposed on indigenous peoples
by conquest without much difficulty. The Bahaya
examples would appear to suggest that the Bahinda and
Babito sometimes faced strong, well-organized opposition by the religious authorities or by Bacwezi
spirit mediums who also may have held local political
authority. This is not to say that it is possible
to write an historical account of religious opposition
to the throne as it is reflected in myth. It is
possible, however, that the structure of pseudohistorical genealogies and the dialectics of the
mythemes therein may provide a culture chronology or
a generalized history of cultural development in an
area. Cohen suggests as much when working with
Kanem-Bornu king lists, and in his discussion of
structuralism, Gilsenan also suggests that with
critical methods the historian can work toward these

goals.[29]

Bahaya oral tradition must also be viewed in conjunction with ritual surrounding the institution of kingship to determine whether some of the structural
oppositions that are analytically isolated in the
oral tradition are also manifest in symbolic activities in political life, and whether all of these
phenomena are the result of historical experience.
The difficulty in this position is that we have not
yet developed the analytical devices for understanding
the degree to which myth development is related to
historical change. As Gilsenan asks, is myth an
epiphenomenon, and can it be manipulated by ideologues
who control oral tradition?[30] The assumption in this
study is that the pseudohistorical genealogical myths
of the Bahaya are interwoven into the political and
social fabric of Bahaya life through time, and that
a structural analysis will reveal unconscious representative structures through time which are tied to
structural change in political life. Most of the
mythemes discussed concern religious opposition to
political form. When that structure changes, the
structure of myth also changes. Thus, by using the
extant mythology, it is possible to arrive at a
historiography of the Bahaya.

The Bahaya, in their own oral traditions and in
interpretative commentary on the traditions, have
themselves suggested some of the fundamental hypotheses
about religious-political opposition. Not surprisingly, many of these suggestions come from the Bakuma
clan to Kiziba, which was at the heart of the magico-
religious and political opposition to the Babito.

After the demise of Lule, the court magician, Mukama
Wanumi encounters direct attack from the Bacwezi
embandwa. Wanumi was vulnerable to attack because
he was not wearing an orugisha, which is a protective
magical necklace worn by the Bakama and conferred
upon them during the installation ritual. Once the
orugisha is given the Mukama, it is then called the
kalinda. The circumstances of this ritual are
particularly germane to this discussion. After the
candidate has been bathed and purified in kishura salt
at specially dug wells, and the new palace has been
constructed, the procession returns to the palace
preceded by trumpters. As the Mukama-to-be nears his
main house, an embandwa is brought to him, and the
candidate ritually kicks the embandwa as a means of
demonstrating that the Mukama has power over the

spirit mediums and witch doctors. The orugisha is
then taken from the embandwa and is put around the
neck of the Mukama.

The origins of the ritual are not known, but the
ritualized opposition of political authority to religious authority is clear. The oral tradition about
Mukama Wanumi would seem to suggest that these ritual
devices were not yet developed, or else the power of
the Bacwezi embandwa was sufficient to incapacitate
the incipient centralized political authority:

> One day Mukama Wanumi went to Bukwali for a hunt
> and while there he saw a very beautiful woman
> cultivating her kibanja. He asked people about
> her and was told that she was the wife of a man
> who was an embandwa of Wamara. The Mukama decided
> that he must have the woman. He approached her
> and tried to make arrangements which did not
> succeed. The Mukama became angry and when he
> went back to hunt, he took all the cattle
> belonging to the embandwa, who then followed the
> Mukama to his kikale and unsuccessfully pleaded
> for the return of his cattle. Finally, the man
> asked for only two cows: 1) Bugonda Kya Mugisha
> (spotted with black), and 2) Kitale Kya Wamara
> (pure white). The Mukama refused to return the
> two cows. When the Mukama turned toward his
> Rwensinga house, the embandwa threw his Kisingo,
> or possession hat, on Wanumi's head. From that
> minute the chief was possessed by Mucwezi Wamara.
> When the Mukama's people looked for the man,
> they found that he had been swallowed by an ant-
> hill, though later he was seen at Bukabuye-
> Kashenkele village, the headquarters for the
> embandwa of Wamura. As soon as Wanumi became
> possessed, another kikale was built for him. . . .
> And as soon as Chief Wanumi was possessed he gave
> up his drum [or, gave up the throne] to his nephew
> Bwanamba. . . .When Mukama Wanumi died, a special
> burial had to be made since he was both a Mukama
> and an embandwa of Wamura.[31]

This variant omits a mytheme that occurs in many other
texts, including the royal versions: Wanumi's advisors
recruit a Mushengya clansman from Bukabuye village,
put the kisingo on his head, and transfer Wamara's
spirit from Wanumi. But even the official version
acknowledges that this strategy was not completely
successful. The nonroyal texts tend to omit this
claim. The arrangements for Wanumi's burial are also
instructive. The dead bodies of Bacwezi embandwa in
precolonial times were considered polluted flesh and

were buried outside the village in the bush. But this
is not appropriate for a Mukama, so Wanumi's body is
wrapped in a cow's skin and placed in the attic of
his gashani burial house.* To this day people are
warned not to look up at the roof of that gashani
house or the spirit of Wanumi will kill them.

The Lwamgira-Mutahangarwa royal version contends that
Wanumi is taken across the Kagera River to Kitara,
where all the Babito kings were buried in their home-
land, but that he is placed on a raised platform in
the manner of burial common to embandwa. The royal
text also mentions that the burial ceremonies were
conducted in this way to avoid further conflict with
the Bacwezi. The gashani house is a symbolic rendering, a mediation between Wanumi's dual status. The
Bakama are buried outside the kingdom, and the
embandwa are buried outside the village; the Bakama
are returned to the earth, and the embandwa are
raised above ground. The binary oppositions in this
case and their mediation by the Wanumi burial arrangement may point to a transition in political life, or
at least a precedent for later change:

	Bakama	:	Embandwa
Burial rites:	Earth	:	Sky ::
Status:	Pure	:	Dangerous
Transformation to:	Sky	:	Sky::
	Dangerous	:	Dangerous

With the burial of Wanumi, there is a resolution of
the dialectic that establishes the capacity for new
political-religious developments that occur four
generations after Wanumi. The new form of the
political-religious opposition has its origins in the
royal acquiescence to Bacwezi power, which first began
during the reign of Wanumi.

The reigns of Matwi, Magembe, Muzinga, and Mwigara are
not marked by any direct interference by Bacwezi
embandwa in the political process. There is, however,
an increasing record of succession conflicts and
warfare among the Bahaya kingdoms. There are no

*A gashani is the house that covers the burial site of
the king's jawbone. It is also a term used to describe
the estate encompassing the area of the former palace
of the king, inside of which the gashani is usually
located.

apparent possessions of royals by Bacwezi after
Mwigara. Only the Lwamgira-Mutahangarwa royal version
and Bernardo Muhambo of Kitobo, Kiziba, maintain that
Magembe (the fifth king) was possessed by the spirit
of Kasa, a stranger from Mpororo. Kasa is killed
because women praise him as more handsome than the
Mukama. His spirit possesses Magembe and is only
appeased after all the cattle of Kiziba are slaughtered
and after the spirit is given Nyante, the daughter
of Magembe. Kasa's origins are unclear, but the demand for cattle appears to avenge Wamara's loss, while
Nyante is also the name of the wife of the alleged
Bacwezi progenitor, Ndaura. This is an ambiguous and
problematical text. It appears that its ambiguity
may be the function of growing suppression of other
oral traditions by the Babito, for it does not have
general currency and it lacks the specificity of previous examples.

During reigns 4 through 7, there is a trend toward
possession by Babito spirits and the renewed help of
Mugasha. In the former case, the son of Magembe,
Kahigi, is killed during a war with Karagwe kingdom.
After his death, his spirit possesses a nephew, who
becomes an _embandwa_. Kahigi's spirit also possesses
people of the Bashasha clan. This is the first
instance of a Mubito spirit medium, and it occurs at
the same time that Mugasha is summoned to help the
Babito dynasty in a war with Karagwe:

> The witch doctors (bafumu) of Magembe then made
> their own divinations and found that they must
> call Mugasha of Isheshe to Kiziba to have him
> fight against Karagwe—and that after Mugasha
> helped them, they must build a house for him at
> Bugundu near Buyango. After being told that
> Mukama Magembe needed his help and wanted to
> make blood brotherhood with him, Mugasha agreed
> to help.

> The third night Mugasha brought much rain. It
> rained very much—as if the heavens had opened.
> The following day Magembe and his allies came
> from Kiziba to fight the Banyambo. . .when the
> Banyambo started to fight they found that the
> strings of their bows would not work properly.
> The Kiziba forces, therefore, were able to kill
> many Banyambo.[32]

When Mugasha is called, it is his spirit which re-
sponds through an _embandwa_. As noted previously,
the Mukama was dependent upon Mugasha and accorded
him a special shrine in the inner courtyard of his

palace. The king's tie to the Mugasha <u>embandwa</u> was
essential for the institution of kingship. While the
king was not a rainmaker himself, the Mugasha <u>embandwa</u>
in his employ performed the necessary rituals to maintain plenty and prosperity in the kingdom. This is
the last official mention of an alliance between
the Babito dynasty and Mugasha, and it also corresponds
in time to a similar alliance effected between the
Bahinda dynasty of Kyamutwara and Mugasha. This is
a period of political consolidation for the Bahinda/
Babito dynasties as they provide increasing protection
to the peoples under their hegemony. There is always
the possibility, too, that the increasing warfare is
fundamentally ritual and that it is a strategy by the
ruling dynasties to gain legitimacy, i.e., they provide effective protection.

Impending change for the acquisition of Babito power
in the religious sector is heralded by the possession
of Magembe and his son Muzinga by the spirit of
Mwigara, the son of the Mukama of Karagwe. They are
able to appease this Muhinda's spirit by arranging
Muzinga's marriage to a Munyambo (Karagwe citizen) and
by naming the baby Mwigara. Muzinga succeeds Magembe
and then is followed by Mwigara. The oral tradition
about Mwigara's burial introduces a new structure to
Bacwezi/Babito relations. The Kiziba oral tradition
is very explicit about the following themes, especially
the royally sanctioned version.

As Mwigara's body is conveyed to Kitara for the usual
burial, his body and boat are covered by an ant hill
and cannot be recovered. His successor, Burungu,
orders people to build a <u>gashani</u> house over the ant
hill and to get soil from the graves of all previous
kings in Kitara. Soil is brought back and placed in
the <u>kikale</u> of each Mukama, a <u>gashani</u> house is built,
and each <u>gashani</u> is staffed with a symbolic queen
mother, a virgin from the last clan the Mukama had
married into, and eighteen cows. When these tasks
are finished, then:

> The grandfathers were pleased, and they started
> to come and possess people.[33]

> After the soil was brought to Kiziba, the spirits
> of the dead Bakama began to possess people. This
> is the beginning of the embandwa for the Bakama.[34]

> What happened to Mwigara's body proved that he
> was a <u>citizen</u> of Kiziba and should be buried
> here—and so should other Bakama.[35]

So Burungu (the eighth king) creates a royal cult of
embandwa possessed by the spirits of dead Bakama.
This results in a new opposition: the spirit mediums
of Bakama supported by the Bakama in competition with
the spirit mediums of the Bacwezi, who depended on the
support of the people. This officially created and
sponsored royal cult brought with it a more elaborate
ritual complex, which needs to be explained because
of archaeological investigation of a gashani complex
in Kyamutwara. The spirit mediums of the Bakama
worked in cooperation with the caretakers of the
gashani, those who maintained the gashani and received
a share of the offerings brought to the gashani for
the king's spirit. These officials also lived at
the gashani.

When a king died, his body was placed in a boat and
left to rot until the jawbone could be removed by
the Bashote clan. The body and boat were then left,
eventually to be covered by an ant hill. Once the
lower jawbone had been removed, maggots were taken
from it and placed in a milk pot. After some time, a
black snake with a white neck ring comes out of the
pot and it is praised as the Mukama. The embandwa
of the Mukama keeps the snake at the gashani, and
the jawbone is buried in the gashani house.

The spirit mediums of the Bakama received official
recognition when a new Mukama succeeded to the kingship. The Mukama would send one cow, one sheep, and
beer (in the twentieth century; in precolonial days,
the cows came in multiples of nine) to the omugurusi,
or caretaker, who would then bring them to the
embandwa in his rubaya room, and say: "This Mukama
has died, have the new one on the throne rule as his
father and grandfather. He should have power over his
people, so give him help (underlining mine)."[36] After
the ritual, both would share the gifts: such offerings
were delivered to the shrines of all dead kings. The
Mukama was responsible for the support of the
omugurusi, embandwa, and all servants.

The establishment of a royal cult was an economically
demanding development. The resources available to
all those who were directly dependent upon the Mukama
on the burial estates were not sufficient to satisy
all the needs of the caretakers and spirit mediums.
Nonetheless, the political advantages accruing from
this development appear to be substantial. No longer
did the Bacwezi possess the kings who had their rival
cult of diviners. However, the Bacwezi spirit mediums
remained at the center of political life, in that
people continued to patronize them and depended on

their divinations.

According to Bahaya living in the Kanyigo area of
Kiziba (where the Babito dynasty was founded), the
Bakama established the royal cult to undermine the
power and influence of the Bacwezi. First of all,
the matters to be divined by a Mucwezi embandwa were
much more serious—for instance, reasons for the
death of a family member. To a Mukama embandwa one
would take a lesser appeal, such as a personal matter.
This dichotomy is similar to political oppositions
discussed, but after Burungu it was expressed exclusively in the religious domain. The royal cult
attempted to emphasize the negative attributes of
the Bacwezi by institutionalizing many opposing
positive functions for Bakama embandwa. The Bakama
embandwa had a petitioner state his problem first
and then an answer was divined; the Bacwezi embandwa
depended strictly on divination devices such as
cowries, sticks of wood, coffee beans, or chicken
entrails. As a consequence, the Bakama embandwa,
limited to lighter problems and given advance warning,
were more often successful in their divinations.
Nonetheless, there remained a demand for Bacwezi
embandwa, especially in highly sensitive matters
such as appeasing the spirits of ancestors who were
troubling a household. These were dangerous affairs
compared to the relatively safe domain of the royal
cult.

The physical structure of both divining houses also
differed. A Mucwezi embandwa had a special room
called Ihangiro on the left side of the entrance and
a special place in omulyango, the living room,
called ekiikaro where the embandwa sits. In a Mukama's
embandwa house, there was no Ihangiro. The embandwa
received his petitioners in the ekiikaro with a small
partition for the spirits' place.

The most important differences between the two cults
are in ease of possession, temperament, cost, and
purity. It is said by some that a Mukama embandwa
can be possessed during the night and day, thus makin-
him more accessible. However, some Bakama spirit
mediums dispute this claim and say that the embandwa
of Kahigi is the only one who is possessed during
daylight hours. Bacwezi are usually only available
during a new moon when the embandwa is possessed.
This is also the time when most Bakama spirits possess;
but when a death occurs nearby, the Mukama embandwa
will be possessed and the Mucwezi embandwa will not.
The Bakama spirit mediums are much more open to the
people.

There is a proverb which illustrates the difficult
nature of a Mucwezi embandwa: Wamara etamarwa, or
Wamara is difficult to satisfy. Essentially, this
means that the Mucwezi embandwa is very demanding for
his services, but a Mukama embandwa is more easily
pleased. Finally, the Bacwezi spirit mediums in
precolonial times were buried in the forest or bush
as polluted flesh, along with suicides, burning and
drowning victims, infertile women, and women who
died in childbirth. However, with the advent of the
new cult, the Bakama spirit mediums were buried in
the villages.[37]

These oppositions in religious life became institu-
tionalized after Mwigara's burial. Strictly religious
domains were involved rather than mixed religious
and political opposition. After Burungu, the fundamental opposition can be summarized as:

$$\text{Bakama} \quad : \quad \text{Bacwezi} \quad ::$$

$$\text{Life} \quad : \quad \text{Death}$$

Previously, the above opposition also existed but
was mediated when death (the ancestral spirit)
possessed the living king and they became one and the
same. After the innovations of Burungu, that capacity
is denied by royal political ritual and its juxtaposi-
tion to times when Bacwezi embandwa are possessed.
The Bacwezi, the death spirits, possess embandwa during the new moon; this is when the embandwa puts on
his possession cap, gives offerings to his Mucwezi,
and is possessed. It is also the time when the
rituals of the new moon take place to renew the
institution of kingship. At that time, the Mukama
wears his kalinda necklace to protect himself, and
he beats his drums to demonstrate that the kingdom,
or engoma (literally, drum), is vigorous, healthy,
and full of life. This political ritual is, of
course, in opposition to concurrent Bacwezi cult
rituals and practices. This opposition is one of
the three remaining vestiges—at a ritual level—of
what was once a real political-religious opposition.

The tertiary opposition is expressed when the Bacwezi
embandwa become polluted flesh upon death. While
their burial outside the village previously paralleled
the king's burial outside the kingdom, Burungu and
subsequent kings maintained a new opposition by the
burial of kings inside the kingdom. This, when added
to the other ritual oppositions, plus an alliance with
Mugasha, effectively neutralized the Bacwezi as a
political-religious force by pushing them into an

exclusively ritual domain. The subsequent ritual
opposition, then, is expressed in burial practices,
during new moon ceremonies, and during installation
ceremonies. The fundamental relationship can be reduced to:

Bakama : Bacwezi ::

Purity : Putrid

and

Safety : Danger ::

Culture : Nature

A number of other themes can be reduced to the same
basic formula, but they all reduce to the Culture:
Nature opposition, which makes the Bacwezi into a
dangerous, uncivilized force. Change toward a ritual
institutionalization of an opposition that had existed
previously for the Babito in political life is documented in the oral traditions. After the reign of
Burungu (the eighth king), opposition between the
Bacwezi and the kings is no longer manifest in the oral
tradition. This marks a period of Babito preeminence.
Thereafter, the structural oppositions can only be
found in the religious domain. Structural analysis
in this case has helped to isolate a period of
radical change in the history of the Babito dynasty
of Kiziba.

The previous discussion demonstrates that the
historian can adapt and modify structural principles
to arrive at a construct of change through time. The
genealogical history of Kiziba has a chronology, but
thus far the chronology cannot be reduced to simple
formula of X number of reigns = Y number years for a
dynasty, or a generation = Z number of years. Data
are not yet available for those types of constructs;
nor, given the predominant mythological form and
content of Bahaya oral tradition until about eight
to ten generations ago, can it be conceived that
they will ever be possible or that they are relevant.

Bahaya oral tradition is a good case study of African
history's overwhelming need for developing methodologies and perspectives that will deal with the writing
of history from myth. Perhaps it must first be done
on a thematic basis, such as the religious-political
history dealt with here. But a thematic history, if
employed with other analytical approaches such as
structural analysis of myth, can lead to diachronic

studies when change in the structure of myth is
isolated and shown to agree with changes in other
cultural phenomena. Archaeology is a necessary adjunct to the endeavor to establish a diachronic
framework.

As a consequence of the study of structural changes
in Kiziba political and religious life, similar
phenomena were sought in Kyamutwara kingdom. It is
known from the Kiziba oral tradition that the Bacwezi
are tied to indigenous social groups that use the
ancestral spirits to harass political opponents. In
addition, the Bacwezi "descendants" have another
important association: some local clans claim that
they are also the earliest iron workers in Buhaya.
In Kiziba, they are called the Bagina, though not
universally. However, the Bagina tradition is a
strong one, and Bike is characterized as both of
Bacwezi descent and as leader of the Bagina.

My work in Kyamutwara touches on questions related
to Mugasha and his recruitment by the Bahinda; the
place of Bacwezi in relating oral tradition about the
history of one king, Rugomora Mahe; and the association of the Bacwezi to iron working. The Bacwezi
religious opposition to the Babito is clearly early,
very likely much earlier than any conventional
genealogy appears to suggest, because of the processes
of telescoping. The Bacwezi/Bagina = early iron
workers theme suggests a very early date for the
peoples who developed the Bacwezi cult. Kyamutwara
oral traditions suggest that Bacwezi spirit mediums
have had close ties to the geographical area and its
technological history for several thousand years.
The history of Kyamutwara kingdom and King Rugomora
Mahe will be discussed in demonstrating these ties.
Analysis similar to that performed on Kiziba oral
traditions shows that the traditions about Rugomora
Mahe have their foundation in myths about the
Bacwezi and Mugasha, and that similar royal Bacwezi
oppositions also existed in early Bahinda history.
These oppositions existed until Mugasha magically
helped the Bahinda seize an important, indigenous
Bacwezi iron-working shrine. The following
chapter establishes why the Katuruka site where
Rugomora Mahe had his palace is so important to
Kyamutwara history—to the early indigenous
clan, Bacwezi spirit mediums from those same clans,
and the Bahinda dynasty.

Notes

[1] John Nyakatura, <u>Abakama ba Bunyoro-Kitara</u>, ed. Godfrey N. Uzoigwe, trans. T. Muganwa, published as <u>Anatomy of an African Kingdom: A History of Bunyoro-Kitara</u> (New York: Anchor Press, 1973), pp. 18-22; and Ruth Fisher, <u>Twilight Tales of the Black Baganda</u>, 2d ed. (London: Frank Cass, 1973), p. 99.

[2] Spirian Lwosa, 5/15/69, in Kigarama, Kiziba.

[3] Nyakatura, op. cit., pp. 24-25.

[4] Fisher, op. cit., pp. 80-122. There are inconsistencies in the genealogical ascriptions of Fisher's texts. For example, Kagoro is referred to as the son of Kyomya (p. 99) and also as the son of Mugenyi (p. 105). It could be that Fisher has confused matters through a literal translation of classificatory kinship terms. Further confusion prevails when Fisher delineates the Bacwezi as the group depicted in the diagram but later calls Isimbwa a Mucwezi (pp. 109, 111).

[5] Ibid., p. 102.

[6] Ibid., pp. 103-104.

[7] Hermann Rehse, <u>Kiziba Land und Leute</u> (Stuttgart, 1910). Translated by V. Luschan and made available in mimeograph form by Israel Katoke, p. 120.

[8]Kuijpers manuscript and Daniel Mugwanzi, 5/15/69, Kyanga, Kiziba.

[9]Bernardo Muhambo, 5/14/69 and 5/22/69, in Kitobo, Kiziba.

[10]Spirian Kyayonka, 5/20/69, in Lushasha, Kiziba.

[11]F. X. Lwamgira, Amakuru ga Kiziba na Abakama Bamu, trans. E. R. Kamuhingire, Makerere University, in mimeograph form, p. 10.

[12]M.S.M. Kiwanuka, "The Traditional History of the Buganda Kingdom: with Special Reference to the Historical Writings of Apolo Kaggwa," dissertation, University of London, 1965, p. 13.

[13]Alfred Kemiti, 5/21/69, in Muhutwe, Kianja.

[14]Kiwanuka, op. cit., p. 13.

[15]Bernardo Muhambo, 5/27/69, in Kitobo, Kiziba.

[16]Manuscript by Dutch White Father, Kuijpers, entitled "History of Kiziba." Held by Father Paul Betbeder, Ngote, Buhaya.

[17]Amakuru ga Kiziba, Makerere translation, p. 42.

[18]Kuijpers mss.

[19]Bernardo Muhambo, 5/22/69, in Kitobo, Kiziba. The version in Kuijpers' mss. is virtually identical, except that Ntare is omitted. Also, Spirian Kyayonka, 5/20/69, in Lushasha, Kiziba.

[20]Amakuru ga Kiziba, op. cit., Chapter VI, phase II, pp. 2-3.

[21]Mutaihwa Lubelwa, 4/9/69, in Kigarama, Kiziba.

[22]Feruzi Kyaruzi Luzigiga, 8/21/69, in Kikukwe, Kiziba.

[23]Petro Nshekela, 8/20/69, in Kigarama, Kiziba.

[24]While the Babito relate a similar oral tradition, the Amakuru ga Kiziba version as compiled by Lwamgira omits this discussion altogether. This is but another example, say the Bakuma, of the bias of Amakuru ga Kiziba.

[25]Bernardo Muhambo, 5/24/69, in Kitobo, Kiziba.

[26]Kuijpers mss. and Daniel Rutamagi, 5/17/69, in Kitobo, Kiziba.

[27]Tibanyendela Kateme, 6/6/69, in Bwanjai, Kiziba.

[28]Spirian Kyayonka, 5/12/69, in Lushasha, Kiziba.

[29]Ronald Cohen, "The Dynamics of Feudalism in Bornu," Boston University Press Papers of African History, Vol. II. Michael Gilsenan, "Myth and the History of African Religion," in The Historical Study of African Religion (Berkeley and Los Angeles: University of California Press, 1972), pp. 50-70.

[30]Gilsenan, op. cit., p. 62.

[31]Fidelis Kyakalija Kachwamiti, 5/31/69, in Kanyigo, Kiziba.

[32]Bernardo Muhambo, 6/11/69, in Kotobo, Kiziba, and Kuijpers mss.

[33]Kuijpers mss.

[34]Bernardo Muhambo, 7/17/69, in Kitobo, Kiziba; Kamurasi Kabuzi, 7/22/69, in Buyango, Kiziba.

[35]Bernardo Muhambo, 7/17/69, in Kitobo, Kiziba.

[36]Ikembwire Rwakairo, 6/27/69, in Bugandika, Kiziba.

[37]I am indebted to Petro Nshekela of Kigarama, Kiziba, for the explanation of differences between Bakama and Bacwezi embandwa. Provided 9/13/69, in Kigarama, Kiziba.

6

The Structure of Kyamutwara
Oral Tradition

The historical perspective derived from the oral traditions of Kiziba can be developed in slightly different form for the oral tradition of greater Kyamutwara,
immediately to the south of Kiziba (see Figure 1,
Chapter 1). Kyamutwara oral evidence does not offer
possibilities for the same kind of analysis, for there
is relatively little mention about Bacwezi spirit
possession of the Bakama. There is also little
evidence for the development of a royal cult of
embandwa. But during the reign of King Rugomora Mahe
in Kyamutwara, there is a similarity to Babito
recruitment of Mugasha and the use of his magical
devices to obtain peace and prosperity in Kiziba
kingdom. If there is any value to gross cross-dating
between royal genealogies, then the general time
period of Rugomora Mahe's consolidation of power by
magical devices corresponds to Mwigara (the seventh
king) in Kiziba history, during which time the Babito
dynasty consolidated its power through a royal cult.
However, a study of Kyamutwara royal genealogy will
demonstrate that it may have relatively little
sequential chronological value and that it has been
widely altered by structural manipulations and
influenced by mythological infusions.

The latter phenomenon, the infusion of mythological
forms, is represented by many examples in the
Kyamutwara genealogy. The point of greatest density
for mythological themes is the reign of Rugomora Mahe.
It is his history which again focuses our attention
on Mugasha and the recruitment of Mugasha by the
Bahinda dynasty, which uses his magical assistance
to reclaim the Kyamutwara throne. The basic structure
of the Rugomora Mahe myth draws heavily from the

structures of myth about the Bacwezi and Mugasha.

Since the most detailed myth about Rugomora Mahe is
provided by Bacwezi spirit mediums, one might argue
that structural similarities to Bacwezi myth are the
result of both oral traditions belonging to the same
verbal domain. This is true, but it is too simple
an explanation. Bacwezi spirit mediums also relate
specific, localized Bacwezi myth in the Rugomora
Mahe tales. The total corpus of myth about Rugomora
Mahe they have always related. The significance in
the Rugomora Mahe myth is the changes introduced,
especially the use of Bahinda names. Furthermore,
the myth about Rugomora Mahe as related by Bacwezi
spirit mediums meets royal approval. The royals consider the spirit mediums the authorities on Rugomora
Mahe, and I have witnessed sessions in which they
heartily approve such versions. It is simply the case
that the royals themselves are not nearly as good at
relating the sanctioned version. It is perhaps
natural that the Bacwezi spirit mediums became the
conveyors of the new, royal version, for, as we will
see in the subsequent archaeological sections, the
royals took over an important Bacwezi shrine and all
of its associated myth. This overpowering of the
Bacwezi and the adoption of Bacwezi myth as an attempt
to gain legitimacy may have carried with it various
concessions—such as allowing the Bacwezi spirit
mediums to become the official keepers of Rugomora
Mahe's history.

The structure of Bacwezi myth which encompasses
themes about Mugasha will now be compared with the
structure of myth about Rugomora Mahe. The structural
comparisons will demonstrate the derivations of many
of the mythemes surrounding the history of Rugomora
Mahe. It is necessary to understand the kingly ritual
relationship with Mugasha (the spirit mediums of
Mugasha), for a description of the rituals associated
with Mugasha will help to explain how a Muhinda king
uses Mugasha to assume control of a sacred shrine and
to consolidate his power.

Bayoza, Bakara, Bagabo, and Bahamba are names used to
designate the former citizens of greater Kyamutwara.
By the late eighteenth century, the kingdom was
divided into four separate minor kingdoms: Kyamutwara,
Maruku or Bukara, Bagabo, and Kianja. The smaller
kingdoms of Kyamutwara and Bugabo were not ruled by
the Bahinda dynasty. An immigrant clan from the
south, the Bankango, had been in varying states of
subordination as tribute payers to the Bahinda, but
the Bahinda became so dependent on Bankango power

that the Bankango were able to establish themselves
as territorial rulers. This was accomplished primarily
by prowess in war and oftentimes at the expense of
the Bahinda, who were then forced to recruit Baganda
assistance.

Local mythology in Kyamutwara universally claims that
the Batundu clan ruled the area before the arrival
of the Bahinda. The Batundu, it is said in most
accounts, were contemporaries of the Bahunga who
were led in the Kyamutwara area by Kashare. Myth in
Kyamutwara tends to be more locally oriented toward
the pre-Bahinda period than the Bacwezi perspective
held in Kiziba myth. A number of variations are
diagrammed below. These examples will demonstrate
that there are multitudinous variants but that the
fundamental structures are similar.

CASE 1

Bahunga rule: Nyango
                                           |
Lushembo, a Mutundu   Kashare/Lushembo
immigrant, arrives and
power is limited to clan
areas. Both are killed
by Ruhinda.[1]
                                        _____

                                        Ruhinda

CASE 2

Bahunga rule: Nyango
                                           |
Mukiza, a Mutundu   Kashare/Mukiza
foreigner, arrives during
Kashare's rule and attacks |
him. The Bahinda then kill |
Lushembo.[2]   Lushembo
                                        _____

                                        Ruhinda

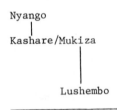

CASE 3

Bahunga rule:

Mukiza, a Mutundu, comes
from the Isheshe Islands.
He effects an alliance with
Lwezangoma by marrying
the Muhunga leader's
daughter.[3]

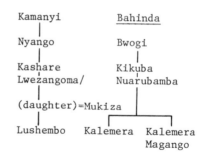

In this case, the Bahinda do
not use force against the
local rulers until the time
of Kalemera Magango.

These three cases show that there was not a hostile
relationship between the Bahunga and the Batundu.
Another alliance with the Batundu was effected later
by Rugomora Mahe. Many Bahaya refer to the Batundu
as originally an *ihiga* (subclan) of the Bahunga;
hence, insofar as the Bahaya are concerned, there is
a close relationship between the two clans. According
to Kyamutwara myth, the leaders of both clans come
into conflict with the Bahinda and are eventually
killed. There are extensive myths about how Bwogi,
the son of Ruhinda, conspires to kill Kashare, and
about the Bahinda use of a Mutundu informant in a plot
to kill Lushembo.

The example cited in Case 3 has Lushembo in conflict
with Kalemera I. According to this version, conflict
develops four generations (possibly five if the
progenitor Ruhinda is included) after the Bahinda
arrival in the area. Cory and Hartnoll cite a
similar example in the case of Kashare, who is deprived of his power by Kalemera.[4] These are not
isolated versions. The Bahaya strongly maintain that
Bahinda consolidation of power did not develop until
the reign of Kalemera. Many oral traditions incorporate extensive lists of local rulers who were killed
and replaced by Kalemera, who is remembered as a
cruel, harsh, and bloodthirsty king. These cases
affirm other themes that occur in the oral traditions,
especially the theme of reaction against Kalemera,
his subsequent difficulties with internal loyalty in
his court, and the temporary loss of power by the
Bahinda. Kalemera's attempt to consolidate power
through force against already well-established and

powerful clans is not successful and leads to opposition.

The themes that can be isolated in Kyamutwara as conveying a general history of Bahinda-local relationships emphasize rainmaking and the power that this ability confers. In this regard, the Kyamutwara oral traditions have close affinities to Kiziba where the Babito rulers have an alliance with rainmakers or the embandwa of Mugasha. The Kyamutwara oral traditions, however, have a different structure from those of Kiziba.

In Chapter 5 (Kuijpers; also text from Daniel Mugwanzi, 5/15/69, Kyanga, Kiziba), Case 1 shows that Kashare, ruler of Bumbuijwa (Kyamutwara), is a son of Wamara—as are Bike, Nkumbia (Nkombya), and Nono of Karagwe. As pointed out previously, there is commonly held myth in Kiziba about descent of an indigenous clan (Bakuma) from Wamara, although the conjugal ties are sometimes seen differently. An abstraction reads:

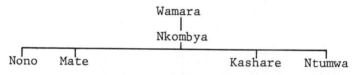

The essential point here is that Kashare is genealogically related to Wamara and is opposed by the Bahinda; as Bike in Kiziba is also linked to Wamara, but killed by his own murderous relatives from Ihangiro; and as Ntumwa of Kiziba is linked to Wamara and his descendants opposed by the Babito. This perspective is also found among the Batundu of Kyamutwara, where a myth establishes the Batundu progenitor as the son of Kasi who appears in most versions (with the exception of Case 2, Chapter 5) as a Mucwezi and as the Bacwezi god of agriculture. It is certainly not possible at this time to attribute any historical value to these claims; the important element is that they exist and that the Bahaya incorporate this linkage into their mythology.

The Bayango and the Bahunga always have been chief advisors to the Bahinda in Kyamutwara. In fact, many nonroyal Bahaya claim that these clans ran the affairs of state with the king performing ritual duties, particularly the new moon ceremonies. It is also clear from the oral tradition that Kashare may have been an important rainmaker before the arrival of the Bahinda, but he appears to have lost that power to the Batundu:

> Kashare no longer had the ability to bring rain,
> and this was one of his failures. Things were
> not well in the kingdom when the Batundu appeared.
> When Lushembo came, he announced that he was
> going to cure the land of its lack of produc-
> tivity. Lushembo brought medicine with him in
> the form of 2 sticks. He dug a hole and buried
> the medicine in it. Then he stomped his foot
> and said, "This medicine will cure you, land of
> the Batundu."[5]

We will see that this is an important theme, for its
basic format is repeated in myth about Rugomora Mahe,
a Muhinda ruler. The Batundu appear to have seized
the power of rainmaking. Other texts are even more
explicit about how they acquired this power. The
specific format is similar to the possession of
Wanumi in Kiziba when he wore the kisingo (possession
hat) of Wamara. In this case, the possession hat
belongs to Mugasha, who tells a Muyozi clansman:

> I have loved you; from this time I will give
> you nine days and I will then pay you a visit.
> When you see that the right day has arrived, go
> and make a kichoko and bear it on your head.
> That will help me to notice that it is you, my
> friend. On the ninth night the Muyozi wore his
> kichoko and his wife greased him up with butter.
> He sat down next to a house post to wait for
> Mugasha. The Mutundukazi when she saw that
> her husband was sleeping awoke her nephew, took
> the kichoko off the Muyozi's head, and made
> the Mutundu wear it. Mugasha arrived and saw
> the kichoko man. He is the one who was possessed
> by Mugasha's spirit. His name was Kibuyza.[6]

The Batundu, then, are the rainmakers, a position which
myth claims they received through sleight of hand.
The Batundu in Kyamutwara (Kianja today) are in fact
rainmakers; their clan spirit is Mugasha, and the
spirit mediums of Mugasha are Batundu. The cult
center for Mugasha's spirit mediums of this clan was
and still is Bwigura village on the shores of Kyasha
Bay, about seven miles south of Kemondo Bay.
Significantly, the clan totem of the Batundu is the
Otter, which is also the totem of the Otter clan in
Buganda. Like Mugasha, the otter clan is associated
with the Isheshe Islands. These relationships are not
coincidental, for the Batundu claim a Buganda origin; [7]
it is undoubtedly the Otter clan from which they are
descended.

Some texts claim that the Batundu came to rainmaking

power before the arrival of the Bahinda, but there
is no substantial support for this assertion. The
above myth continues to explain that the Batundu
were not possessed by Mugasha's spirit until well
into the Bahinda dynasty during the reign of Rugomora
Mahe. This theme will be detailed in a later discussion. Who performed essential rainmaking ceremonies before the arrival of the Bahinda? This question
cannot be definitely answered, but there are mythemes
about Kashare's inadequate job of rainmaking and about
the warm welcome for the Bahinda because "They had
the power of magic to bring rain and much food.
Ruhinda changed the name from Bumwiga to Kyamutwara
(the thing which takes), for it had taken his son.
Bwogi was able to win loyalty because of the desirable
medicine he had."[8]

The Bahinda appear to have used magical devices for
the consolidation of power in Kyamutwara, much as
Kibi used magic he obtained from Mugasha to bring
grasshoppers to Kiziba. Grasshoppers are tied to the
bringing of rain, for the second rainy season in
Buhaya is called omusenene [grasshopper]. Grasshoppers
do not come until the second, short rainy season
in October-November. A Bahinda-Bacwezi opposition is
not apparent at the outset of Bahinda rule in
Kyamutwara—as it is in Kiziba—but it does appear
that much of early Bahinda history concerns contests
for power through the control of rainmaking, which is
essentially a ritual activity controlled by clan
leaders who had social and judicial authority as well
as control over district territories.

The Bahinda claim to have had the early support of
the Bayango clan, who also claim descent from
Ruhinda. Kayango is pointed to as the progenitor
of the clan, and it is said that he accompanied
Ruhinda to Karagwe from where hegemony was established
over Kyamutwara. The descendants of Nkombya in
Ihangiro (see Chapter 5) who claim descent from
Wamara claim to be Bayango. The Bakuma of Kiziba
whose ancestor Ntumwa also has ties to Wamara and to
Nkombya also call themselves Bayango-Bahinda. Thus,
there are genealogical linkages between the Bayango
and Bacwezi. This phenomenon appears to be a
genealogical cemment for a close ritual relationship
between the Bayango and Bacwezi, most clearly
expressed when important Bayango political figures
acted as Bacwezi spirit mediums and overseerers of
major cult shrines.

The Bayango may have been a local clan that was
closely incorporated into the Bahinda governmental

structure and whose name has changed through time because of close royal association. The Bayango in
Kyamutwara were the officials closest to the king.
It is said that Kayango (and all his descendants with
the same name) ruled as virtually a co-ruler with the
Bahinda. He was responsible for laving out the
boundaries of the new kikale (as was the clan head of
the Bakuma in Kiziba), and he was the first to sleep
with a new wife of a Mukama. He also held the royal
spear, a symbol of power, for it was more legitimately
held by one who had an indigenous claim to power.

Some Bahaya go so far as to claim that Kayango was
much more powerful than a Katikiro (chief minister).
One Muyango informant stated; "Kayango was buried as
a Mukama. Until recently when a Mukama died a
descendant of Kayango would be appointed to rule with
the Mukama. And if he died, then he would be buried
as a Mukama."[9] Most Bahaya living in Kyamutwara
state this point of view in very similar terms,
usually saying that the Bahinda and Kayango ruled together and that Kayango was a diviner, spirit medium,
and rainmaker. In traditional times, people would
take gifts or offerings to him so that he would
arrange for rain and thereby produce food for the
people. As Augustine Kaindoa put it: "He could also
turn a dry grasshopper green by putting it in water.
There is little the Mukama could do without calling
on his advice."[10] Kayango had the power to appeal
to the Bacwezi spirits of Kazoba and Ishewanga, and
that very probably means that he was also a Mucwezi
spirit medium.[11]

Other Bahaya oral traditions deny the Bahinda link
with the Bayango. One of these claims that Kayango
came from the south and that he was a smelter of iron:
"Kayango came from Buzinza, smelting iron and shaking
his shoulders. They called him Kayango Kitengya
mabega, i.e., Kayango the shoulder shaker. When he
came he just smelted for Kashare. Then Kayango went
to Karagwe to find the Bahinda."[12] So, Kayango is
associated with indigenous rainmaking, the Bacwezi,
and iron smelting, all of which are pre-Bahinda.

The recruitment of the Bayango into the Bahinda
government, given the probable power of the indigenous
clan, was probably imperative. In fact, oral traditions in Kyamutwara stress that the Bahinda depended
significantly on the Bayango, the Bayozi, the Bahunga,
and other indigenous clans. These clans were particularly powerful in a system of commoner councillors
who decided many court cases and chose the Bahinda
kings.

A further consideration of Kyamutwara oral tradition
indicates that the Bahinda recruitment of Bayango
assistance may have led to a polarization of power.
According to the myths, Kalemera's consolidation of
power by the slaughter of local clan chiefs was conducted with the advice and support of Kayango. There
followed a reaction to Kalemera, so that: "the
Balangira [princes and descendants] became furious and
decided to kill his most beloved son, Kimuli; the
Balangira [made a poison], and gave it to Kalemera's
most beloved wife, saying 'If you refuse to give it
to Kimuli, your child will not become king.'"[13] The
Balangira were able to exploit the jealousy of the
king's wives and kill his favorite son. This resulted
in the king's slaughter of all but one of his sons,
the death of all other local chiefs, and the killing
of cattle until all the blood ran into the Muleleizi
River from a cliff near the king's kikale in Magango.

The upshot was that the king went mad, Kayango was
able to save the remaining son who was blinded and
named Kiume, and the kingdom of Kyamutwara went into
a state of decline manifested by widespread famine,
the latter portion of which saw the exclusive
authority of Kayango.

Turn to Appendix A for the text. A reading of the
text is necessary at this point. For other versions,
including a royal version, see Appendices B and C.

Most mythology about the Bahinda dynasty in Kyamutwara
fails to mention that Kayango was possessed by the
spirit of Kimuli. He is known as Embandwa ya Kimuli.[14]
The structure of Kiziba myth helps to interpret this
phenomenon, for possession of this kind usually occurs
when an attempt is made on the throne. For example,
after Kibi kills Ntumwa, he is troubled by Ntumwa's
spirit. Kayango is represented in the myth about
Rugomora Mahe as the ruler of Kyamutwara during the
absence of Mahe and after the death of Kiume. If
indigenous forces temporarily gain the throne, then
why are there famine and insufficient rain in Buhaya?
The apparent reason is that Kayango, the usurper, is
possessed by the spirit of Kimuli. If he was previously an embandwa of a Mucwezi, then that rainmaking
power would have been eclipsed by Kimuli's spirit.
With Kimuli's spirit, he is incapable of rainmaking
(as Wanumi was incapable of ruling in Kiziba when
possessed by Wamara's spirit). The prosperity of
the kingdom cannot be assured.

When Mahe returns with the magical devices of Mugasha,
he is able to employ Mugasha against whatever indigenous forces were constraining Bahinda power, especially
the power to make rain. The oppositions are structurally similar to what occurs in Kiziba. Rugomora
Mahe recruits Mugasha's support against the indigenous
clans that have opposed Bahinda rule by the use of
Bacwezi spirit mediums.

It will be recalled that the Bahunga clan with Kashare
as clan head was responsible for rainmaking but that
Kashare had not exercised his power adequately. The
same may be true of the Bayozi, from whom the Batundu
foreigners obtain rainmaking powers. The Bahinda,
in alliance with the Mugasha spirit mediums or the
Batundu clan of Kyamutwara, are opposed to the
indigenous clans that recruit the aid of the Bacwezi.
This opposition is structurally represented in the
ritual life of the Kyamutwara kings. They must take
nine black cows and a black goat (or sheep) and other
offerings to the shrine reserved for Mugasha when they
are installed. They must also provide offerings at
the shrine of the Bahunga clan or Kashare's clan where
a white cow (usually in multiples of nine), a white
chicken, and a drum are given. The color white is
symbolic of the Bacwezi, in opposition to the black
of Mugasha.

These oppositions are poignant commentaries on the
structural arrangements of different interests in
the political life of Kyamutwara. While we can not
give them an absolute date, we can say that they
were a historical reality, as the basic oppositions
are so thoroughly expressed in mythology and ritual
life.

The next step in this analytical procedure will be an
analysis of the Rugomora Mahe myth insofar as it
assists in elucidating origins for the oral tradition
and processes involved in the integration of Bacwezi
mythemes into royal genealogy. This will not be a
structural analysis for its own sake. Rather, a
limited, summary analysis will be performed to bring
out (1) structural affinities between Bacwezi and
Bahinda myth, (2) the derivations of Bahinda myth,
and (3) functional aspects of structural similarities
that can be used to delimit archaeological sites.

The first mytheme that can be isolated and designated
as Bacwezi in origin starts with the construction of
a separate kikale for Mwehozi (Kiume) who is blinded
by his father Kalemera, who also kills all his other
children. Kalemera is left with an infirm or crippled

heir who is exiled to a separate kikale. The latter
part of this episode has the same structure as the
Bacwezi myth about Bukuku and Nyinamwiru (see Case 1,
Chapter 5). One-breasted Nyinamwiru is exiled to a
separate kikale. The parallels are:

Bacwezi	Kyamutwara
(Nyinamwiru)	(Kiume)
Deformed:Exiled   ::   Blind:Exiled

In the Kyamutwara myth, Kayango (a nonroyal) interferes
and sends a commoner girl to Mwehozi, who then gets a
child by the servant girl. This is the same mytheme
as the Bacwezi version, wherein Nyinamwiru sleeps with
the foreigner Isimbwa and bears an illegitimate child:

| Bacwezi | Kyamutwara |
| | |
| Royal:Outsider   ::   Royal:Commoner, and |
| | |
| Outsider:Illegitimate   ::   Commoner:Illegitimate |

The next episode in Bacwezi myth revolves around the
king's (grandfather's) attempted destruction of the
illegitimate offspring and the rescue of the child by
a nonroyal, Kibumbi. In Kyamutwara, Mahe's grandfather Kalemera attempts to murder him but is foiled
by Kayango and women in his court.

| Bacwezi | Kyamutwara |
| | |
| Bukuku:Ndaura   ::   Kalemera:Mahe, which is |
| | |
| Grandfather:Grandson   ::   Grandfather:Grandson |

The structural parallels seen above can be found in
other relationships, such as the affinities between
the nonroyals and the offspring from royal-nonroyal
unions:

| Kibumbi:Ndaura   ::   Kayango:Mahe, which is |
| |
| Nonroyal:Royal Candidate   ::   Nonroyal:Royal Candidate |

These parallels point out the processes of kingmaking
by nonroyals in Buhaya, and this structure reveals a
deeper opposition, viz:

| Bukuku:Kibumbi   ::   Kalemera:Kayango, which is |
| Destroyer:Savior   ::   Destroyer:Savior |

Both Bukuku and Kalemera can be characterized as destroyer as they attempt the destruction of their grandsons who are saved by the interference of Kibumbi and Kayango. The cases cited thus far help to confirm the hypothesis that Bacwezi myth is used as a model to convey the themes of indigenous opposition to Bahinda rule. Expression through a Bacwezi structure submerges the themes of political opposition. In this sense, the myth expresses a social dialectic which is mediated by the use of Bacwezi mythological themes that mask the Bahaya sociopolitical realities. After this point, the Kyamutwara oral tradition does not continue the use of the Bacwezi formulations. The next Bacwezi episode, which is the murder of the grandfather by his grandson, is not employed in the Kyamutwara myth about Rugomora Mahe.

The next important episode in the Rugomora Mahe myth is Mahe's transformation from a royal to a commoner—a fisherman, or the lowest possible status. He travels with fishermen on Lake Victoria and behaves like a fisherman, so that he is greeted by Nyamata, the daughter of Muchundu, as a fisherman: she spits at him and denies him milk (a Mukama is a receiver of milk). This is the same structural format as the Bacwezi myth about Mugasha and Nyabibungo, the daughter of Wamara.[15] Nyabibungo spits at Mugasha when he greets her because he is a fisherman. Nyamata does the same to Mahe, the long-haired traveler among fishermen:

Bacwezi		Kyamutwara
Nyabibungo:Mugasha	: :	Nyamata:Mahe or
Royal:Commoner	: :	Royal:Commoner

Mugasha is received as a fisherman, but eventually he is acknowledged by Wamara. Mahe is received by Nyamata as a fisherman, but he is acknowledged by her father as a king. The structures are still parallel, for Mugasha must demonstrate his power to Wamara before he is accepted, so Mugasha is transformed:

Mugasha the Fisherman ——➤ Mugasha the God

So, too, is Mahe transformed in the next Kyamutwara episode which corresponds to the storm episode in the Bacwezi myth:

Mahe the Fisherman ————➤ Mahe the Quasi-God

This transformation is accomplished through Mahe's

superhuman feats of strength—for example, his
transportation of many bundles of wood and his excavation of post holes in rock, both of which create a
status equal to Mugahsa's. The structural parallels
also continue into the next episode, for in the
Bacwezi myth Mugasha attempts an alliance with Wamara
by taking his daughter. The Kyamutwara myth also has
the same theme, as Mugasha offers his daughter in
marriage to Mahe or an alternative, blood brotherhood.
Mahe's alliance with Mugasha is not effected immediately; this is also true of Mugasha and Wamara, who
gives his daughter but not in marriage. Therefore,
the alliance has no ritual bond and can be broken.
Mugasha has no protection. He is hunted down—shot
with an arrow by Kagoro. The alliance is not effected properly until Mugasha comes to live in the presence of the Bacwezi and serves them.

The same parallel occurs in the Rugomora Mahe myth.
However, there are intermediate episodes from the
time Mahe leaves Isheshe until he returns to make
blood brotherhood with Mugasha. These episodes are
not structural parallels, and it is not yet clear if
they are similar to other stereotypes in Bahaya
mythology. The parallels resume with Mahe's return
to Isheshe where an alliance with Mugasha is
effected, but only a blood brotherhood which, despite
prescribed ideals, often is used as a political ruse
in Buhaya. The parallel structures can be diagrammed
as:

<table>
<tr><td>Bacwezi</td><td></td><td>Kyamutwara</td></tr>
<tr><td>Mugasha:Wamara</td><td>:: </td><td>Mahe:Mugasha   or</td></tr>
<tr><td>Receiver of Woman (Life):</td><td>::</td><td>Receiver of Blood (Life):</td></tr>
<tr><td>No Payment of Bride Price</td><td></td><td>Delayed Obligations</td></tr>
</table>

In Mugasha's case, he departs without fulfilling his
contractual marriage obligations to Wamara, and Mahe
departs without fulfilling his reciprocal obligations
to Mugasha—building a special house for Mugasha in
Mahe's kikale.

The episodes in the Mahe myth from the time of Mahe's
second departure from Isheshe to the search by
Kayango do not have structural parallels in myth
about the Bacwezi, but they do have parallels in
early Kyamutwara mythology. Some of the intermediate episodes, such as Mahe's power over divining
magic, can be viewed allegorically—for instance, as

a statement that Mahe is above the power of diviners, especially those who might oppose Bahinda rule through spirit mediumship. Most of these collateral episodes will not concern us here, except when they have clear parallels in other Bahaya myth. One example is the previously cited myth about the Batundu who plant two magic sticks in holes. The same episode occurs in the Rugomora Mahe myth: Mugasha gives Mahe two magic sticks which he then buries in two separate holes during his trek to Katuruka.

The next use of a Bacwezi format is when Mahe's return to Kyamutwara is recognized. The forces of the usurper Kayango fall on Mahe's hiding place. There is a definite adversary relationship between Kayango who hunts and Mahe who hides from the hunters. The parallels in this episode are:

Bacwezi		Kyamutwara
Kagoro:Mugasha	::	Kayango:Mahe or
The Hunter:Hunted	::	The Hunter:Hunted

Both Mahe and Mugasha are outsiders, foreign and dangerous. They are portrayed as wild, uncivil forces. Mugasha is shot by the greater warrior-hunter Kagoro, and Mahe is hunted as a wild animal as he hides in the bush. There is also structural duplication in the Mahe myth when Mahe returns to Kyamutwara. When Mugasha goes to Wamara after the storm, he brings peace. When Mahe returns to Kyamutwara, he brings plenty; he stops famine. As a consequence:

Bacwezi		Kyamutwara
Mugasha:Chaos	::	Mahe:Famine, and
Mugasha:Peace	::	Rugomora:Prosperity

These complementary functions can also be expressed as complementary oppositions:

Chaos/Peace   :   Famine/Prosperity

In the former, Mugasha is the mediator because he can cause both chaos and peace through his power, and in the latter, Mahe can cause both famine (the result of his continued absence) and prosperity (the result of his return).

The episodes that occur after Mahe is hailed as Rugomora (he who satisfies) interrupt the structural

parallels with Bacwezi myth. The parallels to Bacwezi
mythology can be delimited again once Rugomora Mahe
establishes his kikale. The numerous parallel
structures that have been isolated thus far confirm
that the mythemes about Mugasha in Bacwezi myth (in-
jected with other episodes) provide the basic
structure for the saga of Rugomora Mahe. Up to this
point, the Rugomora Mahe myth has incorporated every
major mytheme of the Mugasha myth. It is highly
improbable that the concluding mytheme would be
omitted. It is needed in order to provide a balanced
structure.

In the Bacwezi myth, Mugasha returns to establish his
residence at the kikale of Wamara. There he accepts
Wamara as his father-in-law, pays homage to him, and
becomes a servant. This structure is parallel to the
Kyamutwara myth. Rugomora Mahe returns to Kayango,
who is called Owa Mahe, father of everything, and
establishes residence with him. The parallel is:

Mugasha at Wamara's: Rugomora at Kayango's:
                       ::
Matrilocal Residence   Matrilocal Residence

Kayango, with his Bacwezi connections and as the
strongest leader among the indigenous clans, leads
Rugomora Mahe to the indigenous heartland of
Kyamutwara. The residence of Rugomora is established
on an important Bacwezi shrine of great antiquity.
Kayango or Owa Mahe had been directly responsible
for arranging the union between Mahe's father and
mother, who is from an indigenous clan from Katuruka.
Rugomora Mahe then marries into his mother's clan.[16]
Mahe's settlement on the Katuruka site, an indigenous
shrine, in fact establishes a kind of matrilocal
residence, as does Mugasha's settlement at Wamara's
kikale. Mahe returns to his mother's village and to
a shrine that has symbolic meaning to the indigenous
iron-working clans. As subsequent chapters will show,
this site is a very ancient place where activity areas
that date to more than 2,000 years B.P. are remembered,
particularly by Bayango who are Bacwezi spirit mediums.

The Bacwezi myth about Mugasha does not end until
Wamara dies, whereupon Mugasha departs for Isheshe
where he has other loyalties and obligations as the
god of the waters. This also is paralleled in Rugomora
Mahe myth. Rugomora Mahe has primary obligations to
Mugasha, with whom he makes a contract. Rugomora
Mahe build a residence for Mugasha at Katuruka, which
is clearly the establishment of a shrine. By doing

so, he neutralizes or consumes the symbolic value—
at least for rainmaking—which the indigenous shrine
may have had. This episode has structural parallels
in the Bacwezi myth, for after Wamara's death Mugasha
eats the white cow of Wamara, thus destroying the
symbol of the Bacwezi. Once this event occurs, the
spirits of Wamara and his kin are released and the
Bacwezi possess people.

This structure also occurs in the Rugomora Mahe myth.
Rugomora's primary obligation lies with Mugasha.
After he establishes residence at Katuruka and
neutralizes the indigenous shrine, he reciprocates
by calling Mugasha to his place. At this time, it is
also claimed that the Batundu are possessed by the
spirit of Mugasha: "Kibanza was possessed by Mugasha's
spirit. It was due to the promise that Rugomora
Mahe made to Mugasha, that if he became Mukama, he
would give Mugasha something."[17] However, the obligation which the Bahinda contracted with Mugasha is as
unending as the obligation of Mugasha to his realm:

> . . . the Bahinda were uniting with the local
> clans and offering things to shrines, and look-
> ing after the shrines. That is why the Bakama
> up to this time make their offerings to the
> Batundu, because they fear that if Mugasha is
> not appeased, then he will get angry and bad
> things might befall the dynasty.[18]

The final outcome of the Rugomora myth is an alliance
between the Bahinda and the Batundu (or Mugasha).
The remaining episodes are not found elsewhere in
Kyamutwara or Bahaya mythology. The iron tower
mytheme may have belonged to the indigenous clan
occupying Katuruka. It is a mytheme particularly
well known by Bayango in Kyamutwara. As we have seen,
Kashare is also associated with iron smelting, and
the Katuruka shrine with the iron-smelting myth that
was later incorporated into the myth of Rugomora Mahe.
Certainly, the great detail about the places where
iron was worked seems to suggest that this myth was
associated with the physical place long before the
arrival of Rugomora Mahe.

It has been suggested that the Bahinda dynasty may
have chosen the Katuruka site because it was an
ancient shrine and residence that would impart a
legitimacy to the Bahinda through a tie to the past.[19]
This interpretation also captures a process of
accommodation, for residence at Katuruka would also
have been a major concession. It would have
communicated that acknowledgment of local shrines and

gods was necessary to peaceful rule. Regardless of the
concession by the Bahinda, the move also placed the
Bahinda in a subsidiary religious position which was
mediated by Mugasha, the fisherman/god and conveyor
of Chaos/Prosperity, the surpreme mediator. Mugasha's
mediation is so strong that he helps to reestablish
Bahinda power. After reciprocating, Mahe is transformed:

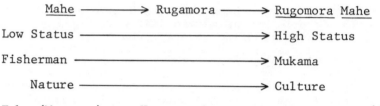

The important aspect of this analysis is that it
focuses attention on Bahinda difficulties in establishing power over local peoples in Kyamutwara. It also
focuses attention on the Katuruka shrine—the symbolic
center of conflict and accommodation between the
Bahinda and indigenous Bacwezi-led peoples. Had it
not been for this mythology, and the subsequent
analysis that led to the delimitation of the Katuruka
gashani, the Katuruka site would not have been recognized as special among scores of other magashani in
Buhaya.[21]

The development of these perspectives was immeasurably
assisted by Augustine Kaindoa, an accomplished oral
tradition historian. His texts about Rugomora Mahe
were much more detailed than those provided by dozens
of other informants. The reason for this is that his
own clan history is intimately related to the affairs
just discussed. He is a Muyango and, consequently,
is more knowledgeable than most Bahaya about the
Bayango relationship to the throne. More importantly,
he is also a Bacwezi spirit medium for the Mucwezi
of Wamara, but through two other Bacwezi spirits,
Kazoba and Ishewanga. As such, he has been invested
with ritual responsibilities to pass on didactic
mythology about the Bacwezi. He is party to the oral
traditions of both the Bayango and Bacwezi. His
perspective employs Bacwezi myth as his fundamental
narrative model, for the model holds structural
principles that are complementary to the Bayango and
the indigenous perspective of Bahinda rule. As an
official keeper of tradition about the Bahinda and
Rugomora Mahe, he operates in both domains, but as a

spirit medium of Wamara, he has a definitely hostile
point of view toward the Bahinda. That bias is
essential for revealing the dynamics of early Bahinda
rule in Kyamutwara. Without the Bacwezi perspective
on history in Buhaya, there is serious doubt that
historians and anthropologists can begin to unravel
early histories and locate important prehistoric
sites. Bacwezi myth and spirit mediumship are the key
elements for writing early Bahaya history.

The shrine that today functions as Rugomora's gashani
is so central to Kyamutwara myth that a visitation to
the site was scheduled to see if neighbors in the
vicinity of the gashani held local folklore about
the history of Rugomora Mahe or his gashani. The
following chapter discusses the results of mythological
investigations into Rugomora Mahe and the archaeological investigations generated by these phenomena.

Notes

[1]Joseph Tegamaisho, 10/11/69, in Maruku-Kizi.

[2]Lugimbana Bandio, 10/10/69, in Maruku-Bukuma.

[3]Bayekela Rusinga, 10/20/69 and 10/21/69, in Maruku-Kakondo.

[4]Hans Cory and M. M. Hartnoll, Cutomary Law of the Haya Tribe (London: International African Institute, 1945), Appendix V, Table 9, footnote 1.

[5]Joseph Tegamaisho, 10/11/69, in Maruku-Kizi.

[6]Jacob Rukebela, 5/3/69, in Muhutwe, Kianja; collected by R. Baguma.

[7]Lugimbana Bandio, 10/10/69, in Maruku-Bukuna.

[8]Bayekela Rusinga, 10/20/69, in Maruku-Kakondo.

[9]Augustine Kaindoa, 10/8/69, in Kanyangereko-Nkimbo.

[10]Ibid., 10/11/69.

[11]Ibid.

[12]Jacob Rukebela, 4/10/69, in Muhutwe, Kianja;

collected by R. Baguma.

[13]Augustine Kaindoa and Paulo Kagasheki, 10/11/69, in Kanyangereko-Nkimbo.

[14]Ibid.

[15]See the text on pp.   in Chapter 5.

[16]Matrilocality is very clear in the case of Rugomora Mahe, for not only is he returning to an area that is the cosmological heartland of the "mother clans" of Buhaya controlled by Kayango, but he also returns to his mother's village, Katuruka. His mother's ihiga or subclan is an indigenous group, as Bayekela Rusinga points out in the Appendix B text (10/22/69). Once in Katuruka, Rugomora Mahe marries into the clan of his mother, the Bankango: "Rugomora Mahe then married his first wife, Mpunga—a Munkango by clan." There is a prescribed rule which prohibits marriage into the clan of one's mother, but Rugomora Mahe's behavior is summed up in the proverb "Ebishanila bilibwa omukama," or, "unedible things are eaten by the Mukama." (Augustine Kaindoa, 10/22/69, in Kanyangereko-Nkimbo). Whatever political alliance may have issued from this "incestuous" marriage did not last, for in the nineteenth century other subclans of the Bankango became the most fierce competitors for the throne and eventually established the separate states of Bugabo and smaller Kyamutwara.

[17]Jacob Rukebela, 5/3/69, in Muhutwe, Kianja.

[18]Edward Kagombona, 4/23/69, in Muhutwe, Kianja.

[19]Robert Jay, personal communication. Professor Jay pointed out that in Java shrines were seized by new dynasties attempting to achieve a tie with the past.

[20]Mahe was known as the "taker" when he stole the walking stick of Mukama Kabula in Igara (Uganda). "The Mukama suspected that Mahe had taken the stick and called him Mutwara (the taker). Kyamutwara is derived from this word and it means to take or steal something. Before the time of Rugomora Mahe the area was known as Bumbuijwa, but only known as Kyamutwara as of Rugomora; Kabula also said that

Mahe's country would be known as Kyamutwara.
Related by Augustine Kaindoa, 10/15/69, in
Kanyangereko-Nkimbo. This text adds further evidence for the consolidation of power and authority
by the Bahinda in Kyamutwara as of Rugomora Mahe's
reign.

7
Oral Tradition and Mnemonic Guides for Archaeological Investigation

During the course of oral tradition research in Buhaya,
I attempted to recognize objects and places used by
the Bahaya as mnemonic devices for oral tradition.
A concrete mnemonic device calls up memory about
virtually any topic of mental image associated with
the mnemonic object. In some cases, the mnemonic is
not an immediate aspect of one's common environment;
then direct reference must be made to the concrete—
be it an object, an incantation, a ritual, or a
song—to call up the associated information. Bahaya
mnemonics assume both forms, but the latter is by far
the easiest to recognize. There is no device among
the Bahaya such as the Inca quipu, which was a series
of knotted cords of different lengths and colors used
to assist memory in oral tradition so that they could
be read as if they were books.

One widespread mnemonic device in Buhaya is the sing-
ing of praise songs or the panegyrics of the Bakama
and Bacwezi. These praise songs, which celebrate the
reigns of the Bakama, are performed to the accompaniment of an enanga (zither). The texts are fixed and
the enanga player may depend on the rhythm of his
instrument as a mnemonic device (see Chapter 4).
This device is widespread but not common, for it was
confined to a select group of enanga experts who in
traditional days spent most of their time in the
Mukama's court playing for his entertainment.

Bahaya mastery of long genealogies and complex
genealogical histories, outside of enanga texts, in
the form of free texts usually is accomplished without
any apparent physical aid. But as one grows accustom-
ed to how the Bahaya relate to their physical

environment and to aspects of their material culture,
it becomes apparent that complex and diverse phenomena
that are ever present in the environment call up
memories of traditions about the past; natural and
man-made features of the landscape are used as
mnemonics. The Bahaya draw on many aspects of their
natural environment as mnemonic devices which are
explicitly tied to folklore, mythology, and political
oral tradition. Fields, cliffs, trees, streams, and
crossroads are among features that have extensive oral
traditions associated with them—ranging from myth
about Bacwezi gods to the origins of villages, many
of which have taken their names from trees. Place
names in Buhaya are very often associated with
historical events, and these names often precipitate
local folklore about the origins of villages. The
former kikale and the gashani of the Bakama are
particularly instrumental in developing stories that
are mentioned only in the presence of the burial site.
Marking trees and other physical structures near the
gashani evoke tale telling. The plentitude and
variability of physical aspects of the environment,
both natural and those modified by man, tied to
mnemonics for oral tradition, are a commentary on the
omnipresence of the past—in myth, folklore, and other
oral tradition—in Bahaya life. These ever-present
mnemonics are essential to an understanding of the
Bahaya world view and historiography.

Most mnemonics are located outside the household and
are usually associated with either Bacwezi or royal
oral tradition. A good case in point for the latter
are the gashani burial estates located in each kingdom.
During investigations of oral tradition in Kiziba,
visits originally were made to the gashani to determine
possibilities of archaeological survey and excavation.
During these visits, it was learned that physical
aspects of the gashani were key sources for further
oral tradition, particularly previously unrelated
folklore and myth about former kings. Those most
familiar with the oral traditions associated with
parts of the sites proved to be caretakers, neighbors,
and embandwa of the former Bakama. If an embandwa
lived near the gashani, his help was sought (not
always successfully), as the embandwa probably are
the people in Buhaya most completely versed in
specific local lore associated with the Mukama or the
Mucwezi by whose spirit they are possessed.

Familiarity with the complexities of gashani estates
as mnemonic objects in Kiziba kingdom prepared me for
the possibility of similar arrangements in Kyamutwara
kingdom. Gashani estates are dispersed throughout each

kingdom and all of Buhaya. They function as mnemonic
objects for tradition relevant to the kingdom in which
they are located, and especially within the neighbor-
hood very close to the gashani. Land adjacent to a
gashani often supports residents who may be descendants
of those who received special appointments and estates
from the former Mukama. As a consequence, the lineage
and clan histories of these people are tied into the
royal histories, and they have a vested interest in
maintaining greater specificity in their oral traditions, especially if their positions are inherited.

After initial recognition that many accounts of the
royal Bahinda genealogy of Kyamutwara had been substantially influenced by mythemes usually related by
Bacwezi spirit mediums, a more thorough inquiry was
begun into the oral tradition surrounding Rugomora
Mahe. Two approaches were used (1) a broader investigation of Kyamutwara genealogy involving more informants, and (2) interviews with Bahaya associated with
or knowledgeable about gashani estates, particularly
with Rugomora Mahe's gashani. The second procedure
concerns us here, for it eventually revealed that the
most elaborate and interconnected set of mnemonic
features (they are devices only in the analytical
sense) thus far recognized in Buhaya are associated
with the history of Rugomora Mahe.

Fortuitously, I lived about half a mile from
Katuruka village in Maruku when I recognized the
mythological nature of Rugomora Mahe's history. Since
the integration of aetiological myths about iron
working was potentially important for any study of
the Iron Age, it was necessary to investigate whether
physical characteristics of the Rugomora Mahe kikale
site functioned as mnemonics for further oral tradition.

The Rugomora Mahe site was first visited with the
brother of the Bahinda clan head in Maruku and then
with a spirit medium or embandwa of the Bacwezi god,
Wamara. Both oral tradition accounts obtained during
these first visits were essentially the same. The
most imposing and obvious physical feature on the
site is a huge, old tree called Kaiija—which means
the place where iron is made. The word supposedly
is derived from Luiija, which is the anvil inside the
small hut in which iron is worked. Measuring 3 x 4
meters at the base, Kaiija tree (see Plate 1) marks
the place where Rugomora Mahe constructed the high
iron tower in order to see above the clouds. During
visits on separate occasions to Kaiija tree, located
on the edge of the former royal compound, the embandwa
and clan head related the iron tower myth with the

following elaboration:

> This is the place where Rugomora Mahe had his
> men make iron to build the high iron tower. One
> of the legs (supports) was located right here
> under Kaiija and another in Nkimbo (a neighboring
> village 1 mile to the southeast). The men who
> were working here, making the iron, were killed
> when the tower finally collapsed and fell as far
> as Katelero. After this Rugomora Mahe didn't try
> to build another tower. Just a few years ago
> there used to be large pieces of iron here under
> Kaiija, but men have taken them away.[1]

The essential aspects of the tradition related at
Kaiija tree are: (1) references to iron production
immediately under Kaiija, (2) the location of the
iron tower support in Nkimbo as well as Katuruka, and
(3) the former presence of iron on the site. These
are components of the basic mytheme only when the
fundamental myth is related in the physical presence
of Kaiija. These more specific oral traditions are
related by those living close to gashani and by other
informants who know the Rugomora Mahe tales and have
visited Mahe's gashani.

A Musaizi clan member whose ancestor had been appointed
to a special position in the king's court resided to
the west of the primary site and related the same myth
and local folklore about Rugomora Mahe. He particularly emphasized the recent presence of iron on the site
but could not say when it was there. This aspect
of the myth was also affirmed by another neighbor,
but no one could document the removal of the iron.

A circle of thorn trees (Figure 1) located in the
center of the royal capital is referred to as the
gashani house area, where the king's jawbone is
buried. The gashani itself is well delimited by
large, old thorn trees among which lush vegetation has
grown. The gashani was not being cared for and had
been in a state of disrepair for some time, according
to local residents. Just to the west of the gashani
was a small clump of marking bushes. When the first
two informants saw this spot, both spontaneously
remarked that it was the burial place for Rugomora
Mahe's body.

It was said that people formerly brought gifts or
offerings for the spirit of Rugomora Mahe to all three
primary structures. These ritual sessions presumably
were guided by the spirit medium who was possessed
by the spirit of the dead Mukama, for ritual life

surrounding the royal spirits was the responsibility
of Bakama embandwa. The real boundaries of the site
extend beyond the presently recognized compound
boundaries, which were used to define the archaeological site.

Just to the southeast of the compound Mzee Augustine
Kaindoa guided us to another physical structure
located next to the entry path to a house (see Figure
1).* It consisted of orange-green (mossy) spots beside the path. Upon seeing it, Mzee Kaindoa said:

> These are the bricks which Rugomora Mahe used
> to build brick houses. After the iron tower fell
> to Katelero-Omungoma, Rugomora Mahe was very
> disappointed, and because of the danger in build-
> ing an iron tower, he began to make bricks. He
> constructed houses from these bricks. Sometimes
> people dig them up in their shambas, so he must
> have built them many places.[2]

This specific folklore had not been previously
collected, even during Mzee Kaindoa's and others'
discussions of Rugomora Mahe. My interest in this
phenomenon and its associated tradition led Mzee
Kaindoa to go to Mugasha's place near the kikale.
There, at a small fenced-off plot at a crossroads,
Mzee Kaindoa pointed out a large laterite rock beside
the path. He then related how Mugasha had made an
oblong impression after stepping on the rock (see
Plate 2) while visiting Rugomora Mahe after the Mukama
had established himself at Katuruka. Mzee Kaindoa
also pointed to the adjacent fenced-off area (see
Plate 3) and said that the area was maintained as a
special place, and that it was the location of the
house that Rugomora Mahe built for Mugasha during
the latter's stay at the kikale. The rock was turned
over and a foot-shaped depression could be observed
on the underside. The sight of the foot-shaped
depression precipitated the following previously un-
recorded tale:

> There was much lightning in Katuruka. Rugomora
> Mahe feared it very much, so he sent to Mugasha
> to ask for medicine against it. But Mugasha
> told Rugomora Mahe's people that it was necessary
> that Rugomora Mahe send a man to learn how to
> stop the lightning. Rugomora Mahe then sent a
> man who was taught by Mugasha how to kill Nkuba
> birds [this is also a word denoting lightning].
> This was done; all the large Nkuba birds were

*Mzee is a term of respect used for those who are
one's elder, particularly men.

then killed to prevent lightning. Mugasha told
the man sent by Rugomora Mahe that he (Mugasha)
would come to visit Rugomora Mahe. When Mugasha
came, he stopped at Rugege before going on to
Katuruka. He stopped outside the kikale, right
where this rock is with his footprint on it. Rugomora Mahe informed Mugasha that there was no
water in Katuruka, and Mugasha was annoyed to
hear that his friend had not told him this before.
Mugasha said, "Tomorrow I will go home, but you
will have water in this village." The next
morning much water was seen at Kyakairabwa, so
much that Rugomora Mahe feared flooding of his
kikale. He sent a message to Mugasha about this,
and Mugasha gave the messengers a piece of
Omuramura tree which, he explained, should be
planted at the edge of the water to stop it.
After the Omuramura tree was planted, the water
receded to a good level. The creek into which
the water flowed was named Katanabwa by Rugomora
Mahe; thereafter he prevented all people from
bathing in this water.[3]

This elaborate mythology suggests a complex system
of mnemonic devices, all of which are interrelated
in subject matter but discrete as functional agents
in calling up specific oral traditions. The only
case in which there is a functional link between
mnemonics is between the fenced-off area delimiting
the house site where Mugasha stayed while visiting
Rugomora Mahe and the "foot-impressed" rock. The
mental image associated with the tradition probably
includes both objects, since they are separated by
only a small path (see Plates 2 and 3).

In all, four sets of primary mnemonics are associated
with the Rugomora Mahe kikale site: (1) the gashani
area, (2) Kaiija tree, (3) the pile of orange bricks,
and (4) the "foot-impressed" rock and fenced-off area
associated with Mugasha. Each of these mnemonic sets
precipitated separate but related traditions. An
encounter with one did not necessitate use of another.
While the fourth set closely followed the third, this
may have been as a result of its location on the path
intermediate between the kikale and the brick pile,
passed during our return to the kikale.

In Africa, characteristics of the landscape, either
man-made or natural, are commonly used as a mnemonic
device.[4] Vansina points out that these phenomena
frequently give rise to local legends which sometimes
seek to explain the origins of the phenomenon.[5]
Vansina cites a Kuba example in which a circular

depression in the plain of Iyool is said to have its
origin when, at the end of hostilities centered around
the throne, people danced with such exuberance that the
ground sank.[6] This kind of tale is aetiological, as
it seeks to explain the origin of a natural or cultural phenomenon.

The mnemonic devices located in and near Rugomora
Mahe's kikale are associated with both man-made and
natural phenomena. Both types are associated with what
I call aetiological-technological myth, a rubric that
will be used to denote myth which seeks to explain
technological phenomena. But exclusively natural
phenomena summon up aetiological myth without
technological themes, such as the myth associated
with the "foot-impressed" rock. Finally, there are
two places, the gashani area and the fenced-off
area of Mugasha's house, where man-made places evoke
myths that elaborate and even introduce new themes
into previously related myths about Rugomora Mahe.

The complexities of the mnemonic devices associated
with oral tradition about Rugomora Mahe can be
explicated by a simple categorization suggested by
the above discussion:

  (1) man-made and maintained features: gashani
      and fenced-off area for Mugasha's house.

  (2) natural objects: Kaiija tree and the "foot-
      impressed" rock.

  (3) possible man-made features: the pile of orange
      "bricks."[7]

The first category is the most explicit and has the
most straightforward function, a device that assists
in elaborating previously independently related myth.
The fenced-off area delimiting Mugasha's house is
functionally ambiguous in this regard, as it is tied
closely to the rock, which precipitates a mythological
tale that is not an elaboration but an entirely new
corpus of myth associated with Rugomora Mahe. A finer
analytical division of these mnemonics would have to
maintain that there are elaborating and supplementing
aspects of man-made mnemonics.

The only mnemonic device that is unequivocally
aetiological is the "foot-impressed" rock, which is
indented because the god Mugasha put his foot upon it.
Its location adjacent to the fenced-off area suggests
that it is an integral part of the Mugasha myth and
that it focuses attention on a second but related

device, the fenced-off area of Mugasha's house.

Myth associated with Kaiija tree, a natural object,
is included under the rubric aetiological-technological
myth, which in this case is a myth that attempts to
explain a cultural phenomenon, iron technology.
Local legend, not myth, relates that there were once
large blocks of iron under Kaiija tree, though these
are not present today. It may be that the origins
of the mytheme about the iron tower are tied to the
pieces of iron and slag which people say once rested
beneath Kaiija, and that the myth was partly
aetiological in that it explained why large pieces
of iron were present at that place. However, local
folklore evoked by Kaiija also claims that Rugomora
Mahe's men smelted iron beneath the tree. Later
excavations of this area confirmed the presence
of iron working—exactly where local folklore said
such activity was carried out. The Kaiija tree device,
then, evokes aetiological-technological myth designed
to explain the cultural phenomenon of iron production.

The man-made or natural properties of the brick pile
were impossible to determine without excavation.
The brick pile was located adjacent to a footpath
and household farm. The local head of household informed me that he had always exercised great care
during cultivation to make certain that he did not
disturb the bricks. Excavation of the features did
not reveal that the bricks were used for house
building, the function suggested by the myth, but that
they belonged to an Early Iron Age iron-smelting
furnace (see Plate 4). Unlike the Kaiija tree
device, the brick pile summoned up myth and local
folklore that were functionally unrelated to its
prehistoric function. It is important to note,
however, that the brick pile device is aetiological-
technological, for it seeks to explain one technological phenomenon—houses of brick—while it was the
physical remains of another aspect of technological
life, iron smelting.

It is difficult to say what may have caused the
transformation of functional explanation in the myth
associated with the brick pile. It is possible to
speculate that Bahaya familiarity with European brick
making came to be a more accepted explanation for a
phenomenon that had its origins far into prehistoric
times. With regard to the brick pile device, it is
important to emphasize that, like the Kaiija tree
device, it is related to iron production.

The mnemonic devices associated with the kikale of

Rugomora Mahe are complex and overlapping. They are
functionally elaborating, substitutive, aetiological,
and aetiological-technological (in both functionally
direct and transformed states). The dynamics of
mythology and local legends about Rugomora Mahe would
have gone unnoticed if it had not been for physical
visits to the mnemonics. The fact that I worked at
the kikale site for two months before being introduced
to the Mugasha rock and house area is a poignant
commentary on the subtledty of some mnemonics and the
necessity for developing a thorough familiarity with
the natural-mythological environment. This latter
recognition led to a further exploration of other
physical places associated with myth about Rugomora
Mahe. As time was a limiting consideration, survey
for other mnemonics was restricted to Kyamutwara
and Maruku kingdoms, where Rugomora Mahe traveled
during his return journey through Buhaya.

Rugomora's route through Buhaya was retraced from
Bukoba town southward, with special attention paid to
physical places attached to his mythology (Figure 2).
During this journey, I was accompanied by two Bahaya
conversant in the oral tradition of Rugomora Mahe.[8]
During the course of this two-day trek, some physical
objects were encountered which functioned as mnemonics.
The journey started south of Bukoba at Kibuye village
(where Rugomora Mahe found iron workers who refused
to acknowledge him, and then changed their name to
Bahuge or "the forgetful ones") and passed on to
Iruhurura and Kyansozi near what is today Rubale
Forest. While in this area, Rugomora Mahe gave cowries (ensimbi) to the Bahimba in the forest; this is
a place for offerings to wild animals, but we were
unable to locate it. From there, according to oral
tradition, Rugomora Mahe traveled to Luiija,where he
planted a tree called Karongo at Maruku-Nkaraba
(Figure 2 and Plate 5). This tree appears to have a
relatively limited mnemonic function. Mzee Kaindoa,
when he saw it, said that Rugomora Mahe had not planted
it himself but had given it to people of the Basingo
clan to plant in the farm of a Musingo.[9] The farm
where Karongo tree stands is today owned by one of
the two Bahaya previously mentioned—the Muhinda
elder.

From Maruku the journey was continued by using a text
previously provided by one of the informants:

> Rugomora Mahe then passed on the Rugege (to
> the east of Maruku), on to Lwamuyonga, crossed
> Kigona stream to Ibaijo (near L. Victoria),
> where he sent some ensimbi to Kyema Forest (to

> appease the leopards), and then passed on to
> Byabumba Isikira. The next morning Rugomora
> Mahe passed through (the village) to a nearby
> field, where he sowed the seeds from Isheshe—
> seeds for trees called Emizinda and Emicwezi.[10]

We passed through this latter village, crossed a
clearing, and came to two gnarled trees at the edge
of a forest. The two trees referred to in the text,
Emizinda and Emicwezi, are mnemonics in this instance,
as this tradition was related only in the presence of
the trees, which appear to have derived their names
from Bahinda and Bacwezi. At the two trees, Mzee
Kaindoa, with Mzee Rusinga's concurrence, said:

> "When I settle, come here and cultivate and then
> many trees will grow to become a forest called
> Ilemera." At this place Rugomora Mahe told a
> Musita that he would be guardian of Ilemera
> Forest. He instructed him, "No one will cut a
> tree in this forest." Then Rugomora also
> appointed a Muhinda as a guardian and said, "If
> a Musita cuts a tree in this forest, the Muhinda
> will tell me; if a Muhinda cuts a tree in this
> forest, the Musita will tell me."[11]

After Ilemera, Rugomora Mahe moved on through Kakoko
to Kazi, which today is a large uninhabited area.
There in the midst of a field, "Rugomora Mahe took a
stone, sat on it, and announced, 'This is my chair
where I will sit.'" This is neither a significant
tale nor an essential part of the whole myth. The
mnemonic object itself is a small white rock set
upon a buried boulder.[12] But the Bahaya have not the
slightest doubt that it is the rock upon which Rugomora
Mahe sat. Its presence gives the area its name and
explains why the stone has not been removed for
house construction. Kazi generally is known as the
place where Rugomora Mahe sat and rested, though in all
collected versions of oral tradition, this aspect was
omitted. According to another text,

> Rugomora Mahe then moved on to Kyemizinga [not
> specifically located] and to Omulutunga Iwa
> Mukara, where he called together all the drums
> to announce his presence. [No mnemonics were
> found at these places.] Then Rugomora Mahe
> continued on the Byamawa Kashoro-Burambizi where
> he built his first kikale. There is a tree called
> Byakashoro marking the site.[13]

No sign of the location of the alleged first kikale
itself exists, but there is a small woods where, it is

claimed, Rugomora Mahe had his first kikale. The area
may be uncultivated today because of its association
with Rugomora Mahe. Byakashora tree may be a functional mnemonic among local people and needs further
investigation. The above account is but one version
of the places where Rugomora Mahe passed through on
his way to Katuruka.

The primary mnemonics associated with the southerly
portion of Rugomora Mahe's journey were determined
through our journey over the same terrain. However,
I visited two other places in Maruku which are
associated with Rugomora Mahe myth. The first was
Kya Rugomora tree in Nkimbo village, about 1 mile
to the southeast of Katuruka (Figure 3). The place
had been mentioned in discussions about Kaiija tree
and the iron working that occurred there. A visit to
Kya Rugomora revealed the tradition that "at this
place men who worked for Rugomora Mahe made iron bars
to make the iron tower,"[14] and that "one of the legs
of the iron tower which Rugomora Mahe built was at
this place, where men made iron."[15] This tradition
certainly is called up by the mnemonic, Kya Rugomora
tree, for in the one case in which similar tradition
was obtained, it was associated with reference to Kya
Rugomora. This is a case of a double-image mnemonic,
where reference to one mnemonic, such as Kaiija, calls
up the other mnemonic, or vice versa—in the case of
this one informant.

The final spot to be visited was Rugege, to the east
of Maruku, through which Rugomora passed on his journey but which is known as the place where Mugasha
stopped after being summoned by Rugomora Mahe about
stopping lightning. There is a large tree at Rugege
(Figure 3), which supposedly marks the spot where
Mugasha stayed. The function of Rugege tree as a
mnemonic is ambiguous, as the same myth was provided
here as when the "foot-impressed" rock was encountered.
The ambiguity about Rugege tree is compounded because
I had to ask specifically if any traditions were
associated with it. Further work is necessary to test
the viability of Rugege as a mnemonic, but it, too,
may be a double-image mnemonic.

Mnemonic devices for oral tradition in Buhaya are
complex sets of interrelated physical and cosmological
phenomena. Shrines to Bacwezi gods, magashani,
technological phenomena, and natural phenomena are a
few objects directly associated with a small sample
of Bahaya oral tradition—the life of Rugomora Mahe.
The Bahaya conceptualization of the past is woven into
their perception of their everyday surroundings. The

Bahaya interaction with their natural and man-made
environment is made up of complex images of physical
objects, such as trees or brick piles, which through
processes of training in oral tradition are associated
with historical explanations for change in the past.
A Muhaya trained in oral tradition and mnemonics
virtually is able to read his culture history by
viewing his contemporary physical environment. So in
fact, the past was preserved by reverence for sacred
places such as shrines that are respected now because
they belong to the past, and not for religious reasons.
The continued presence of mnemonics confirms that
mythology is ubiquitous and functional in some Bahaya
lives.

In precolonial times, much of the training in oral
tradition was a byproduct of didactic myth related
by embandwa during Bacwezi possession sessions. As
an integral part of religious life, sacred mythology
associated with physical places, such as shrines, was
an omnipresent influence in the lives of the Bahaya.
Today, those who are embandwa maintain the most complete link with the past because of their intimate
familiarity with and dependence on mythology. Embandwa
are those Bahaya who most intimately know the
complexities of mnemonics and their linkages to oral
tradition. As a consequence, embandwa are an essential
functional link between the past and present.

Today shrines are not maintained, but then again,
they are not destroyed. Oral tradition is rarely
passed on through embandwa during religious ritual,
as the possession cult is essentially dysfunctional.
But mythology associated with former religious
shrines or other objects continues to be actively
related through embandwa in a nonritual context, via
mnemonic devices.

The physical presence of mnemonic devices, which are
tied so closely to traditional religious life, make
up an important part of the Bahaya cosmology. Bahaya
cosmology in traditional times integrated the past
with the present and, consequently, allowed an
explanation of rapid culture change, especially in
technology, to be drawn from mythological motifs.
As the concrete world changes and as culture changes,
the mythology can be transformed to account for
change. Witness the change in the brick pile mnemonic
from an iron-working function (the real function) to a
brick house-building function. As the physical landscape changes in Buhaya, concomitant changes will
undoubtedly occur in Bahaya cosmology, which is tied
to change in the habitat. Thus far, many mnemonic

devices have remained undisturbed. This may in part account for the strong Bahaya love for ancient stories and traditional material culture, such as the old grass and bamboo houses, in the face of incredible change in their religious, economic, and political life.

The fact that the Buhaya landscape is a collage of mythology, folklore, and local legends of untold permutations may ultimately prove to be a guide for further work in studying prehistoric settlement patterns. It is apparent that some geographic locales have a much heavier density of physical objects and places associated with oral tradition. These areas also are those in which surface survey has revealed the heaviest density of Early Iron Age sites. It may be that a mnemonic density index might be an important key for judging the geographical extent of prehistoric settlement as well as the time depth of interaction with the immediate environment.

Notes

[1]Bayekela Rusinga, 12/2/69 and 1/7/70; Augustine
Kaindoa, 11/21/69 and 1/5/70; Lugimbana Bandio,
1/7/70.

[2]Augustine Kaindoa, 4/13/70.

[3]Ibid. In a prior text, Mzee Kaindoa referred to
lightning but in an extremely shortened version,
viz.: "During these times lightning was killing many
people, so Rugomora told people to kill Nkuba birds,
which people thought caused the lightning. The
people killed all these birds, and lightning stopped
killing people—for Rugomora had learned while at
Mugasha's that the birds were the source of trouble."
Related 10/22/69. A text similar to this one in
content and structure was being related by Mzee
Kaindoa on 7/30/70 (see Appendix A), when, at the
end of his first sentence, an observer pointed out
that Mzee Kaindoa had previously related a similar
story at the brick pile in Katuruka. As a result,
Mzee Kaindoa began again and related the same text
given at the brick pile. That part of the text has
been excluded from the Apprndix A narrative as it
was unfortunately influenced by mention of the
mnemonic. Given the form of its beginning, it would
have resembled the above text.

[4]I. Cunnison, History of the Luapula. An Essay on
the Historical Notions of a Central African Tribe
(Lusaka: Rhodes-Livingstone Papers, 1951).

[5]Jan Vansina, Oral Tradition: A Study in Historical

Methodology (Chicago: Aldine, 1965), p. 158.

[6]Ibid.

[7]These are etic categories that have been created as an analytical device; as such, they do not necessarily bear any resemblance to culturally bound emic categories.

[8]Day one, 9/10/70, was spent with Mzee Augustine Kaindoa and day two, 9/11/70, was spent with Mzee Bayekela Rusinga (A.M.) and Mzee Kaindoa (A.M. and P.M.).

[9]Mzee Kaindoa, 9/10/70.

[10]This is an edited version of the text in Appendix A; provided by Mzee Kaindoa, 7/29/70, in Bukoba.

[11]Augustine Kaindoa and Bayekela Rusinga, 9/11/70. Thus far, not enough evidence exists to claim that these are exclusive mnemonics. Further investigations may show, for example, that variability exists to the extent that specific requests for further information about such places may lead to the recitation of similar texts.

[12]While Kazi stone functioned as a mnemonic at its physical location, the story associated with it is also provided in free texts. See Appendix A for an example. However, it is also the case that only those informants familiar with such mnemonics include associated tales in their overall texts.

[13]Johana Kaga Kubetera, 10/30/69.

[14]Bayekela Rusinga, 9/11/70.

[15]Augustine Kaindoa, 9/11/70.

Plate I: Kaiija tree, at the *Gashani* of
Rugamora Mahe.

Plate II: Mugasha's foot-impressed rock: southeast of *Gashani* compound of Rugamora Mahe.

Plate III: Fenced-off area of Mugasha's house adjacent to foot-impressed rock.

Plate IV: Alleged "house bricks" beside path; archaeologically documented as an iron smelting furnace.

Plate V: Korongo tree in Maruku-Nkaraba village; a magical tree given to Rugamora Mahe and later planted by the Basingo clan.

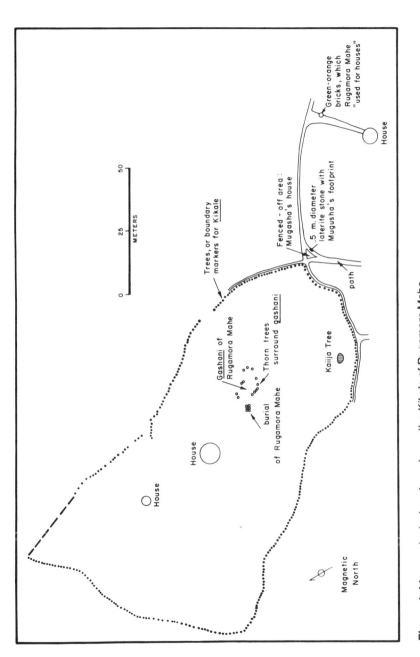

Figure 1: Mnemonic devices in and near the *Kikale* of Rugamora Mahe,
Katuruka Village, Maruku Kingdom.

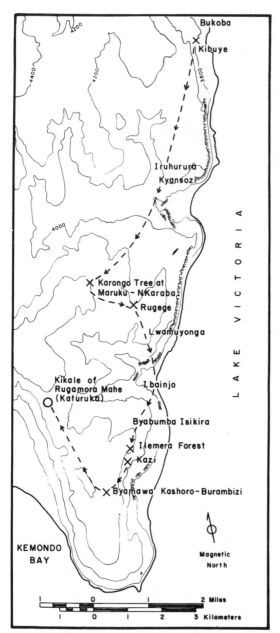

Figure 2: Major place names associated with mythical southern route of Rugamora Mahe; points marked with an x located by reconstructed journey. Other names denote general areas or villages.

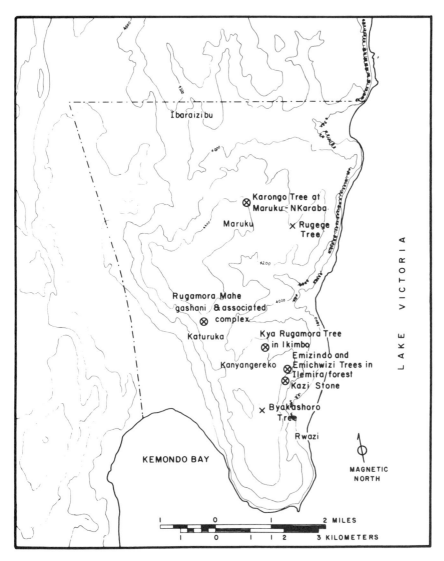

Figure 3: Mnemonic devices in Maruku
Kingdom associated with Rugamora
Mahe oral tradition.
⊗denotes definite device
X denotes probable devices
   other place names are major villages

8

Methodology and Excavation Strategy

The magashani estates of dead Bakama were essential to
Bahaya religious life before European colonization
of the region. They were foci of religious life,
and the embandwa of the dead king often lived near
the gashani or in the area that once held the kikale.
Offerings to appease the spirit of the dead Mukama,
when an embandwa was being consulted, were sometimes
brought to the gashani of the Mukama. Whatever
ritual life was associated with the gashani has now
disappeared. Those spirit mediums who once lived in
the proximity of the gashani have either died, moved
away, or converted to Christianity. Those who have
converted and who have given up their regalia to church
officials are extremely reluctant to discuss their
former livelihood. The disinclination to refer to
spirit mediumship also means noninterference with
archaeological investigation of such sites. To
interfere would be a virtual admission of adherence
to pagan ways or, even worse, to the practices of a
spirit medium, which in the minds of many is now
associated with sorcery.

As a consequence of religious and social change, the
magashani and other places of former ritual importance
have fallen into a state of disrepair. However, the
general poor condition of most magashani does not
diminish their ritual importance to all Bahaya. It
is still in the interests of kings, for instance, to
protect the gashani from depredation, though not
always disintegration. The state of disrepair is
manifest at the gashani of Wanumi in Kiziba. Wanumi's
gashani was particularly well maintained until recently,
a condition that may have been related to Wanumi's
difficulties with local Bacwezi spirit mediums and the

symbolic value of his defeat by a Bacwezi spirit.
When I lived near Kigarama village, Wanumi's gashani
house had collapsed and people openly warned me that
it was treacherous business to visit it, and especially
to enter it, as Wanumi's spirit would obviously be
displeased and might possess anyone who entered. One
does not ignore this explicit advice. The Mukama of
Kiziba made no apparent effort to maintain the
magashani of Kiziba. At the same time, the Mukama
could not be party to any willful destruction of a
gashani. Sentiment for preservation is not strong,
but many Bahaya are keenly aware that magashani are
essential historical documents with mnemonic functions.
F. X. Lwamgira captured this sentiment when he wrote
in the introduction to Amakuru ga Kiziba.

> . . . though our grandfathers never wrote on
> paper, they still were using some signs for
> remembrance. The signs were taught to their
> descendants so that the signs would not be for-
> gotten.
>
> It is then a shameful act to destroy completely,
> say, the worshipping places. I don't suggest
> that you should go to worship or offer sacrifices
> in the gashani, but I mean that you should see
> them as important documents or relics—they act
> as papers bearing special writings of our
> country—and that whoever would destroy them
> would be destroying the origins of all clans
> of all countries.

The former Mukama of Kiziba, Nestor Lutinwa, was
unreceptive to the idea of excavation of magashani,
for he was invested with responsibility for their
preservation. Even though he did not actively execute
this responsibility, he could not support any activity
that might alter the character of a gashani. He made
this position clear through his representative.
Thereafter, archaeological activities were limited
to salvage-preservation operations, such as the
recovery of the royal regalia of Mukama Burungu I
of Kiziba from a collapsed and buried house. These
activities, because of their preservative nature,
were warmly supported by the Mukama.

The Kiziba experience demonstrated that access to the
domain chosen for archaeological investigation, the
gashani of Rugomora Mahe in Katuruka, might be
particularly difficult. If excavation rights were
successfully obtained, then the actual excavation
might create significant problems. If the Bahaya
opposed excavations, the research plan would be dis-

carded for a less sensitive alternative.

Study of the oral tradition of Greater Kyamutwara
continued during October-December 1969. It was during
this time that contacts were established with those
whose influence and kinship affiliations in Maruku
kingdom might help obtain permission for excavation.
As I had been working with several informants from
commoner clans, one of whom was a spirit medium,
it was necessary to gain the perspective of the royal,
family. The newly established, though
uninstalled, Mukama Kahigi was a great help in developing contacts who were knowledgeable in the oral tradition of Greater Kyamutwara and who also had ties to
the throne of Maruku.

Many people had already recommended Mzee Rusinga
of the Bahinda clan (see Appendix B for his account
and Chapter 6 for his other contributions); Kahigi's
recommendation of one of his chief advisors gave the
relationship an official seal of approval. So, too,
my friendship with Mwami Lugimbana Bandio, who was a
chief during the British colonial administration and
who was highly respected in the area, proved to be
essential in preparing the way for excavations of
Rugomora Mahe's gashani. I was particularly fortunate
to have these men as informants and as sympathetic
supporters. Mzee Rusinga's position as a mulangira
and omugurusi of the Bahinda clan opened up a
particularly important avenue of influence.

From the outset, interest in excavating the gashani
was made clear, as was the fact that I had yet to
learn the history of Kyamutwara. Both men were
intrigued by the idea and were eager to see what would
come of excavations. During the month of January,
when arrangements were made for excavations, Mzee
Lugimbana Bandio and Mzee Rusinga offered their good
offices and were the central negotiators for excavation
permission. The Mukama concurred.

Much of the Rugomora Mahe gashani was covered with
dense vegetation, especially the thorn-tree enclosure
delimiting the gashani house. These areas were
cleared of dense vegetation, but much of the site was
covered by grass, banana trees, and vines. The first
stage of the investigation, a comprehensive surface
collection of the site, was clearly impossible, given
the dense vegetation. As a consequence, the surface
collection program was changed from a grid program to
a compass survey working from a central point with
transects laid out at 45° intervals (see Figure 1).

The center point was the alleged burial place of
Rugomora's body—the area west of the gashani house.
The horizontal control used was a dog-leash procedure;
a collection radius of 4.5 meters was employed on the
north-south and east-west axes at an initial interval
of 12 meters and thereafter at 24 meter intervals. The
intervals for collection proveniences on the remaining
axes were 24 meters, until the outer limits of the site
were reached. This collection approach allowed quick
penetration of the vegetation before an established
grid, while at the same time it guaranteed reasonable
area sampling and a controlled collection. The bias
created by the clustering of collection units around
the center point on the north-south and east-west
axes was purposeful.

The original purpose in coming to the palace of
Rugomora Mahe in Katuruka was to attempt to link oral
tradition with archaeological remains. The location
for the center point of survey was adjacent to two
important mnemonic devices. The use of oral tradition
for recognizing the site's importance to the Bacwezi
and to the Bahinda and for recognizing its potential
archaeological importance is itself a highly directed,
biased phenomenon. The survey strategy, then, chose
to complement the physical placement of mnemonics
and the content of oral tradition. Much of the remaining discussion of strategy on this site will relate
how archaeological decisions were made as increasing
correlations were observed between the structure of
the oral traditions and that of the prehistoric
cultural materials.

Even with an hour of collection time within each
provenience unit, the results of the survey failed
to reveal any apparently significant information about
the internal structure of the site, which suggested
in turn that a gridded survey was a difficult investment for a relatively small return. One of the original goals of the research was to see if controlled
sampling (Binford, 1964) would yield data that would
help describe the below-ground structure of the site.
The guiding assumption was that the density, distribution, and spatial relations of certain types of
cultural items would provide the archaeologist with
tentative notions about different economic and social
activities, which could then be tested for by excavation (Struever, 1968:143). It became apparent that
the above mnemonic devices and known ritual areas
were the cultural items more related spatially to
below-ground evidence.

The Rugomora Mahe site demonstrated that conducting

surface collections without previous familiarity with
artifact populations in a region is at best a difficult
procedure. It was discovered that surface artifacts
such as cowries are markers for and correlates of
below-ground archaeological structures and technological
activities that are functionally and temporally very
different from the above-ground markers. However,
once congruence of both is understood, the procedure
can be employed on other sites that demonstrate the
same surface characteristics. The end result is a much
more comprehensive excavation strategy.

A collateral goal of the surface collections phase was
the isolation of an Early Iron Age component. The
results were meager. An upper rim (undecorated because
of weathering), with a double bevel from a small
globular necked pot (clearly common attributes of
Early Iron Age ware known as Urewe or "Dimple-based"),
was discovered at 24 meters on the 160° transect, and
an upper and lower rim of a globular, necked pot with
incised hatching was collected along with two plain
Early Iron Age sherds on the 70° transect at 24 meters.
In the latter case, the collection provenience was
located on the entrance way to the house on the site;
the area was then under deep hoe cultivation and excavation was impossible. (The former area will be
discussed with test excavations.)

The very presence of Early Iron Age ceramics on the
site confirmed that an heretofore unstated hypothesis
that the oral tradition about Rugomora Mahe was about
an early cultural period (of the Iron Age) was in fact
now a testable hypothesis. This was a major development that called for test excavations.

One of the major goals of this study from its inception
has been to make explicit inferences or untested
assumptions as well as to reveal how and why propositions are formulated. This means an explication of
inductive processes as an integral part of any
reconstructed logic. Unfortunately, recent attacks
in archaeological thinking on inductive thought has
not only led to the sometimes mistaken idea that there
is only one correct approach to scientific inquiry
in archaeology, but it has also led to the submerged
discussion about processes of discovery in archaeology.
The processes of scientific discovery, which ultimately
may be guided by a logical positivist format, are
particularly complex in the Buhaya investigations.
Most insights are generated from Bahaya culture and
are distinctively inductive.

The following summary discussion on methodology
provides a reconstructed logic, which will allow an
assessment of the origins of assumptions and a
consideration of the logics of inquiry and justification. A reconstructed logic, it should be cautioned,
is only an idealized version of the logic-in-use
and should be considered only as a suggested model
about the utility of an inductive-deductive approach
in this given case study.

The aim of explicitness in this context is the reconstruction of logic used in discovery and proof,
which will lead to an increased understanding of the
entire process of scientific inquiry—not only the
end results or justification. The basic assumption
in this endeavor is that a more comprehensive study
of the scientific process will lead to the formulation of more significant problems and to more inclu-
sive explanations from archaeological data.

Previous attempts by archaeologists to tie Bacwezi
myth, which is pre-Babito in "dynastic" sequence, with
archaeological remains are suggestive, but they do
not adequately discuss the characteristics of myth
allegedly related to sites such as Bigo (Posnansky,
1966, 1969) and Ntusi in Uganda (Lanning, 1970). Both
Posnansky and Lanning fail to inspire confidence in
their interpretations that archaeology confirms
Bacwezi occupation at Bigo or Ntusi because of their
vague and unsystematic analysis of the myth. They
do not provide texts, nor do they analyze the myth
that supposedly has guided their research. While
in the field, I had not yet developed a critical
perspective on Posnansky's use of myth in his claim
that Bigo and its Bacwezi myth dated to a time period
preceding the Babito dynasties. The Posnansky position,
therefore, was an important germ and an essential
stimulus in the development of my own inquiry.

As the wealth of Bacwezi myth in Buhaya came to be
recognized, a simple association was made between
two sets of data: (1) Posnansky's claim about the
antiquity of Bacwezi myth in Bunyoro, and (2) extensive
Bahaya myth about the Bacwezi. It was generalized
inductively that Buhaya might be an area of early
settlement for "Bacwezi communities" and that Bacwezi
mythology symbolically discussed indigenous, predynastic peoples the descendants of whom later presented their political case—in fact, the case of
their ancestors—against the Babito and Bahinda via
spirit mediums.

As we have seen, the later recognition of Mugasha

mythemes in the Kyamutwara royal genealogy immediately
led to a closer analysis of the mythemes. Rugomora
Mahe's construction of a large iron tower seemed to
be a symbolic commentary on the impact of iron technology on Bahaya culture. After the collection of
oral tradition, the variable stimuli that had impinged
upon me during the previous months appeared to converge
gradually. The methodology devised was to draw on
all of these data and to see if they could be so
ordered that they might lead to a greater comprehension of their obvious interactive quality.

The previous Posnansky investigations, widespread
Bacwezi myth in Buhaya, the opposition of Bacwezi
spirit mediums to the royal dynasties, the inclusion
of myth about Mugasha in royal genealogy, and the
occurrence of myth that appeared to be symbolic discussions of the impact of iron on Bahaya culture led
me to Rugomora Mahe's gashani. There, local folklore
repeated and affirmed the mythology about Rugomora
Mahe and delimited "mythological" activities on the
site. Since myth and folklore were tied to concrete
places on the ground, a hypothetico-deductive proposition was formulated which had its origins in the previous ten months' work: a progression from intuition
to inductive positions that could not be tested but
that were influential in guiding my inquiry toward
the Rugomora Mahe site. The methodology included the
combination of inductive generalizations:

>   (1)   Bigo and its Bacwezi myths, plus the
>   archaeological dating of Bigo to an early
>   period, led to the inductive generalization
>   that Bacwezi myth is about a prehistoric
>   period.

This inductive position allowed the formulation of the
next position:

>   (2)   Bacwezi myth is associated with Rugomora
>   Mahe; thus, the history of Rugomora Mahe may
>   be ancient mythology of a special kind. This
>   assumption is based on mythological evi-
>   dence—the fact that the Rugomora Mahe myth
>   has an identical structure to parts of
>   Bacwezi myth.

The content of the mythology itself suggested yet
another inductively derived generalization:

>   (3)   The possible antiquity of Bacwezi myth, when
>   combined with aetiological myth about a
>   technological phenomenon such as an iron

>tower and with similar local myth and folk-
>lore tied to the Rugomora Mahe royal capital
>site, suggested that the iron technology
>discussed in myths and folklore at the site
>was ancient.

The germ for a testable hypothetico-deductive statement
is held in the last generalization. It needed reformu-
lation into proper hypothetico-deductive form and then
testing by archaeological means. The process of inquiry to this point was a series of inductive generalizations, all of which were interlinked and drew upon
empirical information, both archaeological and ethnographic. In this instance, the interactive process
and feedback between archaeological and ethnographic
data demonstrate how the archaeologist/anthropologist
can use a broad variety of information to come to
testable propositions in archaeology.

The hypothesis formulated out of this complex web of
inductive positions was: If the Bacwezi myth and
aetiological myth tied to the Rugomora site are ancient,
then the parts of the Rugomora site mentioned in myth
and folklore predate the Late Iron Age. Before excavations were started in order to test the proposition, intuition said if there were an early occupation
of the site tied to myth, then probably it would be
Early Iron Age, which at that time had been dated in
East Africa to about A.D. 200-1200. Confirmation of
the intuitive position during survey allowed formulation of the above hypothesis.

Negotiations for obtaining permission for excavation
started in late December, and by the first week in
January 1970 the woman whose son had caretaking rights
to the site had agreed to excavation. The grid system
was started with the datum point located at the base
of Kaiija tree.

The first goal in the test excavations was to see
whether there were prehistoric cultural materials which
were in some way associated with the Rugomora Mahe
myth. Consequently, two systematic or arbitrarily
placed tests were carried out in the gashani house
area enclosed by thorn trees (see tests 100 and 200
in Area 1, Figure 2) after another vertical datum (B)
was established in this area.

Within a week after test excavations at the Rugomora
site began, Early Iron Age pit features and midden
were discovered and defined. The hypothesis was
confirmed, but functionally it was only a heuristic
device for limited inquiry or, in fact, a working

hypothesis confined to one site. It either had to be
modified, or a corollary hypothesis had to be proposed
to include myth and iron technology mentioned in the
third generalization above. While excavation was in
progress, the following adjunct working hypothesis was
formulated, which drew from the results of the first:
If the Rugomora Mahe site associated with Bacwezi myth
is an Early Iron Age occupation, then the aetiological
myths about iron technology that are woven into the
other myths are tied to Early Iron Age iron production.

This later working hypothesis was tested during test
excavations and block excavations. In each case,
it was confirmed where folklore and myth related
directly to the site. Out of more than sixty pit
features on the site, all of the structures that can
be tentatively interpreted as associated with iron
production are Early Iron Age. The following discussions illustrate the testing of the above hypothesis.
The next step in the methodology will be discussed
in Chapter 11.

The first test of the above hypothesis was to determine
whether there was a relationship between the iron
tower mytheme and the prehistoric remains beneath
Kaiija tree. Consequently, three test pits were placed
beneath Kaiija tree (see tests 9000, 9100, and 9200 in
Area 6, Figure 2). Three days later, a heavy concentration of charcoal was found at about -90 centimeters in
test pit 9100. It was possible to define a circular
area with black soil, much charcoal, pieces of slag,
and Early Iron Age pottery. Excavation of the char-
coal-laden feature in test 9100 under Kaiija tree
continued and revealed that the associated Early Iron
Age pottery definitely dated it. The heavy densities
of slag, charcoal, and tuyères suggested a possible
function associated with iron production—either
smelting or forging. The significant aspect of this
discovery was that three informants had stood precisely
where test 9100 was placed and related the iron tower
myth; they had also claimed that Rugomora Mahe had his
smiths produce iron at that very place beneath Kaiija.

Excavations of Feature 6 in test 9100 eventually revealed that the pit, a forge, was an iron-working
structure. The essential link had been established,
and its verification stimulated considerable Bahaya
interest in the research.

The Kaiija tree testing was extended to test 9200, in
which further definitions of the putative iron-working

complex were accomplished. The initial success of the
test excavations led to the conclusion that the area,
because of its artifacts of iron technology and
features, must be opened by a controlled block excavation that would allow a better definition of larger
structures, such as house floors, and that would
determine the spatial relations among formal artifact
classes and the structures. However, the wider goal
at this stage was to sample the variation of cultural
remains on the site, especially the frequency of
feature types and artifact classes. To do so meant
much further test excavations. As a consequence, a
block excavation beneath Kaiija was delayed for two
months.

Test excavations in the gashani house area had shown
that the Late Iron Age deposit there was -35 to -45
centimeters deep, or substantially more shallow than
the -82 to -90 centimeters deep Late Iron Age midden
beneath Kaiija tree. The depositional history of the
site was variable. The deeper deposition beneath
Kaiija was undoubtedly the result of more rapid humus
collection because of the leaf fall. In addition,
the tree's foliage prevented rain bombardment, which
resulted in more rapid organic acretions. With the
comparative depositional evidence available from the
Kaiija and gashani tests, and with the mythological-
archaeological conjunctions established, text excavation proceeded to a mixed random and systematic
program.

The test excavations in the gashani house area had
revealed Early Iron Age features that displayed much
burning activity, as if some part of limited, localized
burning activity had been performed there. During the
testing phase, no Late Iron Age features of consequence
were delimited. Up to this time, oral tradition had
been employed as the means for placement of test pits.
While this method was extremely successful and the
results gratifying, there were no assurances that
other areas in the palace compound did not support
specialized activities, such as cooking, food preparation, food storage, and iron working. The physical
characteristics of the site, which included two areas
with a high frequency of Early Iron Age features
closely tied to oral tradition, created a localized
bias. This bias suggested that a stratified sampling
program was appropriate for the remainder of the site
(Watson, et al., 1971; Rackerby, 1973).

The site was horizontally stratified according to
several criteria: the two areas with mnemonic devices
and associated with oral traditions and ritual life

were designated as two separate sampling proveniences,
Areas 1 and 6 (Figure 2). The intervening territory,
where during surface collections three of the four
Early Iron Age sherds were found, was designated as
Area 2, and the far southeastern part of the gashani,
which was covered in thick vegetation, was mapped as
Area 5. Area 3, to the west of the gashani house and
alleged burial place, was defined as separate because
it supported a luxurious growth of banana trees that
were obviously sitting upon a rich organic deposit.
Area 4 made up the remainder of the site to the west
and northwest of the gashani house. All of the ground
included in Area 4 was under intense cultivation,
much of which was done while we worked on the site;
those sections of the site under crops were excluded
from the testing program.

Testing in these horizontally stratified units proceeded according to both a random and systematic program. Each random test excavation in each stratified
area was selected from a table of random numbers. In
this way, test excavations proceeded at first in Area
3, as Areas 1 and 6 had already been partially sampled
by systematic tests. Once test excavations revealed
new structural or activity data, then the random
pits were followed up by systematically placed tests.
In Area 3, for instance, after randomly placed test
3000 delimited a post hole, another test, 3200, was
placed in the center of the lush banana tree growth
to see if similar phenomena were located there (see
Figure 2). As it happened, test 3200 was placed on
a large pile of laterite blocks. The rock pile and
the post hole evidence needed further investigation.
As a consequence, Block B was started to obtain more
complete definitions of the structural relations between the post hole and the rock pile (see Figure 3).

While block excavation in Area 3 commenced, random
and systematic sampling continued in Areas 5, 2, and
6. Random and arbitrary tests were placed in each
area in a frequency from approximately 0.2 percent
for Area 4, 1 percent for Area 1, to 3 percent for
Area 3. Four random pits were placed in Areas 1 and
5, three in Area 6, and two each in Areas 2 and 3.
Area 4 was more problematical because of congestion
from plantings. Because four tests placed in Area 4
failed to fall above the entrance path to a small
house, two systematic tests were placed in the far
northern area to test for Early Iron Age occupation
in that area.

Random and systematic testing were conducted
simultaneously with block excavations. It was clear

from the outset that the test results in the gashani
house area merited block excavation. Therefore, during
the first month of excavation Block A and Block B
were opened on a controlled basis (Figure 4). Excavations proceeded according to 1.5 meter squares. Each
area was assigned a different thousands place digit
for excavation numbers; for instance, Area 1 is a
1000 sequence, Area 3 a 3000 sequence, and Area 6 a
9000 sequence.

Arbitrary excavation units were used because testing
revealed no distinctive natural stratification of
soil on the site. Most areas had been disturbed by
cultivation and, consequently, the soil was homogeneous in color and texture, with the exception of a
transitional zone immediately before the clay subsoil.
Arbitrary units (spits) of 15 centimeters were used
for the surface unit which contained humus, and
thereafter arbitrary units of 8 centimeters were
employed until the transitional zone was reached.
When the transitional zone was reached, an arbitrary
unit was terminated before completion if necessary,
and a new vertical excavation unit was begun. The
transitional soil was in fact the Early Iron Age
horizon. Arbitrary units were also used to excavate
the Early Iron Age deposit, which varied from 3 to 38
centimeters. It was not desirable to lump all the
Early Iron Age materials together in one stratigraphic
excavation unit because such would have eliminated any
natural, cultural stratigraphy that may have been
retrievable. The arbitrary excavation units, when
used with stratigraphic principles, proved to be
a sensitive approach. It resulted ultimately in the
delimitation of different artifact density zones in
the deposits that otherwise would have been missed.
All excavated soil was sifted through half inch wire
mesh.

Another major goal from the outset of excavation was
to recover subsistence evidence.* It soon became
apparent that bone on the site in recognizable form
was very recent. Decomposition proceeds so quickly
that after several hundred years only traces are left.
Therefore, it was necessary to depend on whatever
charred bone there might be in the proximity of
cooking hearths or other areas where bones may have
been burned. The floral and microfaunal evidence
was recovered by washing or flotation (Struever, 1968c)
of the soil through use of a screen-bottomed bucket
as described and used by Struever. All features were
sampled. A half bushel sample of pit fill was taken
from each and transported to the Lake Victoria shore
where the samples were floated and were later dried
*To be discussed in a separate publication.

and sorted in the lab. The midden was not sampled
because of the high probability of recent disturbances.

As Block A excavations continued, random sampling
continued in Areas 1, 2, and 5. Random test C-1 was
followed by systematic test D-1 (see Figure 2) because of a concentration of Early Iron Age sherds in
C-1 at -48 centimeters. However, the systematic test
failed to recover comparable materials; this finding
may be significant, as we will see in Chapter 10.
Tests G-5 and H-5 showed a very shallow Late Iron Age
deposit of only 25 centimeters depth, with no Early
Iron Age materials present. However, test 5200,
later included in Block D excavations (Figure 2),
was placed in the midst of heavy undergrowth. The
random program had its vindication in test 5200 alone.

Once test unit 5200 had reached -35 centimeters, the
heavy densities of charcoal and slag in the proximity
of what were to be defined as Features 10 and 13 (see
Chapter 9) indicated a cultural deposition of unusual
interest. The outline of Feature 13 appeared in
test 5200 as a black circular outline mottled with
burned orange clay. To the east was a heavy concentration of slag in Feature 10. The associated ceramics
indicated that these were Early Iron Age features,
and the iron-working evidence merited further exploration. Systematic test 5300 was opened to the west,
and in the next two months the remainder of Block D
was excavated. As we will see, some of the most
important evidence for Early Iron Age production of
iron in East Africa comes from the Block D area;
without a random sample program it would never have
been discovered. Further tests, I-5 and P-5,
indicated that the complex defined in Block D did not
extend further to the north or south.

Random testing in Area 2 failed to reveal signs
of Early Iron Age features or a distinct horizon.
However, test F-2 did reveal that a very deep (-90
centimeters) Late Iron Age midden to the east of Area
2. There were signs of much cooking activity, which
are important for interpreting later occupation of the
site. Random tests in Area 1, 1200 and 1275, later
included in Block C (see Figure 2), revealed two
features. Test 1200 was placed directly on Early Iron
Age Feature 21, and test 1275 revealed a stone
structure, including grindstones.

The testing in the southern part of Area 1 demonstrated
a very shallow Late Iron Age deposit on parts of the
site. It was 30 centimeters on the southern border
in this area and gradually deepened to approximately

45 centimeters near Block A. All of it was hoe zone, that is, it had been disturbed by hoe agriculture to the clay subsoil. The highly disturbed soil and the presence of structural features, many of which dated to the Early Iron Age, led to the next major strategy decision after two months of test and block excavations. The highly disturbed soil conditions in Areas 5, 3, and the southern part of Area 1, and the great probability of other Early Iron Age features in the proximity of those already defined, merited stripping operations.

The population of features on the site was dense for the Early Iron Age, but after two months of controlled excavation, approximately one dozen features had been defined. The value of stripping, a widespread technique in North American archaeology, is that it increases the sample of artifacts and features (Struever, 1968a). The spatial relationships among different classes of features is an especially important aspect of this phase. However, in areas of the site where the midden was deeper and where there was no evidence of widespread disturbance, controlled block excavations were used exclusively; Block E is an example of this type of excavation.

Block E excavations were started on March 1, 1970, at the same time that the controlled section of Block C was excavated. The controlled excavations in Block C were performed before stripping because it was necessary to test the assumption that it was a disturbed deposit. It proved to be, as there was a homogeneous mixture of Late and Early Iron Age materials. Several weeks later, test excavations had been completed in Area 4, with the only sign of Early Iron Age occupation located in test L-4 near the path to the small house (see Figure 2). By this time, most efforts had been concentrated on completing Block E and stripping operations in Block C by April 20 (Figure 4). Therefore, the evidence located in test L-4 was not pursued.

By mid-March, the primary rainy season had started and work proceeded in sometimes inundated conditions. A 7 x 7 meter portable corrugated roof shelter was constructed on the site to protect block excavations where features were being excavated. Lab analysis of materials from the Block D area also indicated disturbance in that area, which was borne out by the truncated and partially disturbed nature of some of the Early Iron Age features. The evidence obtained in Block D excavations had been essential for an understanding of Early Iron Age iron production, but

better structural-spatial evidence was necessary.
Therefore, stripping operations started under shelter
in the west of Block D in late March. The results of
this decision were considerable, as two Early Iron
Age putative smelting furnaces and a house floor
were eventually excavated in the western area.

The excavations in Block B were completed on about
March 1. In early April, it was decided to strip the
far northeastern part of Block B solely for a better
definition of the rock structure, Feature 4, located
in Block B (Figure 5). This completed excavations with
the exception of Block E, which continued until April
20. In mid-April, the brick pile mnemonic device to
the southeast of the gridded site was excavated by
two test squares (see Chapter 9). This limited
excavation was conducted to test the oral tradition
associated with the mnemonic.

The use of oral tradition and mnemonic devices as
guides for excavations proved to be a surprisingly
successful device for excavation strategy. A systematic testing program using oral tradition, when employed
with a random program to check the bias introduced by
the oral tradition, provided an adequate and reliable
sample of the site and led to the definition of most
of the major Early Iron Age activity areas. This
strategy, when combined with extensive controlled
block excavations and stripping operations in
disturbed areas, led to extensive spatial definitions
heretofore not available for Early Iron Age structures.

The preceding discussion points out some of the
stratigraphic characteristics of the site. The Late
Iron Age deposit was confined to a soil that was
homogeneous throughout, with the exception of a humus
zone on the surface which varied from 8 to 15 centimeters deep. This zone was black and organic, and
the underlying soil was a dark brown loam of slightly
sandy texture. The homogeneity of this deposit did
not vary on the site except in Block E (Figure 6),
where there were several isolated sandy lenses, and in
test F-2 in Area 2, where there was black greasy soil
with ash lenses (Figure 7). The dark brown loam varied
in depth from 90 centimeters in test N-4 (Area 4),
60 centimeters in Block A, 35 to 40 centimeters in
Block D, to 70 to 120 centimeters deep in Block E.
In all areas except Block C and parts of Block D,
the dark brown loam was situated above a brown-orange
transitional soil with a clay-like texture. In most
cases, this was a stratigraphic marker for the Early

Iron Age horizon. In Block C, the Late Iron Age
deposit rested directly upon the firmly packed orange
subsoil.* This is likely the result of cultivation
which has completely destroyed all vestiges of the
Early Iron Age midden, leaving only features that
cut into the subsoil. The variability of deposition
can be seen in Figure 8, a profile which cuts across
Blocks A, C, and E to Datum. The profile for the
western wall of Block A (Figure 9) characterizes the
general homogeneous nature of the deposits in undisturbed areas. The same profile is applicable for any
section for Block B, except that the transitional
soil begins at -45 centimeters rather than at 60
centimeters. However, the Block B area is virtually
devoid of Early Iron Age artifacts.

Blocks A and E exhibit a cultural stratigraphy that
is unambiguously associated with the natural stratigraphy. The discussion of slag and tuyère densities
in Chapter 10 will demonstrate these characteristics
in the stratigraphy of the Rugomora Mahe site.

*The terms brown-orange or orange-brown correspond to
10 yr 5/6 to 5/8 or yellowish brown on the Munsell
soil chart, while the orange sub-soil is 7.5 yr 6/8
or reddish yellow on Munsell.

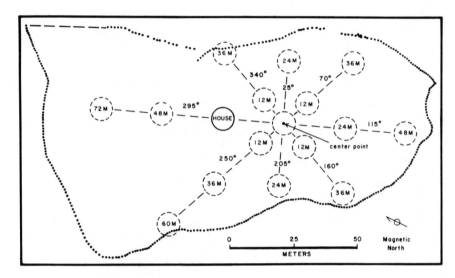

Figure 1: Surface collection areas at
Rugamora Mahe site, Katuruka Village.
Dog-leash method deployed every
45° at 12 m intervals. Center point is
alleged burial place at Rugamora Mahe.

Figure 2: Site stratification and test
excavations. Those labeled with
numbers are tests included in block
excavations; those with letter labels
are extra-block tests.

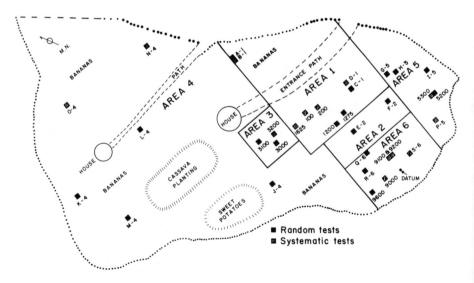

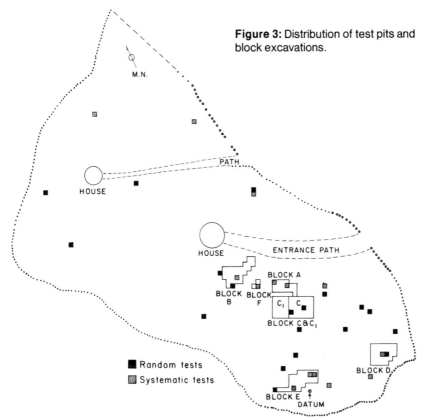

Figure 3: Distribution of test pits and block excavations.

Figure 4: An example of excavation strategy in a highly disturbed area, Block C and C_1.

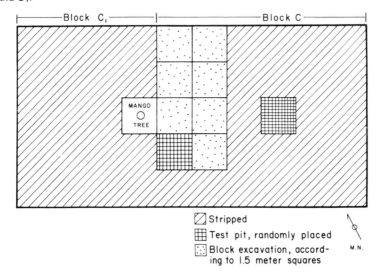

Figure 5: An example of excavation strategy from Block B.

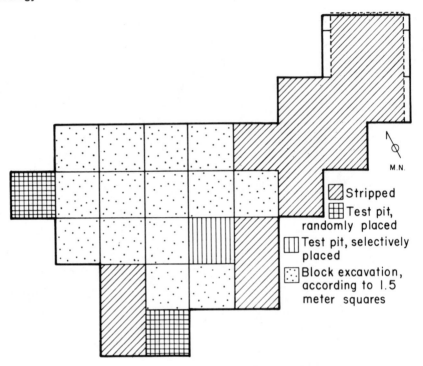

M.N.

⊡ Stripped

⊞ Test pit, randomly placed

▥ Test pit, selectively placed

⊡ Block excavation, according to 1.5 meter squares

Figure 6: The north-south stratigraphic profile in Block E.

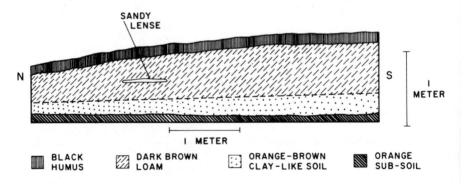

SANDY LENSE

N   S |
                                                                              1
                                                                              METER

1 METER

▥ BLACK HUMUS   ▨ DARK BROWN LOAM   ⊡ ORANGE-BROWN CLAY-LIKE SOIL   ◼ ORANGE SUB-SOIL

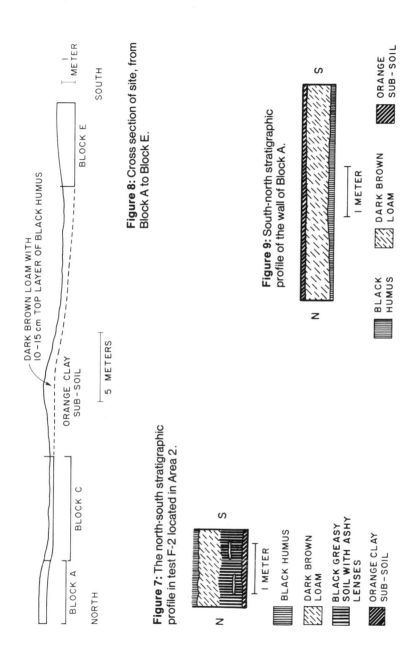

Figure 7: The north-south stratigraphic profile in test F-2 located in Area 2.

Figure 8: Cross section of site, from Block A to Block E.

Figure 9: South-north stratigraphic profile of the wall of Block A.

9
The Results of Block Excavations: Structures and Features

Chapter 8 emphasizes that spatial definitions among
pit features and other structures was a major goal of
block excavations. The color and texture contrast
between pit fill and subsoil, or soil immediately
overlying the subsoil, was extreme and very easy to
recognize. Features were relatively rare in the Late
Iron Age deposits, perhaps as a result of intensive
agriculture on the site. The pit fills in recent Iron
Age features are often exactly the same color and
texture as the surrounding soil. Consequently,
definition becomes difficult. Given these characteristics, a more recent pit feature will only be recognized if it has a high density of cultural remains or
if it penetrates the orange subsoil.

Each floor in every excavation unit was carefully
scraped with a trowel in order to delimit features
and post molds. The archaeological workmen on the
site displayed especially fine prowess with this
aspect of excavation technique. Once a feature was
defined, it was excavated by one of the two excavators
trained to work with feature data, which were then
recorded by a supervisor. If the pit was deeper than
30 centimeters or if it displayed heterogeneous
deposits, it was excavated in stratigraphic or
arbitrary units—whichever were appropriate.

Characteristics of each block will be outlined and
then the features of each discussed. Cross-reference
will be made to features in other blocks when there
are affinities among features, or when it is apparent
that they belong to the same class. The spatial
arrangement of blocks is set out in Figure 3, Chapter
8. Detailed analysis of artifacts other than those

associated with iron working will be published in a
separate study.

The first major block opened by controlled excavation
was Block A, located in the gashani house area. Thorn
trees bordered the excavations on the north, south,
and east; the limits of the excavations were determined
by the placement of the thorn trees. Figure 1 shows
the features defined and excavated in Block A.

The numbering is by sequence in excavation. The Late
Iron Age pits that penetrated the subsoil are confined
to the southeastern portion of the block. The entire
western half is an Early Iron Age domain. As will be
seen in Chapter 10, the upper part of the midden
in this space supported the highest density of ceremonial artifacts on the site, such as cowrie shells
used for currency in precolonial times.

Post molds were not defined in the Block A area, although there were a number of small rodent disturbances, which were rarely encountered elsewhere on the
site. Many of the Early Iron Age pit features were
defined by the presence of small pieces of burned
orange clay, which appears to be the natural clay soil
hardened and discolored by burning activity. The
areas where burning occurred are discrete and clearly
defined. As a rule, the density of artifacts in this
type of feature is very low; in several cases, cultural
material is lacking altogether. This is not problematical for dating, for there are sufficient cases where
there is dating evidence and similarities in
morphology and content. There is no question that
these features are the consequence of Early Iron Age
cultural activity. Interpretation of the associated
activity, however, is sometimes difficult, for function is not always apparent and cannot be ascribed on
an intuitive basis.

Comparative evidence for Early Iron Age settlement
is woefully deficient, and there are few other
archaeologically documented cases that assist in defining Early Iron Age structural phenomena. Interpretations will be based on the contextual evidence,
the spatial relationships to other structures, and the
densities of artifacts in nearby midden. The ceramic
evidence is used for dating as well as for determining
functional nuances. Ceramics will be discussed in a
separate publication, but it should be noted that most
of the well-preserved pottery has been recovered from
sealed features. In this analysis, reference will

be made to pottery only for dating purposes and for
limited functional interpretations.

Feature 1 in Block A, illustrated in Figure 2, is
an Early Iron pit (see Plate 1). No pottery is
associated with the feature, which was defined at -60
centimeters. However, it has a very close resemblance
to Features 2 and 3 in type of pit fill. There is no
question that it is Early Iron Age, for this type of
feature is in fact diagnostic of this period elsewhere on the site. This was the first feature discovered on the site, and its lack of pottery at first
puzzled us. The southern side was excavated first,
and then excavation was suspended for two months until
other similar features were discovered and could be
compared to Feature 1.

The characteristic which first set it off from the subsoil was the inclusion of 1 centimeter diameter lumps
of orange burned clay. The burned clay was mixed
with charcoal in the northern side in a circular
pattern. This 25 centimeter diameter mixture of
orange clay bits and charcoal descended to the
bottom of the pit. The sides of the pit were also
discolored by burning, especially in the proximity
of the charcoal and burned clay concentration.
Trowelling into the side of the pit revealed that
the discoloration penetrated the surrounding clay
approximately 10 centimeters. The extent of the
discoloration may be an isothermal boundary. These
characteristics strongly suggest that burning occurred
in the pit; a fire in a clay bed in open conditions
would perhaps lead to limited firing of the clay
and certainly to discoloration. The fact that
the burned, hard clay is orange shows that the
firing was done under oxidizing conditions. Therefore, the associated cultural activity could not have
been iron smelting, where conditions of reduction
prevail.

The concentration of black soil in the southern
portion had a texture very similar to the soil overlying the feature. However, the inclusion of charcoal and some orange burned clay suggest that this is
a part of the original structure and not a later
disturbance. The most common form of open, concentrated burning would be a cooking fire; the confined
area of burned clay and charcoal strongly suggests
that this may be a hearth, the outer boundaries
of which are difficult to define.

Feature 2 in Figure 3 has fill characteristics similar
to Feature 1. It has no dense concentration of

burned clay, although it does have charcoal-mottled soil in the northern side along with isolated pockets of burned clay. There were three Early Iron Age sherds, one fragment with deep grooving, a common decorative element. One depositional episode appears to be represented in this case. The geographical placement of the burned clay and charcoal within the pit is similar to Feature 1, but the lack of concentrated charcoal and its dispersed nature may mean that the original structure was disturbed or that its terminal function was different from its originally intended function. The clay in the vicinity of Feature 2, however, did not display discoloration, as was evident near Feature 1. The low density of burned clay and a natural clay coloration argue against any function associated with burning.

Feature 3, illustrated in Figure 4, displays extensive signs of burning activity. The pit was set off from the surrounding soil by pieces of orange burned clay. Notice that there are two bulges in the burned clay mass and that within each rounded area there is a concentration of charcoal. Also, the burned clay is a uniformly thick buffer between the charcoal fill and the outer boundaries of the pit; the charcoal fill is encased in orange burned clay. It is also important to note that the area immediately beneath each charcoal mass is deep. Hence, where there is charcoal (or burning), there is also a deeper layering of orange burned clay. These characteristics, when analyzed together, can be interpreted as burning activity confined to the charcoal areas, which causes the surrounding clay to fire so that the burned clay boundary is in fact an isothermal line (Donald Avery, personal communication).

This interpretation is affirmed by the distribution of cultural remains in the feature. Only in the charcoal-mottled spaces and within 4 centimeters of the charcoal was Early Iron Age pottery recovered. The distribution of pottery in the feature and configuration of burned clay around the charcoal masses strongly suggest that the part of the feature with orange burned clay is not part of the original structure, but is simply the extent of clay firing.

Both Features 1 and 3 were extremely difficult to define because of the unfamiliar characteristics of heat boundaries. The pottery from Feature 3 provided a broad sample of Early Iron Age bowl forms— both the small hemispherical bowl with unthickened rims and the large, thick-walled open bowls, both types which occur in low frequencies on other Urewe

ware sites. The functions of these bowls are not
known, but it has often been suggested that the
large open bowls were serving dishes or were at least
associated with food consumption. If so (and the
hypothesis has not yet been systematically tested),
then the presence of bowl forms and concentrated charcoal can be tentatively taken as indicators of cooking activity. I posit that Feature 3 is a hearth.

Feature 5 (Figure 5) has an irregular shape very much
like Feature 3. Defined at -60 centimeters, Feature
5 was black with very slight charcoal mottling.
There were no orange pieces of burned clay or significant clusterings of charcoal. Only two Iron Age
sherds were recovered. The fact that the pit fill
was so much darker than the overlying deposits argues
against this feature being a product of recent
activities. The organic quality of the fill, the
pottery, and the morphology all point to an Early
Iron Age date. Function is not clear in this case,
although it is clear that, regardless of morphological
similarities to Features 2 and 3, there is no
evidence of burning. By inference we may be able to
assign a refuse function to the pit; its organic
qualities and proximity to putative hearths may
mean that it was dug to receive organic waste products from food preparation. This is a tentative
proposition; other features on the site will be
analyzed with this proposition in mind to determine
whether other similar patterns occur with better
contextual evidence.

The remaining Early Iron Age feature is Feature 20
(Figure 6), which was first observed as brown pit
fill with mottling of charcoal and orange burned clay.
Early Iron Age pottery was abundant in the top layer
of the pit fill. Double-bevelled rim forms that
belong to globular, necked pots were confined to
excavation unit A, the top 20 centimeters of feature
fill. The decorative techniques ranged from a zigzag
incising to a predominant incised hatch that had
obliterated the first diagonal hatch applied. There
were also a number of relatively rare forms, such as
inturned rims on small hemispherical bowls with
herringbone design elements above grooving, and fluted
rims, as well as carinated rims.

The feature was excavated in 20 centimeter units. The
feature fill appeared to represent several episodes,
and the excavation units corresponded, by chance, to
the depth of the episodic fill. The top of the
feature (which reached a depth of -148 centimeters
below ground surface) contained most of the globular

pots, but as excavation continued, it was obvious that
the distribution of pottery was relatively uniform.
Of particular interest was the inclusion of very
thick (9 to 13 millimeter) bowl bases. The massiveness of the bases suggests a very large and substantial
bowl form.

From -90 to -105 centimeters there was a very heavy
density of slag, and most of the 2 kilograms of slag
from the feature was within this concentrated mass.
Immediately below the slag was a 10 centimeter thick
layer of charcoal. A C14 sample was taken from this
sealed context under the slag. The date obtained was
120 A.D. + 110 (N-892). In the same level, there
were also a number of small pieces of sandstone that
did not display any signs of cultural modification.
The deepest layer was dark brown loam with very
slight traces of charcoal. This fill extended into
the cylindrical-like hole in the bottom of the pit.

The inclusion of orange burned clay in the upper
levels along with charcoal points toward a function
associated with burning activity. The inclusion of
blow pipes or tuyères that are used in smelting or
forging and large quantities of iron slag (some of
which was unworked bloom) further suggests that the
burning activity was associated with iron production.
Finally, the presence of ironstone or haematite
affirms that an iron production function is probable.
It is unlikely, because of the depth of the pit, that
it was employed as a forge; the sandstone rocks in
the furnace do not show signs of hammering, as they
would have had they been used as anvils. Interpretation in this case is hindered by lack of comparative evidence, for the few reports published on the
Early Iron Age contains virtually no discussion of
structures. Phillipson (1970) discusses some pit
features in his Twickenham Road excavations, but his
illustrations and interpretative discussions do not
elucidate function.

Essentially, then, data are lacking for thorough
archaeological comparisons of Early Iron Age structures. Therefore, structural comparisons must be
carried out with later Iron Age features, in the
hope that this exercise will lead to interpretive
propositions that can be tested in later analysis
and investigations. If the probability that Feature
20 is a forging hearth is low, then what are the
possible alternative functions? The clearest
alternative is that it is a smelting furnace of a
bowl type, as described by the Bahaya during my
study of iron technology (see Chapter 3). The

Bahaya do not mention digging a small hole in the
bottom (Figure 6: west to east profile and Plate 2),
but this phenomenon does occur in Late Iron Age
furnaces in South Africa (van der Merwe, 1971 and
personal communication) supposedly as a place where
magical devices can be placed to assure the success
of the smelt. There is no ethnographic evidence
among the Bahaya to support such ethnographic analogy.

The east side of the bowl is vertical and the west
side is sloped. If the pit was used for smelting,
then the bloom as the heaviest component in the
furnace would run toward the bottom and eastern side
or, in other words, to the lowest part of the furnace.
It may be that the hole in the bottom of the pit was
excavated specifically to receive the bloom or that
the presence of the hot bloom mass at the bottom
of that part of the furnace created an isothermal
boundary that corresponded to the presence of the
bloom (Donald Avery, personal communication).

The inclusion of iron ore in the upper half of the
pit also tends to affirm a function associated with
smelting, for it is probably iron ore that was not
reduced adequately during the smelting process. The
generally dispersed characteristics of burned clay
and charcoal in the upper 40 centimeters suggest
disturbance of the original deposits. The Bahaya
pry the slag and bloom out of their furnaces, thus
destroying the original configurations. Feature 20
with its pottery artifacts appears to have two major
depositions: the lower dark deposits with charcoal;
and the upper, lighter fill with orange burned clay,
ironstone, and charcoal. The uniform inclusion of
pottery sherds and two depositional layers suggest
that there was redisposition in two stages and that
the pit's final function was a refuse dump, especially
for by-products of iron production.

All of the Late Iron Age features in Block A are
located in the eastern section of the excavation.
As Figure 7 indicates, Feature 7 was defined at -35
centimeters in the center of the gashani house area.
This was the most shallow Late Iron Age feature in
Block A, as it occurs at least 25 to 30 centimeters
above the level of the subsoil. The limits of the
feature were very easily defined because of the
heavy densities of charcoal within its borders.
However, the charcoal was confined to a circular
strip of charcoal approximately 10 centimeters wide,
the outer boundaries of which define the perimeters
of the pit. The space inside the circular configuration of charcoal was filled with orange sticky clay

of the same texture and color as the subsoil. The
pit was dug well into the subsoil to a depth of -123
centimeters, and some of the soil excavated to make
the pit was evidently returned to the upper, central
part of the pit.

Note that the charcoal concentration has completely
vertical walls with no signs of sloping. The
arrangement of the redeposited subsoil and the charcoal shows that the charcoal resulted from the burning
of a wooden object placed in the pit and presumably
filled with orange subsoil. The charcoal is 35 to
40 centimeters deep, and it rested on an 18 centimeter thick layer of pure ash. Starting at -81
centimeters, there was orange-brown soil, which is
pit fill made up of topsoil and subsoil mixed together.
On the bottom and on the sides of the pit there was
an eight to ten centimeter thick layer of pottery.

The partial pots recovered from Feature 7 when reconstructed provided good examples of high-necked jugs
and Late Iron Age hemispherical bowls. The partial
nature of the pots may mean that the bottom of the
pit had a refuse function, but the localization of
pottery makes this interpretation dubious. Feature
7 probably has a special function unrelated to exclusively refuse disposal. The pit fill shows three
or four distinct phases of deposition: the placement
of partial pots and orange-brown soil; the deposition
of ash; and the deposition of the orange clay and
charcoal (wood then burned?). The topmost arrangement
may represent the burning of an object with a shape
similar to a drum. We do not know, of course, what
the object was, but the placement of the pit and its
Late Iron Age excavation in an area of paramount
ceremonial importance suggest that a ceremonially
related function is possible.

The Bahaya say that they bury the jawbone of the king
in the gashani house. Thus, a special pit might
have been dug within the area occupied by the
gashani house in order to accommodate the Mukama's
jawbone. There was no sign of bone in Feature 7,
but there was in Feature 16 (Figure 8). In the
center of the gashani there was a 38 centimeter
diameter pit excavated at -45 centimeters but first
recognized at -35 centimeters, the same depth as
Feature 7, 2 meters to the southeast. The pit was
filled with dark brown loam mottled with pockets of
charcoal. The 25 centimeter deep pit had a concentration of bone in the center bottom. Unfortunately, the bone was partly decomposed; it was most
definitely a mandible, but the species could not be

identified. It is noteworthy that bone was the only
material in the pit, that the pit has the same
stratigraphic placement as Feature 7, and that the
Bahaya claim that the jawbone of the king was buried
in that very spot. The burial pit for the jawbone
may be Feature 16, but the absence of teeth, unless
they were removed, is problematical.

In the far eastern section of Block A, there are two
anomalous features, numbers 8 and 11, illustrated in
Figures 9 and 10. Feature 8 was defined at -35 centimeters from the vertical datum and -25 centimeters
from the surface on its southern side. The pit fill
was orange-brown clay, seemingly a mixture of subsoil
and topsoil. This fill was in contrast to the dark
brown midden in which it was located. The top 30
centimeters of the pit was filled with this soil under
which there was a plain brown loam. It is basically
bell-shaped in form, but the form itself does not
suggest any particular function. The fill included
Late Iron Age pottery. There were six undecorated
sherds, one of which was part of a large bowl with
thick char on the inside, which undoubtedly indicates
that it was used for cooking. The one decorated
piece also belonged to an open bowl form with plated
roulette decoration both inside and outside. The
sherds were distributed throughout the fill; therefore, it appears that they were an incidental part
of the fill and were not part of a refuse dump. The
function of this pit is not clear.

Feature 11 at first appeared to be a rodent
disturbance. The lack of cultural material and the
similarity of the pit fill to the upper levels of the
deposit led to the conclusion that it was the result
of noncultural disturbance. However, it was not a
rodent hole, nor was it an Early Iron Age structure.
The fill suggests that it has been introduced by
digging from the surface. This kind of phenomenon
is not unusual on the site, and it may be linked to
the construction of above-ground structures such as
a main post for a house. Until pits of this sort can
be demonstrably related to other structures and
unequivocally dated, they must be excluded from consideration as cultural remains and will be called
features only for analytical reasons.

Figure 11 shows Feature 19 which was defined at -30
centimeters as a heavy concentration of charcoal
and ironstone set in dark brown soil. The eastern
side had large pieces of charcoal set in a concentration of ironstone. The black, organic quality of
the pit fill, the heavy densities of charcoal, and

the presence of iron ore and slag may possibly point toward a function associated with iron production. However, there are no Late Iron Age features on the site that can be unequivocally assigned to iron production. Therefore, any such interpretation is speculative at this time.

If Feature 19 is associated with iron production, however, then the distribution of iron slag in the Late Iron Age deposit may be explained by this function. The difficulty with this idea is that if the gashani house area were in fact a residence, iron working would have been excluded from the inside. Alternatively, Feature 19 has evidence for burning which may be a Late Iron Age hearth, a likelihood increased by the context of the find. Most of the sherds were undecorated, but 40 percent had heavy char on the inside; this evidence tends to support the notion that Feature 19 may be a hearth. Otherwise, the decorated sherds belong to small, delicate hemispherical bowls, one with an everted lip and a globular pot with an inturned rim and plaited roulette decoration.

A general interpretation for Early Iron Age features in Block A must stress the relatively uncharted ground for any functional interpretation. What is clear is that there is considerable evidence for localized burning in what are tentatively posited to be hearths, such as Features 1, 2, and possibly 3. It may be, of course, that the other features are not cooking hearths but that they represent some other activity associated with iron production, such as forging. This alternative is not a testable proposition at this time, as no associated evidence has been found to suggest that it is legitimate. As we will see in Chapter 10, the Early Iron Age horizon in the vicinity of Features 1, 2, and 3 does not have a dense enough distribution of iron-producing artifacts to support this claim.

The Late Iron Age features in Block A can be divided into two groups: 8 and 11 which have unknown functions, and 7 and 16 which may be associated with the ceremonial life in the site sometime during the last 300 years. The internal structure of Feature 7 especially suggests some special function, and the stratigraphic placement of Feature 16, plus its contents, indicate that these features are possibly tied into the Late Iron Age ritual life associated with the gashani house area.

Block B was originally opened and expanded to obtain
better definitions of a stone concentration (Plate 3).
The banana trees growing directly above the stones
were very large and were far more productive than
trees elsewhere on the site. The lush vegetation
first drew attention to the area, which was then
integrated into the stratified sampling system as in
Area 3. Both random test 3000 and 3100 revealed post
molds A and B (Figure 12). A systematic test was then
placed in the middle of the area, and the concentration
of laterite blocks was discovered. The stones were
located between -12 to -40 centimeters deep, with most
about -35 centimeters from the surface.

As excavation of the stone concentration continued,
it became apparent that the fill between the stones
had led to the lushness of the banana trees in this
area. The soil was very black, even greasy in spots,
and was confined to a well-demarcated area. The line
of small parallel lines in Figure 12 shows the
boundaries of the organic soil. The stones in the
western end of Block B were located within the same
boundary. Late Iron Age sherds with roulette
decoration were wedged between the rocks, so it was
documented as a structure dating to the more recent
Iron Age. An Early Iron Age horizon was virtually
nonexistent in this area. Only during the final
stages of excavation, after the stones had been
removed and the soil underneath them excavated, did
we recover several well-weathered Early Iron Age
sherds. This area appears to be peripheral to the
Early Iron Age occupation of the site.

As excavation of the block progressed, post molds
were defined, particularly in the southeastern sector.
The post molds were not dug into the clay subsoil,
which started at -45 centimeters, but were located
at -38 to -40 centimeters, several centimeters within
the Late Iron Age midden. The contrast between post
mold fill and surrounding soil was always easy.
The post mold fill was usually black, sometimes with
charcoal mottling in a dark brown context.

The first clear series of post molds observed was the
A, F, G, H, I pattern, which is illustrated in Plate
4. All of these post molds have the same basic form
and approximately the same depth, which varies between
6 and 10 centimeters. The diameters are all within a
22 to 28 centimeter range. Post molds K, L, P, and

Q also have the same form. While they are somewhat
deeper than those to the southwest, they were also
defined higher in the midden and pedestalled. Post
molds J and O do not appear to fit into this eastern
pattern (see Figure 13). Their diameters exceed 30
centimeters, they do not have flat bottoms as do the
others, and they are twice as deep.

The post molds in the easternmost section, R, T, and
U (S is not a post mold but a disturbed area), have
round bottoms and do not appear to belong to the
previously discussed patterns. At least, it is not
apparent how they might fit in. It is also not clear
how Y, AA, and Z in the southeastern corner relate
to the other post molds. In short, insufficient
ethnographic data are at present available on the
arrangement of posts in Bahaya houses and other
structures to argue by analogy for a particular
structural form. However from observations of Bahaya
traditional houses, it is clear that posts are not
arranged in a circular pattern, such as suggested
by A, F, G, H, and I.

The function of the stone concentration was equally
unclear upon its completed excavation. The Bahaya
who visited the site were asked what they thought
the stones were intended for, because it was obvious
that the stones had been transported there. Several
old men said they were sure that the stones were
intended as fill for a low wet spot. They went on to
explain that it was a common practice to put stones
in a cattle enclosure, particularly if the area was
wet. What with the wetness and the cattle urine, the
place would soon become a mess without a substantial
foundation. They also ventured the interpretation
that all the black soil around the stones resulted
from the collection of cattle manure.

This response was more than a speculative interpretation, for the men said that they had witnessed cases
where stones were added to a cattle compound to
strengthen the footing. This proposition seemed to
be justifiable, for it explained the dense concentration of organic soil and its discreteness, the function
of the rocks, and why the post molds were arranged
differently from Bahaya homes. The remaining post
molds—E, C, DD, D, B, X, W, V, and CC—surrounded
the stone structure. The deeper post molds, such as
D, B, and W, may have been main support posts, while
the remainder may have functioned as dividers or as
intermediate fence posts. There are a number of linear
arrangements, for instance, A-D-B, F-C-BB, G-E-W, and
J-K-CC, with the same orientation, but it is not clear

if these are significant arrangements. We do know
that the Bahaya segregated animals when they kept
animals in their homes in precolonial days. Therefore,
it may be that the area enclosed by post molds A, F,
G, H, I, E, C, DD, and D represents a similar arrangement in a cattle enclosure.

I posit that the double post molds, C-CC and P-Q, are
entrance posts that are arranged in a way to cut off
the entrance path, which appears to be delimited by
the stones running to the northeast. Note that the
stones form two lines (Plate 5) which are approximately
90 centimeters apart. Probing revealed that the stones
continue into the unexcavated area to the northeast.
Contemporary Bahaya will often line paths leading to
cattle enclosures with bushes, cassava plantings, or
stones to prevent the cattle from wandering into the
kibanja and spoiling crops.

This analog was also suggested by informants on the
site who claimed that the rocks to the northeast
were path liners. If this structure is a cattle
enclosure, an interpretation suggested by local people
and affirmed by the presence of cattle teeth and bones
in the deposits, then was it associated with the
alleged occupation of Rugomora Mahe on the site? As
the gashani house is only some 12 to 15 meters to the
east, is it probable that the structure belongs to
the royal occupation period?

Rehse observed in the kikale of the Mukama of Kiziba
that the Mukama's cattle enclosures were very similar
to houses but that they were set apart from the
central residence. Figure 14 (Rehse, 1910:12) shows
that the cattle enclosures (nos. 24-28) were located
some distance from the center of the kikale (no. 1).
This structural arrangement, of course, prevailed
some twenty years into German colonialism. That a
Muhinda king early in the Bahinda dynasty of
Kyamutwara would have had his cattle so far removed
from his personal compound is dubious at best. It
may very well be that the cattle of the king were kept
relatively close to the Mukama's residence 300 years
ago for reasons of security. Alternatively, most
Bahaya informants felt that the putative enclosure
belonged to a more recent period, even though none
of them could personally remember an enclosure at
that spot. This interpretation is less likely, for
the archaeological evidence indicates that the
stones rested almost directly upon soil in which Early
Iron Age pottery was found. Therefore, the stratigraphic placement of the stones, which rested directly
upon the subsoil, argues for their placement there

after the Early Iron Age but certainly much before
the last 100 years. It is highly likely that the
stones are associated with the Bahinda occupation
of the site and that the organic soil, post molds,
bones, and entrance way suggest a cattle enclosure.

As pointed out in Chapter 8, most of disturbed Block
C was excavated with the explicit goal of obtaining
more structural data, especially more complete evidence for the structure of settlement on the site.
Block C was divided into two sections—C1 which was
stripped and C which was excavated first by controlled
excavations and then by stripping operations.
Section C will be discussed first. The most conspicu-
ous feature in Block C is the concentration of sandstone blocks in the eastern sector (Plate 6). Figure
15 shows the original location of each sandstone block,
two of which were well-worn grindstones. Two rubbing
stones were recovered; one was wedged between the
southern grindstone and an adjacent rock. The stones
rested directly upon the subsoil, which was 24 centimeters deep at this point. Most of the stones
varied from -5 to -20 centimeters in depth. The
relatively shallow location of the feature first
suggested that it was a Late Iron Age structure. This
dating seemed to be confirmed by the presence of a
Late Iron Age pit, Feature 51, on the western side.
However, excavation at the base of the stones
demonstrated that it was an Early Iron Age structure,
since exclusively Early Iron Age pottery was recovered
from among the bases of the stones. Feature 51,
illustrated in Figure 16, was dug into the subsoil
and had disturbed the stones on the western side.
Only in the vicinity of Feature 51 were Late Iron Age
sherds recovered from the midden surrounding the
three stones. Feature 51 is Late Iron Age, but its
plentiful organic remains suggest that it may have
had some relationship to the grindstones. The
shallow location of the grindstones may have meant
that they were also used by Late Iron Age peoples.

The function of parts of Feature 30 is obvious by the
nature of the finds, namely, grindstones on which
food preparation such as the grinding of millet takes
place. The function of the remaining stones is
problematical. Fagan (1967a:50) discovered similar
stone circles in the Kalomo culture sites in Zambia
dating to the end of the first millenium A.D. Fagan
interprets the stone circles as grainbin foundations
that normally contain "discarded grindstones, rubbers,
lumbs of granite, and even large fragments of daga"

(ibid.). He does not cite ethnographic data, but he
concludes that the foundation was constructed of
stone to prevent white ants or termites from
destroying the grainbin. It appears that Fagan's
interpretation is a shrewd guess rather than confirmed
analogy, but even so, it provides a useful, tentative
proposition for future investigations. The stone
circle is the same size as Fagan's IP/GBF/2 example;
it also includes grindstones, and it has an open
space in the center. All of these similarities in
structural attributes strongly suggest that the
phenomena are the same. Figure 17 shows that the
stone feature is surrounded by a group of post molds:
post molds I, C, H, R, S, and T have a mean diameter
of 21 centimeters. R appears to be the only post
mold that might be questionable insofar as form is
concerned (see Figure 18). Since the post molds in
this group did not have associated cultural material,
we cannot date them. However, those mentioned appear
to articulate with the stone atructure. This may
mean that if there was a grain storage bin located in
the vicinity of Feature 30, it may have been built on
poles. It seems unlikely, however, that the grinding
of grain was performed under a storage bin. The post
mold configuration may indicate that a circular
structure was built over the grain grinding area as
protection, but then again, this idea can only be
offered as a speculation.

The lack of post molds to the east of Feature 30 may
partly be a function of black organic soil that covered the block east of the stone feature. There was
an abrupt sloping of the subsoil clay at this point,
and the deposit was uniformly excavated no deeper
than -30 centimeters to expose the subsoil. Figure
17 also shows that there are other groupings of post
molds in the Block C area. For instance, there is
the D, E, F, G, J, K group, with Feature 33 in the
middle. According to form, especially width and depth,
D and E belong with A and B, which makes two groupings
of four. Post molds L, M, N, O are also clumped together and have a similar morphology (with the exception of M) and similar fill. Pottery in M and O
indicate that these post molds date to the Late Iron
Age. There is yet another clustering further to the
south: post molds P, Q, W, and V, which also date to
the Late Iron Age. Of the four, only Q appears to
differ in form. It is not clear what these post mold
clusterings represent, but their regular form, fill,
and close spatial relationships suggest that small
structures were built in the vicinity of Feature 30.
The remaining post molds cannot be fitted into any
discernible pattern.

On the north side of Block C, there was a black,
heavily charcoal-mottled area delimited at -28 centimeters. Part of Feature 34 (Figure 19) extended outside the block excavations. The top 20 centimeters
of this pit was filled with black soil and large (2 to
3 centimeter) chunks of charcoal. It was excavated
into the orange subsoil and dated to the Early Iron
Age.

At about -45 centimeters there was a gravel concentration in the middle of which was a mass of burned
orange-red clay. The burned clay was surrounded by
the gravel and by charcoal. The clay was formed
into two mounds and extended to the floor at -59
centimeters on the west and north sides. It was then
followed by dark brown loam in the center of the pit
for another 7 centimeters to the bottom, a depression
in the center. The density of pottery was light
throughout the fill; pottery was not found in the
burned clay and gravel. Early Iron Age sherds were
recovered from the upper 30 centimeters along with
charred seeds.

The two mounds of burned clay were not fired to a
hard form but were porous and easily broken. No
artifacts from iron production were associated with
the pit. Hence, even though ironstone is present,
it is difficult to claim that the function is associated with iron working. Several Bahaya immediately
suggested that the feature was a hearth and that the
two burned clay areas were the remains of two out of
three clay rests used to hold cooking pots over a
fire. This proposition seemed as reasonable as any
other, and it is certainly enhanced by the presence
of carbonized seeds. However, in Feature 34 there is
a 10 to 15 centimeter thick layer of solid but porous
burned clay which is surrounded by ironstone. If
Feature 34 was a reduction furnace, then its internal
structure might be explained by the smelting process.
A poor smelt or unsuccessful smelt may have led to the
reduction of ironstone only in the center of the
furnace where the fire was hotter. The localization
of heat would have led to only limited firing of the
clay, which then may have been heaped up as the bloom
was removed. A relatively poor smelt would also have
left some ironstone in the furnace in an unreduced
or partially reduced state—as it was arranged in
Feature 34. As a consequence, the clay below the unreduced ironstone would not be fired. This hypothetical construct is technologically possible and
may explain the structure of the feature, but it also
lacks substantiating evidence such as tuyères and
slag. Our state of knowledge about Early Iron Age

technology is so limited for Africa, however, that
all possible hypotheses should be explored through
future investigations. It is not possible to assign
a function to Feature 34, but it is possible to test
two hypotheses in the future about the function of
this structure and similar structures, as we will see
in the discussion of Features 21 and 23.

Although the contextual evidence for iron production
in Feature 34 is lacking, there is further structural
evidence which tends to support an iron production
function. Feature 27 (Figure 20) was located adjacent
to Feature 34. It was larger than Feature 34 but
was devoid of cultural material. The fill was dark
brown loam with occasional flecks of orange burned
clay. The northwestern side of Feature 27 tied into
the southeastern side of Feature 34. They were
joined at the bottom (Plate 7). The lack of cultural
material in Feature 27, which extends to -68 centimeters and its connection to Feature 34, suggests
that Feature 27 may have been constructed to tap bloom
from a bowl furnace or to create a natural draught
vent. If the latter was the case, it would explain
the lack of tuyères in Feature 34. The tentative
proposition, then, is that the two features are
functionally linked and interdependent.

The testability of this interpretative proposition
is enhanced by the presence of Feature complex 21/23,
also located in Block C. Figure 21 shows that both
Features 21 and 23 are also linked at the bottoms
by a passage similar in form to the Feature 34/27
relationship. Of the two features, Feature 23 was
the more difficult to define, for it first appeared to
be a layer of gravel on the orange subsoil. Both
features were first recognized at -30 centimeters
and had been excavated into the subsoil. The top of
Feature 21 was characterized by brown fill mixed with
ironstone and charcoal. Within the top 15 centimeters
of Feature 21, a base of a dimple-based pot, one of the
longest known diagnostic attributes of Early Iron
Age pottery, was excavated. The brown fill continued
to -73 centimeters, which was the bottom of the pit.
The north side of the pit was filled with ironstone,
and the density of cultural material was relatively
high. A total of 2.1 kilograms of slag was recovered
from the midden immediately above Feature 21. Besides
the dimple-base, there were four rim sherds, two of
which represented small globular pots with incising
on the upper rim. There was also a hemispherical
bowl with a triple-bevelled rim and a small globular
pot with an inturned rim. The distribution of pottery
in the fill indicates that the pit was intentionally

filled with refuse and soil. The adjoining Feature,
23, was completely filled with ironstone to a depth
of -70 centimeters. There were two Early Iron Age
sherds in the fill, one of which was decorated with
grooving filled with herringbone-like incising.

The ironstone, charcoal and slag in Feature 21 are
not sufficient to argue for a function associated
with iron production, but the structural characteristics may provide further evidence. First, the slope
of the pit toward the passageway connecting the two
pits may have been intended to direct slag toward
Feature 23, from which place the slag and bloom of
the smelting furnace could have been tapped. Interpretations of prehistoric iron-smelting furnaces are
usually extremely difficult (Goghlan:1956), for the
upper portions of a bowl furnace are usually destroyed
when the bloom is removed. In Europe, where there is
widespread documentation for prehistoric iron production, there are ongoing disputes over whether or not
pits adjoining smelting furances are used for roasting iron ore, for tapping bloom, or for a variety of
other tasks. In terms of technological logic, the
structure of Feature 21 would encourage the runoff
of a fluid slag. It is difficult to speculate about
the connection between the two pits as a tapping area
for bloom, for the ironstone fill precludes a
tapping function. However, if the passageway was left
open during a smelt in Feature 21 and the top of
Feature 23 blocked off, then the reduced atmosphere
and the heat might have been sufficient to cook
some of the oxygen out of the iron ore, that is, to
roast it in preparation for smelting. It may be that
the adjacent pit has a roasting function and that
Feature 27 near Feature 34 has had its iron ore removed for smelting.

The structural relatedness between features in both
groups, the internal structure of both Features 34
and 21, and the presence of partially reduced ironstone all suggest that a function as smelting pits
is a testable hypothesis; if so, its vigorous testing
by archaeological data may lead to more acceptable
interpretive positions in the future.

The remaining features in the eastern side of Block
C are Features 32 and 33, illustrated in the Figure
17 plan view. Both are located in the midst of a
separate post mold configuration. It is not clear
if this arrangement has significance. Feature 32
was filled with an organic, humic soil and had three
undecorated Late Iron Age sherds. Because this
feature and Feature 33 cannot be definitely linked

to a specific cultural activity, I am forced to
speculate that they do not represent intentional
cultural activity, but that they are most probably
a byproduct of agricultural activity. Their placement in the midst of post molds is enough to warrant
their description as features. However, hoeing on
the site for agriculture has most probably created
these depressions in the subsoil; the cultural
material found in each was likely derived from the
midden above. The fact that Feature 32 sprouted grass
one week after its exposure supports this allegation.
Banana sprouts when they are planted require an excavated hole from 30 to 45 centimeters deep. Features
32 and 33, then, are most probably the result of
agricultural activity on the site.

The only other feature in the eastern side of Block
C is Feature 26 (see Figure 17 for plan view). It
was first observed at -30 centimeters and pedestalled
as excavation continued around it. The bottom two-
thirds of the pit was dug into the subsoil. It had a
dark brown fill in contrast to the orange-brown clay
in which it was set. The depth, width, and cultural
inclusions suggest that the pit is more than an excavation for a banana tree planting. The fill was
very humic. Given the size and volume of the pit,
the density of cultural material was high—certainly
higher than the Late Iron Age midden for the area.
There were eleven undecorated sherds, many of which
are from large, thick bowls tempered with hunks of
slag. One rim sherd was decorated by the plaited
roulette technique. Pottery was concentrated at the
bottom between -50 and -55 centimeters. The high
density of pottery in the pit and the concentration
of sherds in the bottom suggest that Feature 26 may
be a refuse pit dug to receive broken pottery and
perhaps organic refuse. It appears that there is one
fill episode associated with the refuse disposal.

Evidence obtained in test excavations in Area 4
indicates that the Bahaya dig refuse pits in their
agricultural plots to accommodate nonorganic and
organic waste. In test 0-4 we opened up a refuse pit
that neighbors dated to 1968. In it we found broken
jars, pottery, bits of clothing, and organic waste—
probably banana peelings. Thus, one way of disposing
of refuse is to dig pits for it. The other more
common means is to scatter it in the farmed plot,
especially if it is organic. Pottery is also disposed
of by throwing it among the banana trees or behind
the nyaruju (main) house. It is not clear what kinds
of conditions must prevail before a refuse pit is
excavated, but there may be a threshold point beyond

which surface garbage is not tolerated. Closer
observation of refuse behavior in Buhaya in the
future may lead to ideas that can be used in formulating propositions for explaining pit features thought
to contain refuse.

To the west of Feature 26 in Block C there was a
black charcoal-mottled area (Figure 22), with a
circular and dense concentration of charcoal lumps
in the center. This was designated as Feature 39
and can be dated to the same time period as Features
37 and 38 further to the west. The large charcoal
mass extended to the bottom of the 16 centimeter
deep pit, which was defined at -40 centimeters. The
basic morphology of the feature first suggested that
the central portion might be a post mold with the
charred remains of a post in situ. The full extent
of the feature could not be defined because the
eastern pit had been cut off in previous block
excavations. There were four Late Iron Age sherds
with impressed cord decoration; all had very large
(3 to 5 millimeters) slag tempering, as did one rim
sherd from a hemispherical bowl. Of the seven
undecorated sherds, one was an Early Iron Age sherd
that was probably introduced when the pit excavation
cut through the Early Iron Age midden. The function
of this pit is not clear, although its structure
indicates either a hearth or a burned post. It is
quite possibly not a hearth because no ash is present,
which may indicate that the burning took place in a
reduced atmosphere (such as a buried post) and left
only charcoal.

Adjacent to and immediately to the north of Feature 39
was another feature mottled with charcoal and orange
burned clay. Figure 23 shows that Feature 38 was a
shallow, 8 centimeter deep, saucer-shaped pit. At
this point in Block C, the midden was 15 centimeters
deeper than the area to the south; thus, Feature 38
was defined at -45 centimeters. The black charcoal-
mottled soil with orange burned clay did not appear
to be directly related to an activity associated with
fire, but rather appeared to be the refuse from a
fire combined with organic, domestic refuse. The
pottery in the pit was more plentiful than in Feature
39. There were twenty-six undecorated sherds, of which
four dated to the Early Iron Age. Two of the five
Late Iron Age sherds were decorated with a plaited
roulette. One of the two rims was from a globular
pot with an inturned rim and plaited rouletting.
The other rim had a massive lip and was from a very
large open bowl. The remainder of the sherds were
decorated by a twisted grass roulette. There was one

Early Iron Age rim—a hemispherical bowl form; this,
like the undecorated sherds, was included as a result
of the disturbance of the Early Iron Age midden.
Feature 38 may also be a refuse pit, as the density
of the sherds indicate that they were intentionally
placed in the pit. However, the 75 centimeter
diameter indicates much work to bury so little refuse.
This observation and the fact that these pits are so
shallow may mean that the upper portions have been
destroyed by hoeing on the site.

Feature 37 (Figure 24) was located to the west of
Feature 38 and may form some sort of activity complex
along with Features 38 and 39. Feature 37 was located
at -45 centimeters and was spotted as a black charcoal
mass 70 centimeters in diameter. The top 2 centimeters
of the pit had large lumps of charcoal, which then
were underlaid with a black soil with many charcoal
inclusions. At -54 centimeters in the center of the
pit was a crescent-shaped mass of compactly packed
ash mixed with orange burned clay. The pit was excavated in 15 centimeter spits, which agreed with the
natural stratigraphy of the pit (see Figure 24, north-
south profile). The ashy mass included decomposed
bone and some bits of charred bone. Immediately
underneath the compact ash was another layer of large
charcoal pieces. At this point, the sides of the pit
began to expand.

The pit fill from -75 to -105 centimeters changed to
a plain black, very soft, and loamy soil with a much
lower density of pottery. At -105 centimeters the
charcoal mottling abruptly ceased and the soil
continued as a soft loam with very little pottery.
At -115 centimeters there was a 15 x 15 centimeter
square laterite block underneath which there was a
concentration of charcoal. From the bottom of this
charcoal concentration to the bottom of the pit at
-165 centimeters, the fill remained virtually free
of artifacts and was very soft. Multiple episodes
are represented in the fill deposition. The pit
fill in the bottom 60 centimeters is homogeneous,
with the exception of the laterite block and charcoal
mass beneath. The charcoal appears to have been
placed in the dark brown soil and then the rock placed
over it. In the bottom of the pit (excavation units,
E, F, G, and H), there are only eight sherds weighing
42 grams, or 3.5 percent of the total weight of all
sherds from the entire pit.

The bottom fill represents one episode with two
phases. The fill from -75 centimeters to -105 centimeters represents another episode. The top 30

centimeters of fill in Feature 37 has 75 percent of
the pottery by weight, and it has a structure somewhat
similar to Feature 7 in Block A, in that the fill
in the upper center had vertical sides, as the orange
clay and charcoal fills did in Feature 7. The ash and
charcoal layers appear to have been deposited after an
excavation of the black soil which surrounds it. It
would appear that there has been burning in place
after the upper pit was reexcavated where the ash and
charcoal mass were located.

It is difficult to know what kinds of activities may
have been associated with this pit, but the structure
of its fill, which in its bottom and top portions
resembles Feature 7, seems to suggest that it may have
a function tied into the ceremonial life associated
with that area. The thorn trees of the gashani are
but 1 meter north. It certainly is not a refuse pit
or a hearth. Furthermore, because of its lack of
characteristics associated with the productive
technology or domestic life, a tentative interpretation should be ventured that it has ceremonial import.

Feature 37 cuts into the outer boundaries of Feature
45, an Early Iron Age feature illustrated in Figure
25. On the periphery of the pit there is a 3 to 5
centimeter deep layer of orange and brown burned clay
set in reddish and tan soil. Within this 1.6 meter
long area, there was an oblong pit with large pieces
of charcoal and burned clay in its fill. The dating
of the feature is slightly ambiguous, for only three
undecorated sherds were recovered. Two Late Iron Age
sherds were located on the top of the peripheral
burned clay deposits, and one Early Iron Age sherd
was located in the bottom of the pit feature itself.
However, the morphological similarities of this
structure to Feature 55 (Early Iron Age) in Block E
means that the date must be tentatively set in the
Early Iron Age. There was no significant localization of charcoal, except that most of the large
pieces were found in the top 7 centimeters and on
the bottom in the southern portion of the pit. The
boundaries of the pit were extremely difficult to
define because of variable discolorations due to
heat. The bottom at -87 centimeters was undoubtedly
more an archaeological creation in this case than the
actual, natural limits of the pit. The evidence
predominantly points to burning, which partially
fired parts of the subsoil. However, the underlayer
of burned clay on the east and west sides of the pit
is predominantly dark brown, which may mean that most
of the clay was fired in a reduced atmosphere. The
context for such activity would likely be limited to

pottery or iron production. But there is no evidence
to suggest either function. Burning with a reduced
atmosphere may also indicate that the prehistoric
peoples experimented with a variety of structures for
iron-smelting furnaces. Whatever the case, it can be
concluded that the feature supported a fire, most
probably in a reduced atmosphere.

The function of a group of features in the southwestern sector of Block C is unclear. Figure 26
shows that Feature 43 along the southern wall has
been disturbed by recent agriculture. The feature is
25 centimeters deep, and from -31 to -46 centimeters
the pit fill has been removed and replaced by topsoil.
It is often the case that during cultivation features
are discovered, and cultivators will attempt to bring
the dark, organic-appearing soil of features up into
the cultivation zone; such appears to have happened
to Feature 43. The bottom 10 centimeters had all the
cultural material, seven Late Iron Age decorated
sherds, nine undecorated, and one intrusive Early
Iron Age sherd. The concentration of sherds in the
bottom, along with a decomposed bone, points to a
refuse function.

Feature 44 (see Figure 17 plan view) was located at
-45 centimeters and was 27 centimeters deep with a
flattened bottom. The pit depth effectively excludes
it from consideration as an agricultural disturbance.
There were only four Late Iron Age sherds in the fill,
which was a dark brown loam—similar to topsoil. Its
function is not clear. Features 46 and 47 were also
delimited at -45 centimeters and had fill identical
to Feature 44. Both pits have the same fill form.
These similarities and the basic resemblance to other
Late Iron Age pits suggest that both were likely Late
Iron Age in origin. However, analysis of the ceramic
evidence shows that Feature 46 was Early Iron Age and
47, Late Iron Age. The inclusion of five Early Iron
Age undecorated pottery sherds in Feature 46 appears
to be more than coincidence. It is possible, of
course, that Feature 47 also dates to the Early Iron
Age and that the two undecorated sherds recovered
from the top two centimeters of the fill have been
introduced by recent disturbances. Identical form and
fill and spatial arrangement all suggest that the pits
date to the same period. Function in these cases
remains an interpretive problem which can only be
solved as more settlement data are acquired.

Figure 27 illustrates one of the two most important
features on the site in terms of dating the activity
complex associated with the major occupation during

the Late Iron Age—namely, the occupation of King
Rugomora Mahe. Both Features 41 and 42 are somewhat
similar in form and fill and are located between
Feature complex 46/47 and 37/38/39. Feature 41 was
delimited at -43 centimeters as a dark brown oval in
orange clay. The fill was excavated in 15 centimeter
spits which happened to correspond to major episodes
of fill. The top 15 centimeters was a layer of brown
loam, at the bottom of which (in the center of the
pit) was a group of highly decomposed, powdery bones.

At approximately -58 centimeters the fill changed to
a black soil mottled with charcoal and small bits
and pieces of bone in a similar state of decomposition. This deposit continued to -88 centimeters.
Given the large amounts of decomposed bone, at first
it was thought that the pit might be a grave. However, the random distribution of broken pottery in
the pit tends to point more strongly to a refuse
function. There was also a cluster of bone at
approximately -100 centimeters. The bone was mixed
with large pieces of charcoal, some of which were
taken for a C14 sample. This sample was dated to
1700 A.D. + 100. This dating generally agrees with
genealogical information about the time of Rugomora
Mahe's occupation of the site.

None of the Late Iron Age pottery in this pit has
plaited rouletting, and most of the decorated sherds
are decorated by separate impressions of twisted
grass rather than by a roulette technique. The impressed technique is not a common form on the site,
and it may be that it is in fact a mixture of styles
representing a distinct temporal period. Furthermore,
many of the pottery forms are large open bowls, some
of which have burnishing on the inside; again this
is a relatively rare decoration in the Late Iron Age.
There was also an unusual flat-bottomed bowl. The
pottery densities were heaviest in excavation units
A, B, and D, which marked the beginning of the char-
coal-riddled bottom layer. The small 62 x 75 centimeter opening and 70 centimeter depth from subsoil
level suggest that Feature 41 is a refuse pit with
two discernible depositional episodes: (1) the -88 to
-118 centimeter fill with charcoal, pottery, and bone,
and (2) the -58 to -88 centimeter fill, which is
black soil with some charcoal and pottery in the top.
The top portion of the pit fill was disturbed; most
of the pottery from unit A was located from -53 to
-58 centimeters, and the brown soil could possibly
be a recent introduction.

Feature 42 to the southwest of Feature 41 was

stratigraphically higher in the Late Iron Age deposit,
as it was located at -35 centimeters in orange-brown
soil. The opening was 91 x 65 centimeters, and its
axis was oriented north-south compared to the east-
west orientation of Feature 41. Figure 28 shows that
the fill from -35 to -80 centimeters is predominantly
dark brown loam with occasional lenses of charcoal-
mottled soil.

The Ankole-type spear illustrated in Chapter 10
(Figure 13) was recovered from the very top of the
feature and first drew attention to the fact that
there was a pit beneath. While this artifact might
cause some to jump to inductive conclusions about
northern origins for the Bahinda, I attach no
particular ethnic significance to only one datum,
and an undated one at that. The density of pottery
is not as high as Feature 41. The pottery is also
different in form and decoration; the decoration is
twisted grass rouletting, and the predominant form
is a large, open-mouth jug or storage jar. The
differences point to the inclusion of distinctly
different functional categories of pottery, or
possibly a different time period. Both possibilities
may be the case. At -80 centimeters, there was a
2 to 3 centimeter thick layer of ironstone (laterite
gravel), under which there was black soil with charcoal and decomposed bone. It appears that the
gravel was added to seal the deposit from -83 to
-92 centimeters. The possibility that this intentional sealing may be associated with a jawbone burial of
the king comes to mind but is dispelled by what
appears to be an overall appearance of a trash pit.
Function cannot be fixed, but, as it is similar in
form to Feature 41, it is probably similar in function.

The Block C excavations resulted in the retrieval of
essential settlement data, especially for domestic
activities such as food preparation and possibly
cooking. In addition, structures possibly associated
with iron smelting during the Early Iron Age were
discovered. The Late Iron Age materials recovered
were crucial for understanding the refuse behavior
and possibly ceremonial life of Late Iron Age
occupants of the site. It must be remembered that
Feature 37 in Block C is only 2 meters from Feature
7 in Block A and that both have very similar form,
fill, and unique internal structures that may tie into
the ceremonial life of the area. The contrast
between Features 7/37 and 41/42 is clear and suggests
that the latter two belong to an altogether different
activity complex.

Block D is an especially important area for understanding the production of iron in the Early Iron
Age. The first feature to be defined was Feature 10
in test 5200. Feature 10 was a collection of slag
and charcoal resting on the transitional orange-
brown clay at -36 centimeters. The slag was concentrated to a circular area 25 centimeters in
diameter (Figure 29). There are no associated Early
Iron Age artifacts.

To the west of Feature 10 was an oblong 64 x 80
centimeter pit with charcoal flecks and orange burned
clay at -38 centimeters. As excavation started on
this pit feature, it was immediately apparent that it
contained a wealth of pottery and other artifacts
(Figure 30). There was an iron bracelet-like piece
within the top 2 centimeters of fill, and there was
iron slag as well. The pottery was clearly related
to Urewe ware and demonstrated great variety in
decoration and form. The pottery was incised and
grooved and belonged to what were whole and well-
represented portions of pots and bowls. The yield
of pottery from the first two excavation units exceeded the total for all other Early Iron Age features
in the site. The sides of the pit were easily defined,
as the brown and black pit fill were set in compact
orange clay.

At -134 centimeters, the soil became much darker
and the flecks of charcoal in the soil increased.
The pottery density remained very high, and the walls
of the pit began to spread out so that at -164 centimeters the pit was 50 percent wider than the opening.
The fill remained uniform until -165 centimeters,
where it changed to a dark brown loam. There was an
especially heavy density of Early Iron Age pottery
in the lower levels, between -165 and -204 centimeters. A charcoal sample was taken from the south
side of the pit at -175 centimeters; there was a
small pocket of charcoal immediately underneath
part of the dimple-base pot (illustrated in Plate 7).
This sample was submitted for dating and a date of
60 A.D. + 115 (N-891) was obtained. This date falls
into the same range as the date for Feature 20 in
Block A.

The bottom of the pit was reached at -2.27 meters,
where there were large sandstone blocks lining the
east, north, and south parts of the pit (Plate 8).
The sandstone blocks had been intentionally placed;
the stones had Early Iron Age pottery between them and

under them in several instances. The enormous
amounts of pottery, along with slag, tuyères, and
iron, suggest that this pit functioned as a repository
for a broad spectrum of artifacts. The pottery was
broken before deposition, for we found fragments of
pots scattered throughout the fill. For the most
part, however, the fragments were localized within a
particular type of pit fill. For instance, the
globular pot illustrated in Plate 7 was located mostly
within excavation unit E. This particular pot was
the only reconstructable pot recovered on the site.

The fill appears to have been of the three basic types
illustrated in Figure 30. The scatter of sherds
belonging to the same pots throughout the pit fill
and the inclusion of orange burned clay throughout
suggest that the pit was filled over a relatively
short period of time. The function of the pit after
the deposition of the material excavated from it most
likely was a refuse dump. However, this proposition
does not include possible prerefuse functions.
Certainly, it is unlikely that a pit would be lined
with sandstone blocks to receive refuse or that it
would need to be excavated in a bell shape. The pit's
original function probably was altogether different
from a garbage dump.

Summers (1958) has reported bell-shaped storage
pits at Inyanga dating to Ziwa 1 and Ziwa 2. Nothing
in the fill characteristics indicates that the pit
was used for storage of grain crops. However, the
use of the sandstone liner seems to point to an
attempt to prepare the bottom of the pit in some
special way—perhaps as a way of sealing the pit
against rodents. Summers' data and the structure
of Feature 13 allows the hypothesis that this
feature was originally a storage pit. This proposition should not be taken as an interpretation, which
for the moment is limited to the final function—a
refuse dump.

To the north and south of Feature 13 are two Early
Iron Age features that are anomalous. Feature 17
(Figure 31) was located at -38 centimeters, the same
depth as Feature 13. Feature 17 is a good example
of an Early Iron Age feature which, like Feature 61 to
its east, has been disturbed by cultivation. The
dark loam in its upper portions has been recently
introduced. The incidence of cultural material is
very low throughout, even in the plain brown fill
from -58 to -70 centimeters; there were sherds only
in the bottom fill. There are insufficient data to
justify a proposition about function in this case.

The same situation prevails with Feature 12 to the
south of 13. Feature 12 was filled with a dark brown
soil that has slight charcoal mottling. Three
undecorated Early Iron Age sherds were included in
the fill. The irregular boundaries and light density
of cultural material make interpretation of this
feature problematical. Functional attributes of
features in this class are not apparent at this stage
of investigations into the Early Iron Age.

The Early Iron Age midden in the area between Features
17/13/12 and Features 61/62 has much higher densities
of iron production artifacts such as tuyères, slag,
and fired brick than the area to the west (see the
Chapter 10 discussion on slag and tuyères). This may
mean that Features 61 and 62 had some relationship to
iron production. This notion, however, is not confirmed by any of the formal structural attributes of contextual evidence for Features 61 and 62. Feature 61
(Figure 32) was delineated at -40 centimeters as a
black round spot of loosely packed loam. It was 57
centimeters in diameter and was excavated as one unit.
At the time it was not recognized that black loam
with high humus content, when located in the upper
portions of Early Iron Age pits, means recent
disturbances. A mass of charcoal was located at -50
centimeters in the center of the pit; this extended
to a depth of -62 centimeters, below which there was
a dark brown loam. In the dark brown loam, there were
two undecorated Early Iron Age sherds. Microscopic
analysis of two other undecorated sherds, presumably
from the upper level, shows that they have slag
tempering and are unequivocally Late Iron Age. This
finding indicates that the feature was disturbed
during the Late Iron Age or that it dates to the
Late Iron Age.

A charcoal sample was taken from the charcoal mass,
and a C14 date of 1080 B.C $\pm$ 110 (N-897) was obtained.
This is clearly a contaminated date, obtained from
charcoal recently introduced into the pit. Another
charcoal sample to the north of Feature 29 was taken
from a charcoal mass lying directly on the sterile
subsoil. The charcoal was dated to 1470 B.C. $\pm$ 120
(N-899). This charcoal significantly predates Iron
Age occupation of the area, and it is stratigraphically
located below the Early Iron Age midden. It appears
to be the remains of noncultural burning—perhaps from
a forest fire. Undoubtedly, some of this early
charcoal was introduced into the Early Iron Age pit
when it was originally excavated or when it was later
disturbed by Late Iron Age activity on the site.
The N-899 date, then, helps to explain the process of

contamination for the date obtained from Feature 61
and also Feature 48 in Block E.

The attributes of Feature 61 do not suggest any viable
proposition about function. Feature 62 (Figure 33)
is also difficult to interpret. Only three undecorated
Early Iron Age sherds, tuyère fragments, and 58 grams
of slag were included in its fill. The latter two
categories may mean that Feature 62 has a function
associated with iron production. While the fill is
uniformly dark brown loam throughout, so too is the
fill of Feature 27 in Block C. Furthermore, the form
of the pit in profile has affinities to Feature 34
in Block C, and we have seen that it is possible that
Feature 34 may have an iron production function.
While ethnohistoric data indicate that smelting
furnaces were often cleaned out and reused, the lack
of fired clay on the pit borders denies, for the
time being, the testability of any proposition about
iron smelting in regards to this type of pit.
Therefore, functional interpretation is not possible
until more complete archaeological data and/or ethnographic data are obtained.

Before discussion of Features 28, 29, 60, and 63, it
is necessary to discuss several features in Block D
that do not figure prominently in our discussion
of Early Iron Age settlement. Feature 30 is an
agricultural disturbance. While the overgrown area
where Block D was excavated has not been cultivated
recently, it was cultivated at some time(s) during
the Late Iron Age. Figure 34 indicates that
Feature 36 is an Early Iron Age pit discovered at
-43 centimeters. The contrast between the black,
charcoal-mottled pit fill and the orange subsoil
was severe and easily defined. In the pit fill from
-43 to -56 centimeters, there were several pockets
of orange burned clay with several small pieces of
slag; there was only one Early Iron Age sherd. The
presence of burned clay and slag seems to suggest
that material from another area (for instance, a
smelting furnace) was redeposited in Feature 36.
Since there is no evidence to suggest burning within
the pit itself, a refuse function is tentatively
posited at this time.

To the east of Feature 36 is Feature 29. Figure 35
shows that this pit was defined at -30 centimeters.
This is higher in the midden than most other Early
Iron Age pits, but the pit starts at the top of the
marker soil for the Early Iron Age midden. The
highly compact brown soil from -30 to -50 centimeters
indicates that the fill was not disturbed. There were

several small pockets of burned clay, and the northern
side of the pit floor was lined with burned clay—
along with parts of the southern side. One of the
most distinctive attributes was the central depression
in the bottom of the pit. The cylinder-shaped hole
was 10 centimeters deep and filled with black soil
riddled with charcoal.

The pit fill included two pieces of slag, three
fragments of tuyère, and five undecorated Early Iron
Age sherds. Upon excavation nothing in the form or
contents of the pit was recovered to suggest any
particular function. However, upon comparison to
other pits, it appeared that Feature 36 may at one
time have been similar to Feature 29 but perhaps had
the top 15 centimeters (or the bowl-shaped portion
of the pit) removed by cultivation. As we shall
see, evidence elsewhere on the site points strongly
toward iron production as a function for pits with
similar size holes in the pit floor. Certainly,
the inclusion of slag and tuyères suggests such an
interpretive possibility.

Feature 28 was located several meters to the south of
Feature 29 at approximately the same depth, -28
centimeters. Figure 36 shows that its form is very
much the same as Feature 29. The pit appeared as an
oblong, brown and dark brown stain in orange-brown
clay. It was 85 centimeters wide on its north-south
axis, only 5 centimeters longer than Feature 29.
Like Feature 29, there was iron slag in the pit
(three pieces) as well as fourteen undecorated Early
Iron Age sherds; there was one Early Iron Age sherd
with circular grooving. It was also similar to
Feature 29 in that burned clay was on the northern
floor and some burned clay was against the walls of a
cylindrical depression in the center of the pit (Plate
9). This attribute is identical to the one in
Feature 29.

The fill displayed no signs of recent disturbance.
The inclusion of partially reduced ironstone in the
top center fill and in a pocket on the west side,
along with the other evidence, suggests that it may
have had a function tied to iron production. These
propositions will be explored further in the section
devoted to comparative analysis.

Feature 63 (Figure 37) was located several meters to
the south of Feature 28. It was defined at -40
centimeters as a mass of burned clay and black soil
with charcoal mottling. The resemblance to Feature 45
in Block C is obvious, for the burned clay on the

eastern side of the pit was predominantly dark brown
and set in tan soil. This, then, immediately appeared
to be a pit feature near which or in which there had
been firing under reduced conditions. There was an
apron of brown burned clay on one side, as there was
on both sides of Feature 45.

The top 20 centimeters from -40 to -60 centimeters
was a homogeneous deposit made up of black soil with
some charcoal and orange burned clay. The top 20
centimeters of the fill is a distinct episode and
represents a refuse phase in the pit's overall
functional history. Seventy-five percent of the Early
Iron Age pottery by weight was located in the top 20
centimeters. There were sherds from large jars with
Early Iron Age grooved design elements, pieces of
four globular pots, and bits of small delicate bowls.
The eleven sherds in the bottom two excavation units
represent a more normal, incidental deposition of
pottery in nonrefuse pits.

The burned clay at the bottom of the feature was not
altogether orange but was mixed evenly with brown
pieces of fired clay. It lined the northern and
southern floors and part of a central depression. At
its deepest point, the pit reached -112 centimeters.
While the associated artifacts do not indicate iron
working, the reduced, burned clay and the central
depression may suggest iron smelting, as we will see
in the discussion of Feature 100 in the next section.

The morphology of Feature 63 in its west-east profile
strongly resembled Feature 20 in Block A, a putative
iron-smelting pit. In its north-south profile,
Feature 63 resembled Features 28 and 29 in its bottom
25 centimeters. The fact that Features 28, 29 and 63
in Block D have burned clay on the floors suggests
possible burning activity within the pit; these burned
clay deposits are in situ.

At about the same time that Feature 63 was being
excavated in Block D, the excavation of the brick
pile mnemonic took place to the southeast of the
gridded site. The bricks protruded above the soil
level and were covered by moss. After 2 to 3 centimeters of soil had been removed from the bricks,
their orientation was plain. It was clear that a
house structure was not the structural phenomenon
with which the bricks were associated, as the oral
tradition had claimed. The bricks were mixed with
pieces of slag and partially reduced ironstone. The

circular outline illustrated in Figure 38 represents
a later excavated pit outline. (See Appendix D for a
summary of the brick dimensions.)

At -10 centimeters from the surface level, the outline
of a circular pit became discernible. At this depth,
large quantities of slag were defined in the eastern
sector of the pit as illustrated in Figure 38. There
was also another layer of bricks at the -10 centimeter
level. The bricks, then, were mostly confined to the
western part of the pit and the slag was concentrated
in the eastern part. Once it was defined at -10
centimeters, the pit was excavated in separate units.
The next 20 centimeters was excavated as unit B. This
unit contained most of the bricks in the feature. In
the upper fill in units A and B, there was 0.66
kilograms of tuyères and over 90 percent of the 10.351
kilograms of slag in the feature. There was 0.1
kilogram of tuyères located in the bottom unit, which
was a cylindrical depression very similar in placement and in form to the holes in the bottom of pit
Features 20, 28, 29, and 63.

As Figure 39 indicates, the hole in the bottom of
Feature 100 is slightly off center, as it is in
Features 28 and 29 in Block D. Burned clay was
scattered throughout the pit fill and mixed in with
the slag and fired bricks. The floor on the north
and east sides was lined with a thin layer (2 to 4
centimeters) of burned orange and brown clay pieces.
A similar finding was discovered in the bottoms of
Features 28, 29, and 63. It should be pointed out
that the burned clay is not a pavement of hard baked
clay, but a collection of small nodules that are
fired. The contextual evidence, slag, tuyères, and
bricks all suggest that this is a smelting furnace.
However, consulting metallurgists are perplexed by
the clean appearance of the furnaces and the apparent
lack of a fired clay pavement.

Before moving further from a consideration of iron-
smelting furnaces, it is necessary to discuss
comparative evidence that has been obtained in
archaeological and ethnographic investigations
elsewhere in East Africa for iron smelting. The
inclusion of fired bricks with flat and curved sides
in Feature 100 was at first taken to be the strongest
empirical evidence for generating a hypothesis about
an iron-smelting function for the pit. This argument
is based on Hiernaux and Maquet's (1960) recovery
of similar bricks during their investigations of the

Early Iron Age in Rwanda. They illustrate bricks
that are identical in form to the bricks recovered
from Feature 100 (Plate 10). They note that the
Rwanda bricks, which they date to the Early Iron Age
by associated ceramic evidence, have impressed finger
marks, as do the bricks recovered from the brick pile
mnemonic (Feature 100) at the Rugomora Mahe site
(Plate 11).

However it is also plain that Hiernaux and Maquet
do not attempt to verify their interpretation, which
apparently is based on surface finds and observations.
In the Katuruka case, undecorated Early Iron Age
sherds were recovered from each level of pit fill.
Moreover, a charcoal sample was taken from a sealed
context below slag at -22 centimeters and dated to
170 A.D. + 100 (N-898). Given the standard deviation,
this date agrees with the date obtained for Feature
20 in Block A and for Feature 13 in Block D.

Insufficient comparative and in situ evidence for the
use of fired bricks inhibits attempts to interpret
their possible function in smelting furnaces. But
we can say that the lack of slag runnings on the
bricks and their spatial location above and to the
side of the slag argues against any proposition that
they form a hearth floor.   .

Other excavated furnaces from the Early Iron Age in
East Africa do not have individually fired bricks.
Soper (1971d) excavated a putative iron-smelting
furnace of uncertain date at Chobi along the Victoria
Nile. He recovered lumps of clay with finger impressions, but it is not clear if these are in fact
fired clay bricks. Significantly, Soper apparently
had difficulty defining the bottom limits of the pit.
This was also a difficulty in archaeological definition
of the Katuruka furnaces, and it suggests that the
eventual limits are ambiguous because they are
isothermal boundaries.

Posnansky's (with Grinrod, 1968) excavation of an iron-
smelting furnace in the highlands of Kenya constitutes
altogether different evidence. He found that the
bottom of the furnace was a solidly fired clay mass
or pavement and that there was a vitrified clay cap
on the top of the furnace. This example is clearly
Late Iron Age, and in form it does not explicate the
pit features found at Katuruka. Most of the furnaces
found elsewhere in East and Central Africa do not
have characteristics that help to explain the structure
of the archaeological cases in Buhaya. However,
evidence from North Africa greatly assists attempts to

interpret the possible function of bricks in the
Early Iron Age furnaces of East Africa.

The evidence recovered by Shinnie for Early Iron Age
iron production at Meroe provides important clues
for the use of bricks in furnaces. Plate 12 (by
courtesy of Peter Shinnie) shows an Early Iron Age
furnace excavated at Meroe during 1969-1970. Meroe
has long been known as a huge center of iron production
during the Early Iron Age in the middle Nile region.
The illustrated furnace, which appears to be a shaft-
bowl type, has vertical walls constructed of bricks
that are approximately the same size and form as
those excavated from Feature 100. Also note that
there is a hole in the bottom of the furnace floor.
Four dates are associated with this complex, ranging
from 210 A.D. (HAR -348/II) to 520 A.D. (RL-286)
(K. Robertson, personal communication). The oldest
date for iron production at Meroe thus far obtained
is 514 B.C. $\pm$ 75 (Birm. 97) (Willet, 1971).

The hole in the bottom of the furnace floor, the form
and arrangement of the bricks in vertical walls, and
the dating all suggest that the Meroe furnace may
bear close affinities to the less completely preserved
cases in Buhaya.

Archaeological data for Meroe and Buhaya cannot be
compared, however, without detailed evidence from both
areas. For example, the furnaces excavated by Shinnie
may be Roman influenced, and they have slag tapping
channels (Tylecote, 1975), a feature not represented
in the Katuruka furnaces. Hopefully, further
investigations at Meroe, in the areas between Meroe
and the interlacustrine area, and in East Africa will
lead to more substantial analysis and interpretation
about possible technological ties between the two
areas. For now, it appears that technological life
during the Early Iron Age in Buhaya may have close
parallels and affinities to contemporary technological
life in North Africa.

If the Early Iron Age peoples of the Buhaya coastal
belt built furnace walls of brick, what happened to
most of the brick? The amount of brick deposited
in Feature 100 was not sufficient to build a wall
higher than, say, 25 to 30 centimeters. There is
always the possibility that if bricks were difficult
to make, then they may have been reused; today in
other parts of Africa tuyères are reused when they
are not destroyed. Local folklore in Katuruka about
other "house" bricks suggests that Early Iron Age
furnaces are probably scattered throughout this and

neighboring villages.

A structure of considerable significance in Block D
was Feature 60, located at -40 centimeters as a black
greasy soil set in orange subsoil. Figure 40 shows
that the black stain was approximately 2 meters in
diameter and had an elongated section that ran a meter
to the southwest (Plate 13). The soil within the
oblong area was very organic looking and had a
greasy texture. It was heavily mottled with charcoal,
which in good part contributed to the organic qualities
because of the fine pulverized nature of charcoal. On
the periphery of the dark stain, there were seven
small circular stains with charcoal inclusions. Inspection of these stains on the scraped floor showed
that these might have been post molds; this assumption
was verified by excavation. Within the black circular
area were three smaller areas with higher densities
of charcoal. When the larger feature was excavated,
these areas were given separate attention and were
also found to be post molds.

The feature was divided into three excavation sections
from north to south, and all artifacts were individually plotted. Excavation revealed that the deposit
was 10 centimeters deep at the deepest point and that
the depth averaged 5 to 6 centimeters. The density
of artifacts was low. Six tuyère fragments were
located in the bulge on the east side, and these
were accompanied by four undecorated Early Iron Age
sherds immediately to the north of post mold J. In
excavation unit B, there were seven undecorated Early
Iron Age sherds, three of which were located 3 centimeters west of post mold B. Excavation unit C yielded
six undecorated sherds and one sherd with a grooved
design element. All but one of these sherds were
located in the elongated area to the southwest and
to the south of post mold E. Slag was excavated in
units A and B; two pieces were with the tuyères on the
east side and two pieces to the northeast of post
mold B.

Excavation of the post molds (Figure 41) revealed
considerable variability in form. Morphologically,
post molds A, C, E, and M belong to the same category,
as do J and K, and F and B. Both J and K are located
within the borders of the larger feature and have
shallow profiles 11 to 13 centimeters deep. G does
not belong to the southern cluster because its diameter
is small, it is spatially separated, and its morphology
does not fit the other patterns. Of the post molds

surrounding Feature 60, H and I appear to be divergent
in form, but in fill type and in spatial orientation
they definitely belong to the complex of post molds.
There was uniformity of fill in all cases, with charcoal fill, which perhaps indicates burned posts, and
in three instances (E, B, and C) the inclusions of
Early Iron Age sherds.

The spatial articulation of the post molds to Feature
60 and the characteristics of Feature 60 strongly
suggest that this structural complex is a floor. It
is impossible to tell by the arrangement of the post
molds what form the structure may have had, but there
is an elongated quality, for instance, H-J-B-M-F and
A-E-C, which suggests a structure departing from conventional house forms. The darkly stained area is
too small to argue that it is an area of human
habituation or a house. Certainly, a nuclear family
could not be accommodated in such a small space.
Even then, the elongated area to the southwest that
resembles an entry path was an arrangement closely
resembling the structure of Bahaya traditional houses.
In addition, small temporary dwellings are built in
Buhaya by transient populations; these small grass
huts are at least 4 meters in diameter.

The elongated post mold pattern and the distribution
of artifacts in the fill suggest instead that this
structure is a special structure used to protect a
task area. The artifacts within the floor fill were
all located in the vicinity of post molds or were
discarded on the periphery of the structure, such
as in the putative entry way. The inclusion of slag
and tuyères in the floor fill and the large concentration of smelting furnace bricks to the northwest of
the floor suggest that there may have been an activity
associated with iron production under a shelter, whose
axis had a northwest-southeast orientation. The
inclusion of much pulverized charcoal also suggests
the proposition that the structure is associated with
the processing of iron. I propose that the floor
and post molds associated with Feature 60 represent a
structure that sheltered a special task area where a
phase of iron production occurred.

Ethnographic data from Buhaya show that there are
presently long open-ended structures with large center
posts and smaller side posts used as iron-forging
huts. The general dimensions of these structures fit
the size of Feature 60 arrangement. These archaeological data are important for understanding the settlement history of the site and contribute to our understanding of Early Iron Age technology in East Africa.

The spatial arrangements of Block D features also tell
us much about Early Iron Age technology and the
behavior associated with it. Feature 13 was situated
equidistant from the smelting furnaces, Features 29
and 28. It is 50 percent further from Feature 63,
which is also a putative furnace. Signficantly,
the area between Feature 13 and the other three
features was virtually clean of Early Iron Age artifacts. The floor of the shelter was also relatively
clean, but it was clear that whatever refuse remained
was tossed to an out-of-the-way place, beside a post
or at the edge of the enclosure. The exception is
the brick concentration, which appears to be outside
the primary work area. The lack of iron production
material in the furnaces and around Feature 13 likely
is a result of the refuse function of Feature 13.
It evidently received waste products resulting from
activities to its west. This interpretation will be
developed further in Chapter 10.

The excavation of Block E contributed substantially
to (1) the settlement history of the site, and (2) the
development of propositions for explaining the behavior
of iron production during the Early Iron Age. Its
added importance, of course, lies in its confirmation
of the historical value of myth about iron smelting
at Kaiija tree. The Block E excavations also have
enormous importance for establishing the antiquity
of iron production in the Buhaya area and in East
Africa. These contributions when viewed together mean
that mythology in an African culture has helped
locate the earliest known Iron Age site in East or
Central Africa and that mythological systems appear
to have the capacity for a documentary, historical
continuity that may extend over more than two
millennia.

Figure 42 shows the configuration of both Early and
Late Iron Age features and post molds in the block
excavation. The spaces labeled areas are concentrations of charcoal that are related to the activity
complex represented in Features 6 and 55. The Late
Iron Age midden in Block E is approximately 82 centimeters in depth, which makes it the deepest deposit
on the site—with the exception of parts of Area 2.
It is clear from the illustration that there have been
both Early and Late Iron Age activities in the area,
for pit Features 49, 50, 52, and 54 cut through the
Early Iron Age deposits into the subsoil. A feature
of essential interest is Feature 6, which was located
exactly where local mythology said Rugomora Mahe's

men had produced iron. The important focus for discussion in Block E is the complex of features associated with iron production during the Early Iron Age. In order to concentrate on that aspect of the archaeology, Late Iron Age features will be discussed first.

Several Late Iron Age features are similar in pit fill and anomalous in function. Features 50 and 52 (Figure 42 plan view) were located in the western part of Block E. Feature 50 was delimited at -75 centimeters along the northern wall. It appeared as dark brown soil in the context of orange-brown clay. The pit fill was very loosely packed and loamy, which suggested relatively recent excavation and deposition. The cultural material within the pit, which was only partially excavated, confirmed this impression. There were only three undecorated Late Iron Age sherds. The pit does not appear to have been dug for refuse disposal, for the ratio of artifacts to volume is about the same as the Late Iron Age midden. The function cannot be established. The same characteristics are displayed in Feature 52 to the southwest of Feature 50. Feature 52 contained one roulette decorated Late Iron Age sherd and three pieces of slag weighing 32 grams. The date for this feature is Late Iron Age by pottery and fill type. The iron slag could easily have been introduced from the midden in this area. The function cannot be determined.

Feature 54, illustrated in Figure 43, was located at -104 centimeters, which in this part of the block is slightly above the subsoil and within the Early Iron Age midden. The pit had very heavy densities of charcoal in the top 5 centimeters. Its stratigraphic placement and the fact that an area of disturbance was not observed above it in the orange-brown clay suggest that this is an Early Iron Age pit. However, only two sherds were recovered—an undecorated Early Iron Age sherd and a roulette decorated sherd of Late Iron Age date. As a consequence of this ambiguity, the pit has been placed in the map as a Late Iron Age feature, but it may be Early Iron Age. The function is unclear.

In the center of Block E there was a large intrusive feature. Feature 49 (Figure 44) was defined at -96 centimeters as a round spot made up of black organic soil very similar to the top soil on the site. Mixed in with the black fill were several pockets of laterite or ironstone. The fill was extremely soft and uniform throughout. In excavation unit A, there was a heavy density of large roulette decorated sherds. Within

the next excavation unit, the sides of the pit started
to slope in and the number of pot sherds dropped off
radically to two. The bottom part of the pit fill,
which went to -140 centimeters, was sterile. Feature
49 does not appear to be limited exclusively to a
function as receptacle for refuse. The limitation
of most pottery, which comes from several large jars
with large (5 to 6 millimeters) slag tempering, to the
top 15 centimeters argues against its excavation for
refuse alone. The deposition of the partial pots
appears to have been secondary to the primary function,
as the bottom of the pit did not receive refuse. The
location of this feature at the center of an important
ceremonial area may mean that the feature was originally dug to serve some related function and was then
filled with refuse and soil to cover it up. This is
purely a speculation and does not merit conversion
to a proposition, for there are insufficient data.

The pit features of the Early Iron Age are essential
to archaeological investigation of the Early Iron
Age and to the development of new approaches to African
history. The evidence has far-ranging implications.

Feature 6 (Figure 45) was discovered by testing in the
first month of excavation—exactly where myth suggested we would find evidence for iron working. Indeed,
all the evidence from Feature 6 suggest that iron was
produced in the pit or in its immediate proximity.
It was first defined as a mass of charcoal pieces
up to 3 centimeters in diameter. The charcoal
mass formed an apron around the north, east, and west
borders of the pit, the outlines of which were delimited 5 centimeters below the -98 centimeter level
of charcoal. The charcoal mass extended from the
edge of the apron, across the lip of the pit, and
over the pit fill. The charcoal is an integral part
of the pit. There were twelve pieces of slag weighing
176 grams in the top 20 centimeters of pit fill. It
is from this level in a sealed context that a charcoal
sample was taken in association with the slag for C14
dating. In this same level there was an open-mouth
bowl with sloping walls and a thickened lip supporting
six bevels. This was the only example of a bevelled
rim with more than four bevels on the site. The area
below the bevels had a 2.5 centimeter band of
incised cross-hatching. The rarity of this type
of Urewe ware on the site and its association with
this feature is particularly noteworthy, considering
the date for the feature.

The result of C14 dating was 450 B.C. + 115 (N-890).
This date first appeared to be too early, for other

dating in East Africa had indicated a later date for the Early Iron Age. For instance, Soper (1967) has defined a regional Early Iron Age pottery in western Kenya and Tanzania; Kwale ware has been dated to 220 A.D. ± 115 (Fagan, 1967b; Soper, 1967); and Soper has also obtained dating for Urewe ware in the Kavirondo Gulf area of western Kenya. The Urewe type site has been dated from 270 A.D. ± 110 (N-435) to 390 A.D. ± 95 (Fagan, 1967b:157).

The Feature 6 date and its departure from the generally accepted notions for the antiquity of the Iron Age in East Africa (100-200 A.D.) required further confirmation. Given the excellent context from which the charcoal was obtained, further testing seemed appropriate. A further sample was submitted to Radiocarbon Ltd. for testing from Feature 6. The results confirmed previous conclusions; a date of 520 B.C. ± 110 (RL-406) was obtained. This strongly suggests that the Iron Age was established much earlier in Buhaya than elsewhere in East Africa. As a further check, a sample was taken from the center of Area C, a charcoal mass located to the east of Feature 6.

The arrangement of charcoal around Feature 6 suggests that it was associated with a phase of iron production that called for great quantities of charcoal. To test this idea, and to see whether or not the charcoal was the result of independent and earlier, noncultural burning (everything about context denied this), the Area C sample was submitted for dating. This sample was dated to 600 B.C. ± 100 (RL-405), which is substantially within the range of the Feature 5 date.

The second set of dates from Feature 6 and Area C confirms the first dates and buttresses the argument that the Iron Age in the Buhaya area is at least as old as 500 B.C. The other date for this area is also from the same time period; Feature 58 has been dated to 500 B.C. ± 115 (N-895). The recent results show that the Early Iron Age in East Africa dates as far back as the Nok culture in Nigeria. It must be recognized, however, that such dating is isolated to one area and needs to be confirmed by similar dating from other sites. It is possible, for instance that the charcoal used in and near Feature 6 was made of old wood, thus skewing the dates. Therefore, further evidence is necessary to determine the range of variability for Early Iron Age dates.

The bottom portion of Feature 6 had bits of burned orange clay in the center. As the bottom was approached, the burned clay became more dense until

charcoal or artifacts were no longer present. The
northern, eastern, and southern parts of the pit
had at least a 5 to 10 centimeter thick layer of
burned clay, a deposit that indicates burning inside
the pit. A small pit to the west of Feature 6 was
excavated as part of Feature 6 (Plate 14). Several
undecorated Early Iron Age sherds were included in
the predominantly charcoal-filled pit. The scatter of
charcoal around Feature 6 may mean that charcoal was
excavated from the large pit and thrown around its
edges. This activity might have taken place after
a smelt when the bloom and other materials were removed from the broken-up furnace. But the distribution
of charcoal with a low density on one side highly
resembled a forging furnace in contemporary Buhaya.
In this case, there appears to be real utility in
ethnographic analogy based on data obtained during
ethnoarchaeological study of forging. Some of the
charcoal areas had deep deposits; Area A, for example,
was 20 centimeters deep and parts of Area B were 15
centimeters deep. The scatter of materials from iron
production, such as slag, also was dense around
Feature 6. While the charcoal was distributed to the
east, slag was concentrated to the west (see Chapter
10). The charcoal areas are also where tuyères tend
to be concentrated; the behavioral implications of
these differential spatial distributions are not
known.

Part of the activity complex associated with Feature
6 is Feature 48 which is located 1 meter to the
northwest (Plate 15). Feature 48 was delimited at
-96 centimeters, or -66 centimeters from ground level,
which slopes downward on this side of the block. As
Figure 46 indicates, it was defined as an irregular,
funnel-shaped collection of ironstone mixed with dark
brown soil. In the top 12 centimeters of the pit,
there was a profusion of iron slag, 0.69 kilograms.
The slag was located in the center of the pit, which
appeared to have been disturbed, and some pieces were
sitting on top of the pit fill. Most of the pit
fill was ironstone, a type of fill that made it easier
to define. However, where there was no ironstone, the
limits of the pit were difficult to establish. The
incidence of cultural material was very light for the
first excavation unit.

At -111 centimeters, the pit fill changed to slightly
darker soil with charcoal mottling. A mixed sample
of charcoal was collected from this zone and submitted
for dating. The date obtained was 1250 B.C. ± 120
(N-894). This is an aberrant date that appears to be
the result of a later intrusion into the center of

the pit during which time foreign charcoal was introduced. The density of iron slag in this part of the
fill decreased to 75 grams, or approximately 10 percent of the total slag in the pit.

In the top two excavation units, there was one piece
of undecorated pottery. From -131 to -141 centimeters
there was a centralized concentration of pottery in a
black, charcoal-mottled spot 15 centimeters in diameter. One grooved decorated and sixteen undecorated
sherds came from this limited area. In excavation
unit D, immediately below the area discussed, we recovered three undecorated and one incised rim sherd
dating to the Early Iron Age; the rim sherd came from
a large, globular pot with a heavy and high upper
rim, an unusual attribute. The ironstone pit fill
then continued to -162 centimeters, where definition
of the feature outline was very difficult.

The arrangement of fill suggests at least three episodes of filling: (1) the bottom portion was filled
with ironstone, (2) the middle part with charcoal
and ironstone, and (3) the top 12 to 15 centimeters
with ironstone and slag. The localization of slag
and charcoal in the center of the top deposit and its
vertical placement above the pottery concentration
in unit C suggest that there has been later excavation
into the pit fill for refuse deposit, with pottery
placed in the bottom (unit C), foreign charcoal in
the intermediate zone, and slag in the topmost portion.

Because of its slag and ironstone content, this pit
appears to have a functional relationship to Feature 6.
There is not sufficient evidence to argue that Feature
48 had a smelting function, but its ironstone content
and close proximity to a possible furnace (Feature 55)
and a forge is reminiscent of Feature 23 in Block C.
It is possible that ironstone was prepared for smelting
by roasting in the pit, but there is little contextual
evidence to suggest this alternative. Possibly, the
pit may have been a storage pit for ironstone to be
used in smelting. Analysis of ironstone samples taken
from the edge of Feature 48 shows that the ironstone
has been partially reduced, a finding that may be
support for a roasting function. The slag in the pit
most probably came from iron production carried out
in the Features 6 and 55 complex.

Feature 55 (Figure 47) was located to the east of
Feature 6 with charcoal deposits between. It was
delineated as a concentration of brown and orange
burned clay. The clay was exactly the same color as
in Feature 45 in Block C and Feature 63 in Block D.

Definitions of the pit boundary proceeded according
to the distribution of the orange and brown burned
clay. There was no cultural debris. Several thick
layers of charcoal were mixed in with the burned clay,
especially at -128 centimeters on the south side,
where there was a 20 centimeter wide and 8 centimeter
deep pocket of large charcoal lumps. It is
important to emphasize that a good portion of the
burned clay was dark brown and mixed with a darker
soil; the brown clay was concentrated in a layer from
-112 to -128 centimeters. The pit was probably the
location of a fire burned under reduced conditions,
namely, a smelting operation. The layer of brown
clay, I propose, was the area exposed to reduction
(along with the north wall); the lower areas were
fired but were too deep to be exposed to a highly
controlled reduced atmosphere. The hypothesis
offered for function in Feature 45 and 63 is partially
confirmed by the remains in Feature 55. It can also
be observed that the basic forms of Features 45, 63,
and 55 are very similar; also, all have aprons of
burned clay on the edge of the pit.

The location of Feature 55 near Feature 6 suggests
related activities associated with iron production.
There is good evidence that Feature 6 was used for
forging. The orange burned clay in the bottom of
Feature 6 shows that firing in that particular pit
was done in an oxidizing atmosphere—probably an open
fire. In addition, the scatter of slag and charcoal
around the pit (rather than in the pit as in Feature
100) suggests activities different from smelting. It
is my suggestion that the arrangement of Features
48, 6, and 55 represents a smelting-forging area;
Feature 6, even though it lacks an anvil, appears the
likeliest possibility as a forge.

The other Early Iron Age features in Block E also
appear to have some relationship to the complex just
discussed. Pit Feature 53 illustrated in Figure 48
was located to the southwest of Feature 48. It was
defined at -100 centimeters in the subsoil. The fill
was black, included charcoal, and extended to -114
centimeters. There was one Early Iron Age sherd and
several pieces of slag weighing 43 grams. The sherd
is particularly noteworthy, for it displays distinctive
spatula marks, a decorative characteristic otherwise
unknown to Early Iron Age ceramics. The inclusion
of slag probably means some function tied to the
primary complex. Feature 56, (Figure 49) was located
25 centimeters to the southeast of Feature 53 at the
same depth. The fill was made up of dark brown soil
with some charcoal and ironstone. The small pit was

22 centimeters deep. Its shape is very similar to
Feature 53 except for the northeastern bulge. There
was one Early Iron Age sherd. The function of both
of these small pits is not clear at this time.

The remaining two Early Iron Age features are Features
57 and 58. Feature 57 is located several centimeters
south of 48. It was located approximately 5 centimeters into the subsoil and was the same form as the
small pit located to the west of Feature 6. There
were large charcoal lumps on the north side, and dark
brown loam and charcoal in the center and south side.
No pottery was recovered, but the stratigraphic
location and spatial relationship with the other
features show that it is an Early Iron Age pit.

In the southeastern corner, there was a large black
stain, which at first was not recognized as a possible
pit because of its massiveness. Figure 50 shows that
Feature 58 was the largest feature on the site, with
a total volume of 1439 liters. The pit was defined
at -93 centimeters in orange-brown clay. It was
excavated in 15 centimeter units. The top 30 centimeters of the fill was dark brown and very loosely
packed. Thereafter, the color changed to black,
included flakes of charcoal, and remained uniform to
-195 centimeters, the bottom of the pit. There was
slag weighing 103 grams in the top 30 centimeters of
fill along with one undecorated Early Iron Age sherd.
The fill was then sterile until -150 to -158 centimeters, where we recovered two undecorated and one
grooved Early Iron Age sherds. The charcoal density
was sufficient at the level for a charcoal sample.
The C14 date obtained was 550 B.C. + 115. This date
is very close to the Feature 6 and Area C dates. As
pointed out previously, more recent dating results
have confirmed that the dates for Features 6 and 58
are accurate and acceptable.

The function of the large pit with stepped sides is
not clear. By inference, it might be argued that the
stepped sides were intended as steps to facilitate
descent into the pit. If so, it could next be
inferred that the depth and the steps might mean a
water hole. This sequence of speculation, of course,
cannot be legitimized by any empirical data. For the
time being, functional interpretation of features
like 58 must await further evidence. The dearth of
material culture in this pit suggests that it was
filled by natural means, perhaps by erosion of charcoal
and soil around Features 55 and 6. The top deposition,
however, indicates intentional filling with soil and
refuse slag.

The final structure to be discussed is Block E has major implications for ties between myth, place names, and archaeological data. Figure 51 shows Block E Early Iron Age features and post molds. The post mold data are particularly important, even crucial, to an understanding of the Kaiija tree oral tradition. First, the post molds, which were defined at -80 to -90 centimeters toward the top of the Early Iron Age midden, were arranged in a circular pattern: A, B, C, D, E, F, G, H, I, J, M, and N surround the iron production complex—Features 6, 48, and 55. All but one of the post molds were filled with small ironstone (laterite) pebbles. The exception is I, which was filled with charcoal. In some of the post molds, the pebbles were confined to their periphery (such as M), so that it appeared that the center had once been occupied by a post. The form appears reasonably uniform with the exception of A, which was sunk on the periphery of Feature 48 and which had charcoal inclusions. C and G are also deeper than the rest, but they were defined 5 centimeters higher (-77 centimeters) than any of the other cases (Figure 52).

It is clear that all of the post molds with ironstone inclusions belong to the same class. They have been dated to the Early Iron Age by stratigraphy, by spatial articulation to the feature complex, and by ceramics recovered from C and H. The remaining post molds, T and U, are isolated from the group, and post molds Q, R, and S date to the Late Iron Age. Post mold L might have been an interior support post for what appears to be a circular hut used as a shelter for the iron production complex.

In Chapter 7, it was pointed out that the word Kaiija is derived from luiija, which is a hut and the anvil used by iron workers. It is said that the tree takes its name from the hut built at its base by iron workers. The archaeological results demonstrate that a hut was in fact built at that spot to shelter an iron production complex and that it was a hut built from posts that were held in their holes by an ironstone packing. These data are the final confirmation that the mythological and place name information at the Rugomora Mahe site in Katuruka have astounding value as historical documents for Early Iron Age activity.

The final block of three squares was opened to the west of Block A to determine whether the physical marker for Rugomora's burial place and the dense scatter of ceremonial artifacts, such as cowries, were also markers for Early Iron Age structures—as they had been elsewhere on the site. The association between surface ceremonial artifacts and below-surface Early Iron Age features was established in the three squares of Block F. In the western side of Block F at -47 centimeters, we discovered a dark brown circle (Figure 53) with orange clay in the center. The pit was 97 centimeters west to east and extended to -134 centimeters. The distinguishing characteristic was the 30 centimeter circle of subsoil clay set in the top center. In this respect, the pit resembled Feature 7 in Block A.

At -47 centimeters on the east side of the clay, there was a partial pavement of sandstone blocks. The pottery recovered at this depth from the pit was all Late Iron Age; there were twisted grass, roulette decorated sherds as well as sherds decorated by stamped grass (cord) impressions. Fifty-four percent of the pottery by weight was recovered from the top 15 centimeters. The bulk of the remaining pottery (30 percent) came from -70 to -85 centimeters within a charcoal-mottled pocket of black soil. At -87 centimeters there was another pavement of sandstone blocks which were placed so that their flat sides were on top. A charcoal sample was taken from below the sandstone blocks at -105 centimeters. The date obtained was 1645 A.D. + 120 (N-898). This date agrees very closely with the date obtained in Feature 41 in Block C. In addition, there were also grass-impressed sherds in Feature 41, which may indicate that this was a temporally bounded decorative technique during the Late Iron Age.

The remainder of the pit fill in Feature 59 was sterile. It is not clear what the function was, but the inclusion of sherds with thick char and the stone arrangement at first pointed toward a possible hearth. But sufficient charcoal and ash were lacking, and there is little to justify the claim. The date and ordering of fill—especially the rock pavement which, as a sealer, resembles the ash in Feature 7—suggest that this feature is related to the activity complex to which Feature 7 and 41 belong. These pits were constructed in the late seventeenth century, and their creation appears to coincide with the occupation (and possible death) of King Rugomora Mahe on the site.

The other feature found beneath the marking trees for Rugomora Mahe's "burial place" was Feature 64 (Figure 54). This was an Early Iron Age pit discovered at -60 centimeters and defined as a concentrated mass of orange burned clay mixed with charcoal. The main pit floor extended to -83 centimeters, and the bottom

of a hole on the southeast side went to -103 centimeters. A plentitude of Early Iron Age pottery was
found in this pit. Flared-rim bowls and pieces of a
groove-decorated, large globular, necked jar were
recovered. The curvature of the sherds from the large
jar suggested a jar at least 40 to 55 centimeters in
diameter, which is much larger than any other pot form
heretofore recovered. There was also a base of a
globular pot without a dimple. The distinctiveness
of the pottery forms suggests that this pit may either
include pottery from a distinct time period or that
another functional category of Early Iron Age pottery
has been discovered.

The pit itself shows signs of oxidized burning only.
The small size, characteristics of burning, and the
pottery all suggest that pit Feature 64 belongs to
a functional category different from the other Early
Iron Age structures on the site. I propose that this
pit was a cooking hearth. The pottery forms associated
with it range from possible cooking to food storage
vessels, and the pit size and fired clay also suggest
an open-hearth fire.

The Block excavations revealed a broad variety of
feature types and activity complexes. Of essential
importance is that the two activity areas associated
with iron production in Blocks D and E are the first
activity complexes for iron production documented
for the Early Iron Age in East Africa. The excavation
results also show that the site was predominantly
an iron production area and that iron production took
place on the site during two distinct periods of the
Early Iron Age. The first period was 400-500 B.C.,
thus far the earliest documented iron working in the
Buhaya area. The Block E excavations confirm the
historical accuracy and value of mythology about this
early period, regardless of changes it experienced
under Bahinda manipulations. The second period of
iron production took place about 50-150 A.D. The
activities associated with this period have been
archaeologically documented in Blocks A, D, possibly
Block C, and Feature 100, which helped to demonstrate
further the archaeological utility of mnemonic devices.

There are relatively fewer data to argue for a general
occupation of the site, although the facilities for
food preparation in Block C (Feature 30) and the
putative hearths in Block A and F suggest that
domestic life may have been located in the northern,
unexcavated part of the site. The inclusion of

domestically linked pottery in Feature 13 refuse also suggests the existence of domestic activities on the site, the vestiges of which have been partly obliterated by efficient refuse collection.

The Late Iron Age structures also help to explain the distribution of ceremonial activities on the site. Because of the correspondences between the C14 dates and genealogical information, we are assuming that the pits very tentatively interpreted as ceremonial are tied into the occupation of Rugomora Mahe or his subsequent veneration. It is certain, however, that the dating for the 1650-1700 period documents an intense utilization of the site by Late Iron Age peoples, presumably the Bahinda who seized the Bacwezi shrine, its mnemonics, and its associated oral traditions. Finally, there is a correlation between the distribution of ceremonial artifacts such as cowries on the surface and the density of Early Iron Age features on the site. On other sites of like structure, it should be possible to test the hypothesis that if there are physical structures and artifacts of a ceremonial nature, then there will be Early Iron Age structures below ground in the same areas. This is a testable hypothesis; its viability has been affirmed by the Rugomora Mahe excavations. It also stands as testimony to the fact that the Rugomora Mahe results have helped to develop new investigatory and explanatory procedures for Early Iron Age and Late Iron Age lifeways.

Plate I: Block A from the east with Feature 7 pedestalled on the left.

Plate II: Feature 20, Early Iron Age smelting pit from the west with Feature 7 (Late Iron Age) in background.

Plate III: Feature 4, Block B, Late Iron Age; this was a concentration of laterite blocks; viewed here from the east in initial stage of excavation.

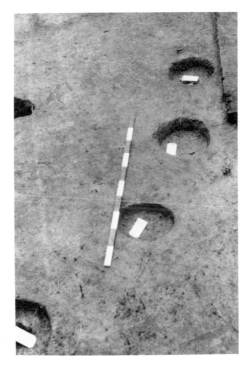

Plate IV: Post molds F, G, H, and I to the west of Feature 4 in block B; these post molds are Late Iron Age.

Plate V: Parallel lines of stone, Late Iron Age, Block B; this is the northeast extension of Feature 4; view from the southwest.

Plate VI: Block C excavations from east with stone concentration, including grindstones in foreground. Block C_1 is in background behind mango tree.

Plate VII: Features 34 and 27, Block C, Early Iron Age; viewed from the south after excavation.

Plate VIII: Dimple-base pot, Feature 13.

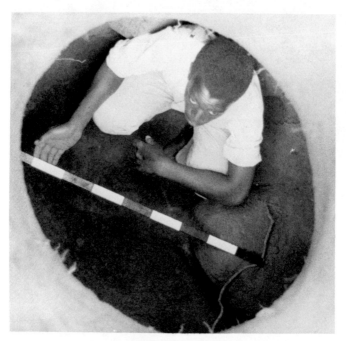

Plate IX: Sandstone block in bottom of Feature 13.

Plate X: Feature 28, Block D, an Early Iron smelting furnace viewed from the south after excavation.

Plate XI: Molded, fired brick from iron smelting furnace, Feature 100.

Plate XII: Finger impressions on bricks from Feature 100.

Plate XIII: An Early Iron Age furnace excavated by Peter Shinnie at Meröe, Sudan.

Plate XIV: Block D, Feature 60, Early Iron age shelter floor from north.

Plate XV: Feature 6, from the west after excavation of the pit and surrounding charcoal concentrations.

Plate XVI: Block E from west; Feature 49 right foreground; Feature 48 left center; Feature 6 right rear; Feature 55 left rear.

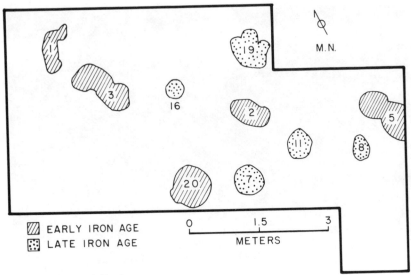

Figure 1: Block A Features.

Figure 2: Feature 1, Early Iron Age (Block A).

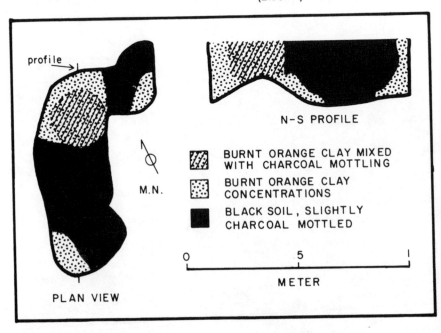

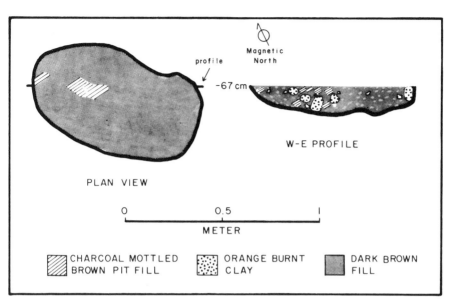

Figure 3: Feature 2, Block A, Early
Iron Age.

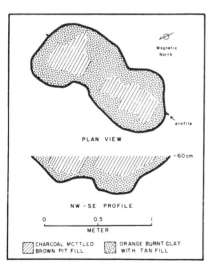

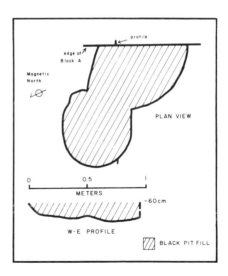

Figure 4: Feature 3, Block A, Early
Iron Age; interpreted as a possible
hearth.

Figure 5: Feature 5, Block A, Early
Iron Age; function is unclear, but it is a
possible refuse pit.

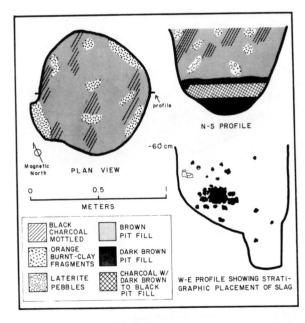

Figure 7: Feature 7, Block A, Late Iron Age; note the circular configuration of charcoal in plan view and its distinctive boundaries in profile.

Figure 6: Feature 20, Block A, Early Iron Age; probable iron smelting furnace; dated to 120 A.D. ± 110.

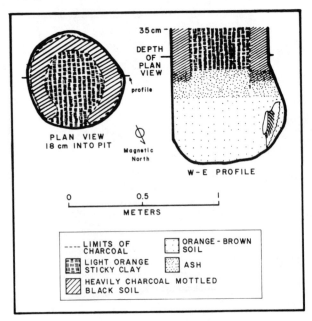

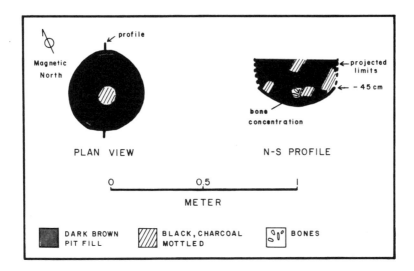

Figure 8: Feature 16, Block A, Late Iron Age; located in center of Block A and stratigraphically equivalent to feature 7.

Figure 9: Feature 8, Block A, Late Iron Age; the function of the bell-shaped pit is not clear.

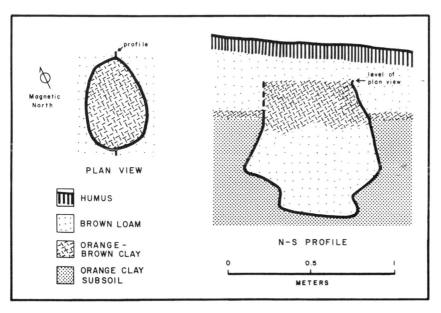

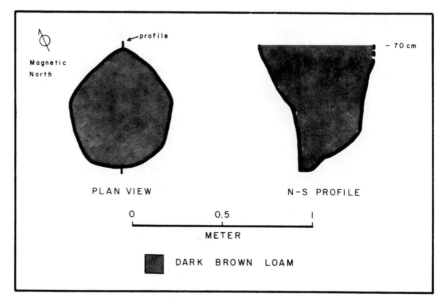

Figure 10: Feature 11, Block A, Late Iron Age.

Figure 11: Feature 19, Block A, Late Iron Age.

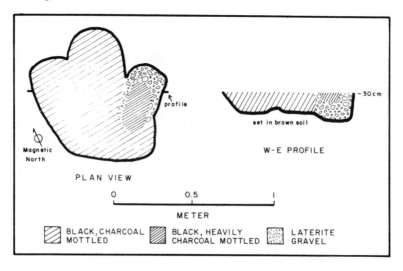

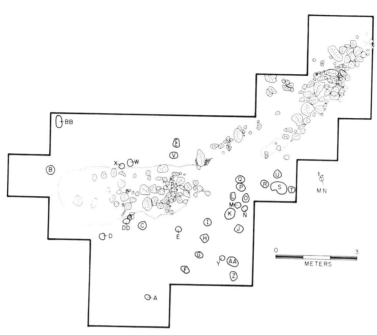

Figure 12: Block B: Feature 4 and post molds. Post molds are marked with letters.

Figure 13: Block B post mold from Late Iron Age; profiles are north-south unless indicated.

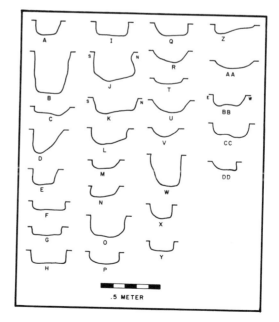

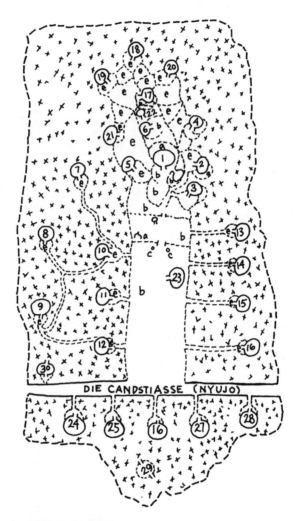

Figure 14: Hermann Rehse depicted
the structural arrangement of a
Mukama's *kikale* during the early twentieth century in Kiziba kingdom. The
cattle enclosures are in the lower portion of the picture and area numbered
24-28. The shrine for Mugasha (a) is
left of the gate in the first enclosure off
the main avenue.

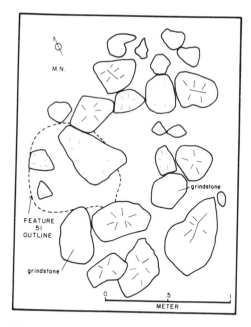

Figure 15: Feature 30, a rock circle including grindstones. Dotted outline de-
limits Feature 51, located beneath
grindstones; it is located in eastern
part of Block A and dates to Early Iron
Age.

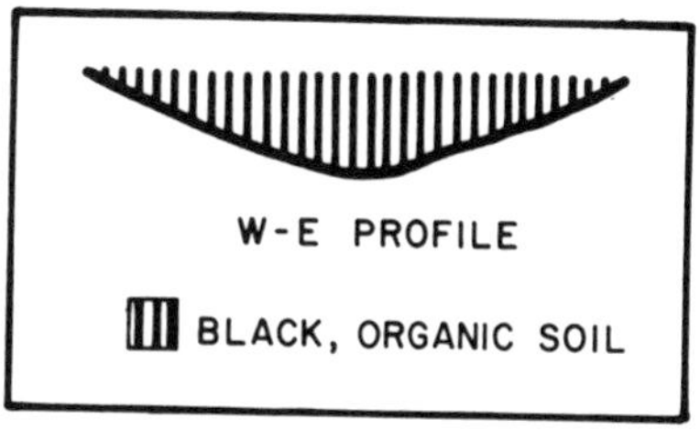

W-E PROFILE

III BLACK, ORGANIC SOIL

Figure 16: Feature 51, Late Iron Age;
located beneath Feature 30.

Figure 17: Block C features and post
molds. Post molds are marked with
letters.

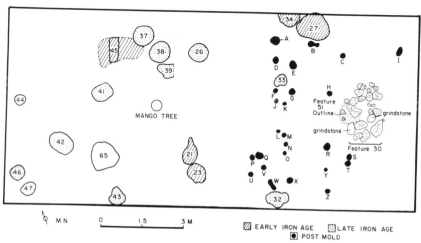

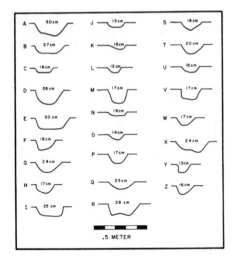

Figure 18: Block C post mold profiles, with north-south profiles.

Figure 19: Feature 34, Block C, Early Iron Age. This pit is located contiguous to and west of Feature 27.

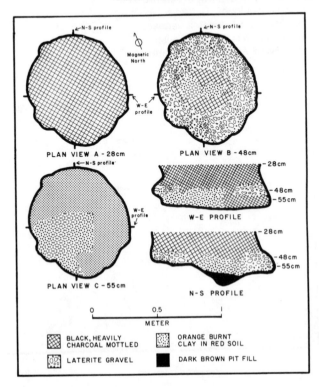

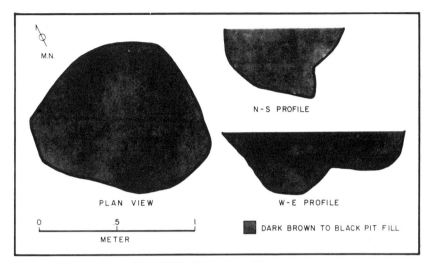

M.N.

N-S PROFILE

W-E PROFILE

PLAN VIEW

0   .5

METER

■ DARK BROWN TO BLACK PIT FILL

Figure 20: Feature 27, Block C, Early Iron Age; it is possible that this feature has a functional relationship to 34 which is similar to Feature 23's relationship to 21, also in Block C.

Figure 21: Feature complex 21, 23, Block C_1. This Early Iron Age complex has a possible function related to iron production.

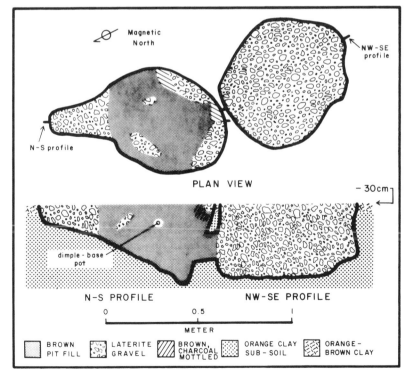

Magnetic North

NW-SE profile

N-S profile

PLAN VIEW

-30cm

dimple - base pot

N-S PROFILE   NW-SE PROFILE

0   0.5   I

METER

BROWN PIT FILL   LATERITE GRAVEL   BROWN, CHARCOAL MOTTLED   ORANGE CLAY SUB-SOIL   ORANGE-BROWN CLAY

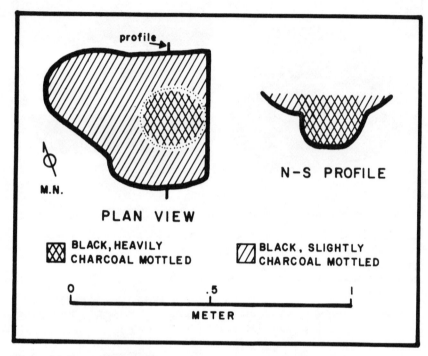

Figure 22: Feature 39, Block C₁, Late
Iron Age.

Figure 23: Feature 38, Block C₁, Late
Iron Age.

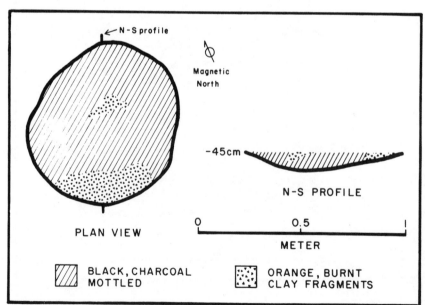

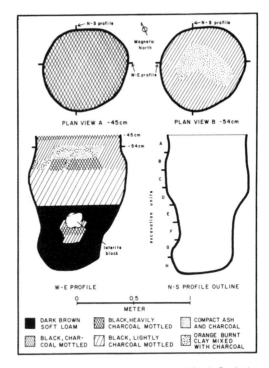

Figure 24: Feature 37, Block C₁, Late Iron Age; note the similarities in upper fill to Feature 7 in Block A, 2 meters north.

Figure 25: Feature 45, Block C₁, Early Iron Age. The east-west profile (not shown) and the burnt clay apron resemble Feature 55 in Block E.

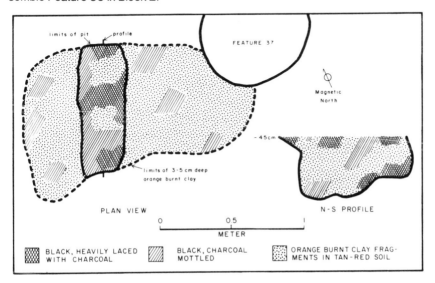

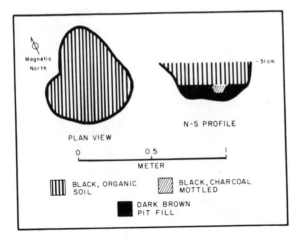

Figure 26: Feature 43, Block C₁, Late Iron Age.

Figure 27: Feature 41, Block C₁, Late Iron Age. This feature appears to be a refuse pit. Nonetheless, it should be considered contemporary to Features 37 and 42 (Block C₁) and Feature 7 (Block A).

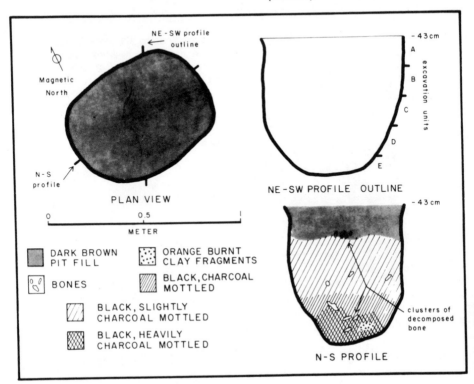

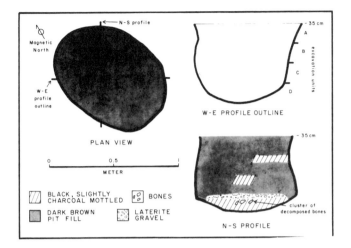

Figure 28: Feature 42, Block C$_1$, Late Iron Age. This pit is C 14 dated to 1700 A.D. ±100, which is the approximate period of Rugamora Mahe's reign according to genealogical evidence.

Figure 29: Features and post molds in Block D. Early Iron Age features are hatched. Solid spots are post molds.

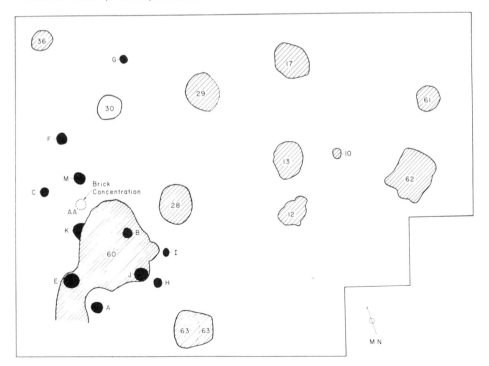

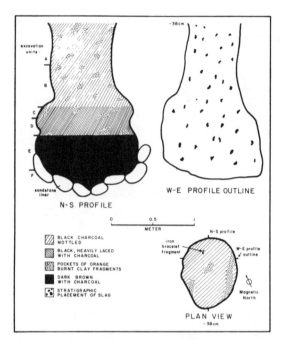

Figure 30: Feature 13, Block D, Early
Iron Age. This pit was a refuse receptacle for pottery, slag, tuyères, brick,
and iron. Dated to 60 A.D. ±115.

Figure 31: Feature 17, Block D, Early
Iron Age; topmost portion has been
disturbed, probably by hoe agriculture.

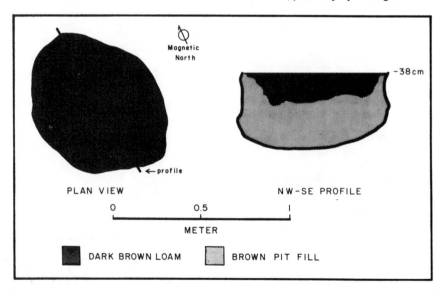

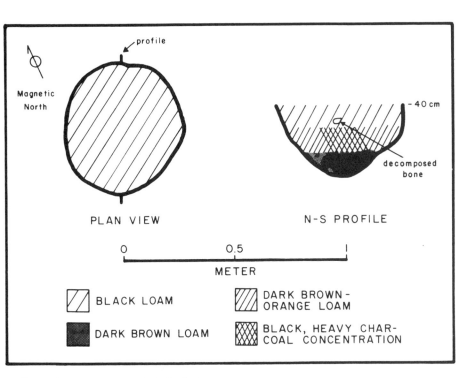

Figure 32: Feature 61, Block D, Early
Iron Age. The top two-thirds has been
disturbed, with foreign charcoal introduced.

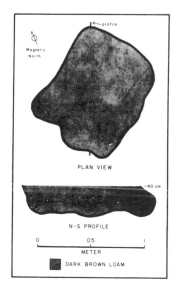

Figure 33: Feature 62, Block D, Early
Iron Age; note the similarities in form to
Feature 27, Block C.

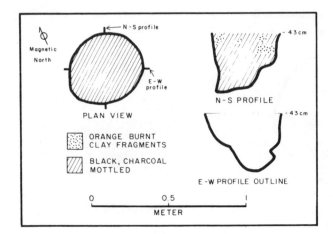

Figure 34: Feature 36, Block D, Early Iron Age.

Figure 35: Feature 29, Block D, Early Iron Age; based on similarities to Feature 100, an iron smelting furnace, the feature is probably the lower portion of an iron smelting furnace-- presumably cleaned out.

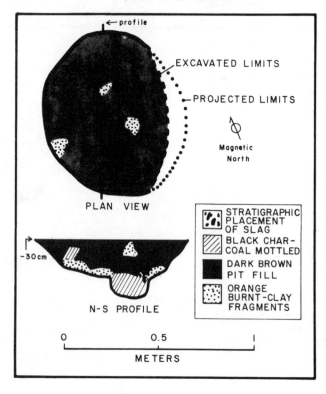

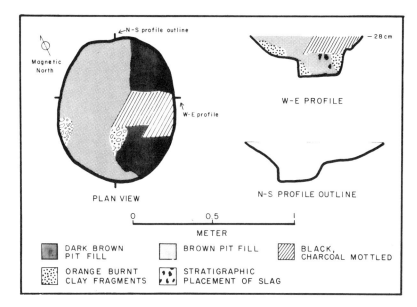

Figure 37: Feature 63, Block D, Early Iron Age. Note the similarities to Feature 20, Block A and Feature 45, Block C. This is probably a smelting furance which has not been truncated by hoeing.

Figure 36: Feature 28, Block D, Early Iron Age. This feature is highly similar to Feature 29 and Feature 100. It is probably an iron smelting furnace of bowl type.

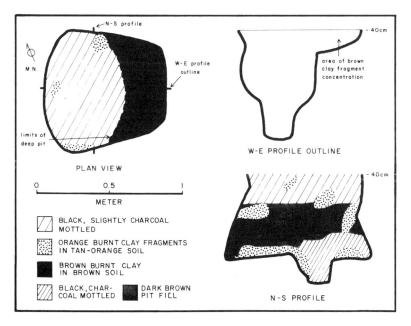

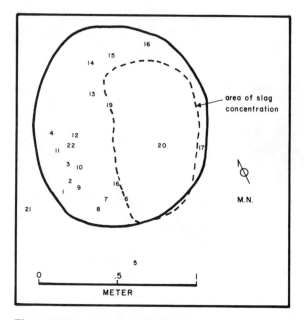

Figure 38: Feature 100; brick pile
mnemonic. Location of angular bricks
at −10 cm, or beginning of excavation
Unit B. Area of slag concentration is
distinct.

Figure 39: Feature 100, Early Iron
Age. Smelting furnace profiles after
excavation. Dated to 170 A.D. ±100.

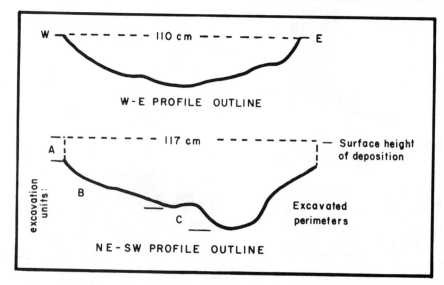

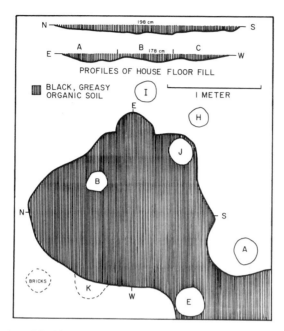

Figure 40: Feature 60, Block D, Early
Iron Age shelter floor; labeled circles
are post molds.

Figure 41: Block D post mold profiles,
north-south.

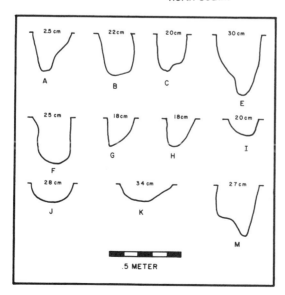

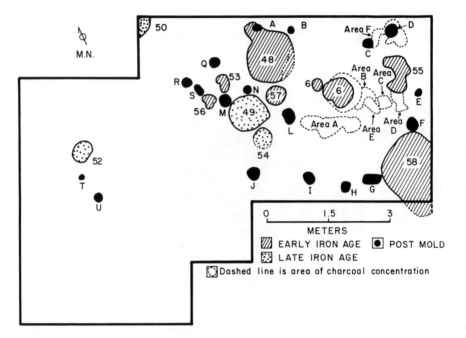

Figure 42: Block E features, post molds, and areas of charcoal concentration.

Figure 43: Feature 54, Block E; part of Early Iron Age feature complex.

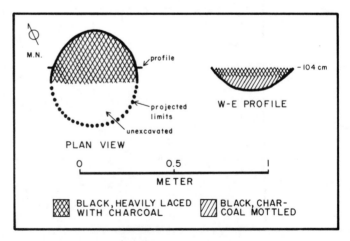

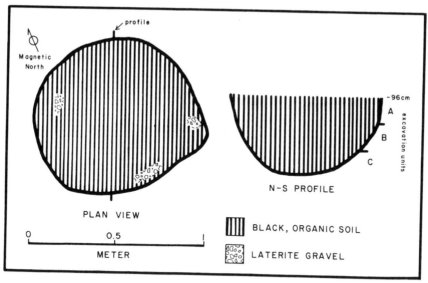

Figure 44: Feature 49, Block E, Late Iron Age. This is the largest intrusive feature under Kaija tree. The impressed grass decoration on the pottery indicates it dates to the same period as Feature 42, Block C$_1$.

Figure 45: Feature 6, Block E, Early Iron Age. This Early Iron Age forge (an interpretation based on ethnographic analogy) is closely linked to oral traditions about iron production beneath Kaija tree. The small pit to the northwest may have held the anvil. Charcoal samples have been C 14 dated to 450 B.C. ±115 and 520 B.C. ±110.

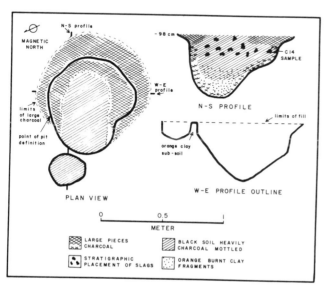

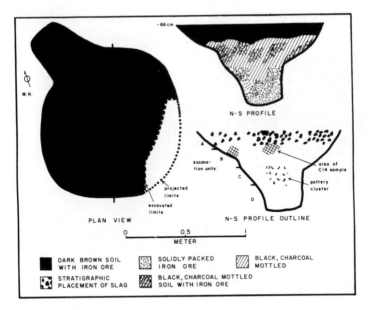

Figure 46: Feature 48, Block E, Early Iron Age. The dark, upper zone is disturbed, and it is from this zone that foreign charcoal was taken for a C 14 test. This was probably an iron ore storage pit.

Figure 47: Feature 55, Block E, Early Iron Age. This possible smelting furnace is located to the east of the forge in Block E and in a dense concentration of slag. It resembles Features 45 (Block C$_1$) and 63 (Block D).

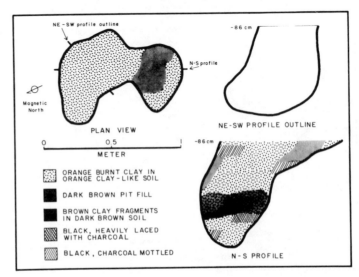

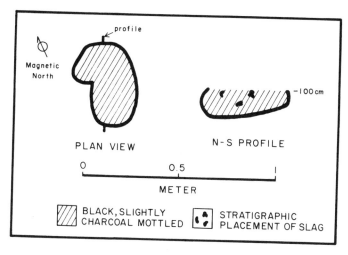

Figure 48a: Feature 53, Block E, Early Iron Age.

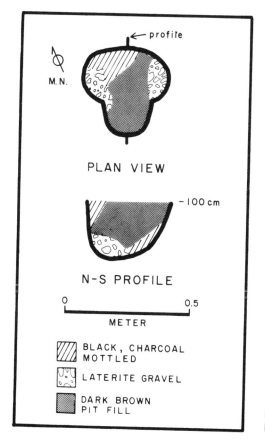

Figure 48b: Feature 56, Block E, Early Iron Age.

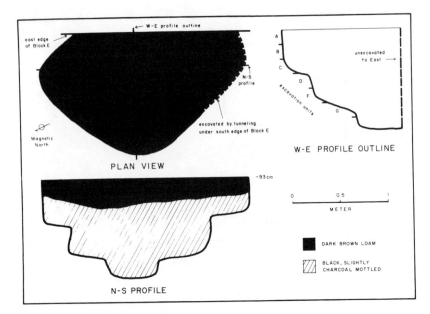

Figure 49: Feature 58, Block E, Early
Iron Age. It is possible that this feature
is part of the iron production complex
in Block E.

Figure 50: Block E; Early Iron Age
features, post molds, and charcoal
concentrations.

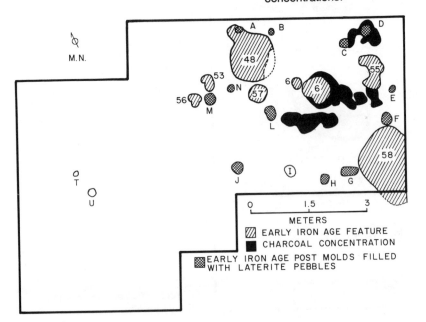

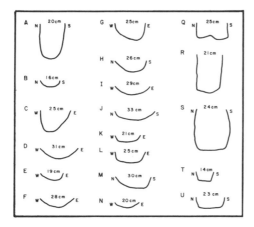

Figure 51: Block E post mold profiles.

Figure 52: Feature 59, Block F, Late
Iron Age. The pit was located
immediately beneath the trees marking
Rugamora Mahe's alleged burial place.
A charcoal sample was dated to
1645 A.D. ±120, which is the
approximate period of Rugamora
Mahe's occupation of the site.

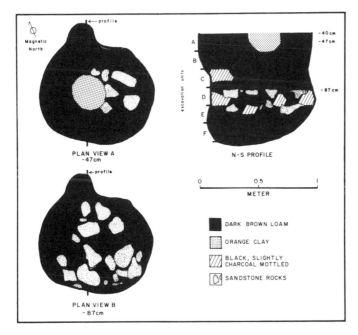

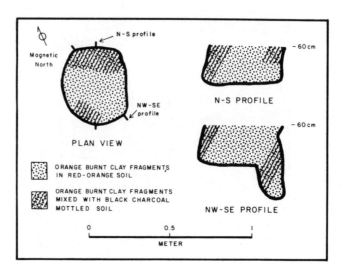

Figure 53: Feature 64, Block F, Early
Iron Age.

10 _____ Iron-Working Evidence

Iron Age smelting technology in Africa is a direct
or bloomery process that results in a sponge iron
(bloom) that can be forged into implements. The end
product is wrought iron, which when observed micro-
scopically displays fine, internal slag splinters.
Hammering in the forge removes most but not all of
the slag. The essential procedure in iron smelting
is to reduce, usually, an oxide ore such as haematite,
limonite, or magnetite by depriving it of its oxygen
and leaving the metallic iron (Goghlan, 1956:38).
This result is obtained in the reduction furnace by
burning charcoal, the carbon of which combines with
oxygen in the iron ore to release metallic iron
(ibid.). The key to the success of the process is
the maintenance of carbon monoxide, which takes the
oxygen to produce carbon dioxide. If carbon dioxide
is allowed to predominate because of insufficient
charcoal and carbon monoxide, reduction of the iron
ore will not take place.

Also essential to the process is a high temperature
and exclusion of oxygen from the ore. It is common
in primitive smelting that much of the iron is lost
to the slag, sometimes so much that the slag can be
profitably resmelted to make iron. The disappearance
of the iron or slag mentioned in folklore from beneath
Kaiija tree might be explained by resmelting; such
an explanation is offered by Bahaya living in the
immediate area. Slag is the waste product of iron
smelting. It is a glass-like substance, sometimes
very porous, formed after a combination of earthy
matter in the ore with the flux. It is highly
fusible, and its relatively low density allows the

escape of liquid metal. The variability of slag
characteristics on one site, or even in one furnace,
may be considerable. Also, differential production
of carbon monoxide, which may vary with the amount
of placement of charcoal, might lead to the production
of widely different slags in the same furnace.

The physical location of tuyères in a furnace is
another essential variable in iron smelting. For
example, if the tuyère does not penetrate the furnace
but terminates at the wall, the ore immediately in
front of the rush of fresh air will be deprived of
the reduction agent, carbon monoxide. The slag
produced in this area will probably have a higher
percentage of metal content or will remain as partly
reduced ironstone. These are but a few of the
variables affecting the production of bloom and slag.
This inherent variability makes slag analysis
particularly difficult and virtually eliminates the
possibility for chronological dating of slag through
a study of constituent elements (Donald Avery, personal communication). However, study of slags from dated
furnaces might establish limits of variability for the
types of ore and flux used during different cultural
periods. Analysis of slag must be performed with good
contextual and chronological controls. These conditions have not yet been obtained in an African culture
area, but the groundwork has been established in
Buhaya.

If comparative data are not yet available for iron
production in the Late and Early Iron Age, then
what kind of analyses are appropriate for slag?
Donald Avery and I have attempted to ask questions
of the data that are appropriate for developing
related questions about prehistoric conceptualizations
about the technological process. Experimentation
started with the goal of hypothesis formulation rather
than analysis for the sake of analysis, that is, to
simply produce another dry technological analysis as
an appendix to an archaeological report.

Heat tests were conducted on slag from Early Iron
Age Features 6, 20, and 48. The goal was to
determine at what temperatures the slag slumps or
becomes spongy, or its original condition in the
smelting furnace. The working assumption is that the
slag slumping point provides a kind of thermometer
for the temperature of the original furnace. At the
same time, we recognized that the slag had been
subjected to heavy leaching since its Early Iron Age
deposition. This meant that in the cases where the
slag was porous it was possible that the alkalies or

flux that had been introduced to the smelting furnace
to increase fusibility at a lower temperature would
have been lost by leaching. Consequently, in a heat
test the porous slag, deprived of its flux, would
slump at a higher temperature than the one at which
it was originally formed.

To avoid the possible bias which a leached, porous
slag would introduce, we selected highly fused, fluid-
looking slags for analysis. Once slag is fused to a
glass-like state, it is stable and cannot lose flux
elements to leaching. The results of the tests, which
are ongoing, are provocative and important. The testing temperatures in the furnace were increased at
50° intervals, and the slag was tested with tongs to
see if it had reached a spongy state. The tests were
conducted over a forty-eight-hour period, with a
sufficient time at each gradient to establish if the
spongy state had been reached. The results were:

> Feature 6
> > 1350°C
> Feature 48
>
> Feature 20   1400°C

Given the probability that deposition for 2,000 years
in a heavily leached soil would have led to some
leaching of even the most fluid-looking slag, these
temperatures may be too high, but at this time, there
is no adequate scientific control to determine standard
of error.

Ironstone has been found to reduce at temperatures
ranging from 1000°C to 1150°C. Significantly, the
sample from Feature 20 was the most highly fused,
glassy sample of the three. One might expect that,
if the others were more porous and had lost some of
their alkalies, they would have produced even higher
temperature results. Further constituent analysis
will tell us if there are alkalies in the fused
samples, for there is always the possibility that the
flux is low grade or that the addition of a flux per
se is lacking in the Buhaya area, as it was in some
instances during the Roman period (Goghlan, 1956:41).
Ethnohistorical research indicates that a flux was not
used by the Bahaya smiths. Certainly, if a good flux
material such as limestone or fluorspar is lacking
in an area, as is the case in Buhaya, then the smelting
may have relied on other techniques for slag separation, such as hammering or higher reduction temperatures.

The primary question resulting from the experiments is: How were the high temperatures in Early Iron Age furnaces obtained? One possible technological procedure is to preheat air used in the blast in order to obtain higher iron-smelting temperatures. This technique was perfected in the mid-nineteenth century by Siemans but was not unknown to earlier peoples. Europeans found that the addition of more fuel to the smelting process did not necessarily result in higher temperatures, although it did produce more heat. The European developments, however, were related to production of steel by increasing the carbon content of iron at higher temperatures. At first thought it seems unlikely that this was an explicit goal of the prehistoric smelters in the Buhaya region, but investigations during 1976 suggest that the contrary is true, that the Bahaya smiths developed a technology particularly suited to increasing carbon content at high temperatures.

The presence of fluid-looking slag in the Early Iron Age structures would appear to confirm the notion that slag separation may have occurred at high temperatures, but the external appearance of slag is insufficient evidence for preheating. If preheating is in evidence during the Early Iron Age, then it is necessary to formulate hypotheses that seek to explain how it was done.

After examining other evidence associated with the production of iron at the Rugomora Mahe site, we concluded that a hypothesis about preheating was testable. The presence of bowl furnaces and the occurrence of tuyère fragments that were highly vitrified and fused with slag suggested to us that the tuyères had been passed through the wall of the furnace and through the charcoal mass. If they were inside the furnace, they would have been subjected to reduction and, in many cases, would have become highly vitrified and encased in slag. A quick review of the tuyère evidence showed that a number of tuyères even had fluid-looking slag on the inside. This phenomenon suggests that the tuyère was in the midst of a highly fluid slag, a condition usually not possible in forging. Furthermore, the angle of the slag drip on the outside of the tuyères was extremely low and usually combined with a glassy quality, which show that very hot conditions predominated around such tuyères.

This evidence suggested a hypothesis: If the furnaces were preheated, then their preheating was achieved by running tuyères inside the furnace and through the charcoal and slag mass. The evidence to confirm the hypothesis could not, however, be the presence of highly vitrified and slag-encased tuyères, for this data had contributed to the generation of the hypothesis. However, to assess the testability of the hypothesis we needed an internal, subsidiary hypothesis, the test of which would demonstrate that the tuyère fragments had adequate properties for a tuyère placed inside a furnace. We reasoned that a fairly substantial proportion of the tuyère, approximately 35 to 45 percent, (this is an arbitrary determination also open to testing) would have to protrude inside the heat zone of the furnace. Therefore, if there was a similar proportion of vitrified slag-encrusted tuyères on the site—particularly in the furnace or in the areas surrounding the furnaces—the hypothesis would be justifiable in an independent experimental or ethnographic context.

Several other subsidiary observations and assumptions in this specific experiment need explication. All of the tuyères at the Rugomora Mahe site are fragments; none was recovered with a complete circumference. This is probably the product of two processes:

(1) continual bombardment by agricultural tools for two millennia, and

(2) the fragmentation of tuyères when they were hammered away from the slag and bloom as the furnace was opened. If they protruded inside, they would have been fused with the slag and then broken away to get to the bloom. This procedure, of course, is costly because new tuyères must be made, but this drawback would be offset by the increased bloom production.

The preheating of air is based on the technological argument that if a temperature of 1150°C is reached with a draught blast of cold air through tuyères, then air passing through heated tuyères embedded in the furnace will exit from the tuyères as hot air, which will raise the temperature of the furnace. For example, if the air issues from the tuyère at 300°C, then the temperature of the reduction zone will rise sufficiently to produce slag and bloom more efficiently at, perhaps, temperatures indicated in the slag tests. These assumptions must be tested experimentally by measuring the temperature of air throughout an embedded tuyère. Hamo Sasoon's study (1964) of iron smelting in Sukur, Northeastern Nigeria, shows that even today African peoples may practice a form of preheating (Plate 1).

It is not clear if this form of tuyère placement outside the charcoal would in fact constitute sufficient
preheating to significantly raise furnace temperatures.

If inserted tuyères were employed in the Rugomora Mahe
furnaces, there may have been a corresponding need for
an excess of charcoal. The excess charcoal would have
been necessary to produce more carbon monoxide to
offset the oxidizing effect of air entering directly
into the smelting area (Goghlan, 1956:106). The
implications of higher temperature smelting by preheating and the need for more charcoal are considerable. But this argument appears insubstantial when it
can also be argued that preheating with its greater
efficiency and its compensation for heat radiated and
lost up the flue would mean less consumption of charcoal; the effect of preheating on charcoal consumption
can only be understood under conditions of controlled
experimental testing. In any case, the effects of
regular smelting would have been felt in exploitation
of the forests. Charcoal demand for regular bloom
smelting are high without preheating. Pleiner's
experiments (1969) with charcoal production, ore
roasting, and iron smelting in Zelechovice-type
(bowl-shaft) furnaces in Czechoslovakia revealed that
400 kilograms of wood produced 70 kilograms of charcoal
which, when combined with 44 kilograms of ironstone,
produced 5 kilograms of workable bloom.

This is a ratio of 80 kilograms of wood for each
kilogram of bloom and it is easy to see that the
exploitation of the forests in Buhaya during the
Early Iron Age may have been intense. It is clear that
forest clearance for charcoal production to maintain
a special iron technology, when combined with forest
clearance for agricultural purposes, would have
rapidly consumed most of the high-climax evergreen
forest that had been extant in the Buhaya area circa
1000 B.C.

It is impossible to reduce what must have been a
complex interaction between land clearing for
agriculture and charcoal production to simple principles, but needs for charcoal could easily have
interfered with a fallowing cycle and prevented
secondary growth forests from reaching maturity. The
next step in the logic of this argument is that iron
production has contributed to the laterization of soil
in Buhaya because of its demands on the forests and
its possible interference with fallowing cycles. This
is a fruitful hypothesis for future testing.

The tuyères from the Rugomora Mahe site in Katuruka
were analyzed to determine to what degree they
demonstrated properties for inclusion in the smelting
furnace. Evidence that partially confirms this hypothesis and shows that the main hypothesis (preheating)
is testable under experimental controls has three
forms:

(1) Tuyères without vitrification or slag
     encrustation but with a black or very dark
     exterior. The black exterior is the result
     of reduction, and the orange interior results
     from oxidation or exposure to fresh air.
     It has been assumed that this kind of tuyère
     has been included in the charcoal mass but
     not exposed to the slag.

(2) Tuyères with vitrification. Exposure to
     intense heat causes the formation of glass-
     like substances from silicas present in the
     tuyère and in the furnace.

(3) Tuyères with slag. The slag on tuyères is
     fused and extremely smooth, which indicates
     that the tuyère was in the midst of highly
     fluid slag.

The gross percentages by feature and by block excavation will be discussed first to see if there is
evidence that denies or substantiates the testability
of the preheating hypothesis. Then, the spatial
distribution of all conditions of tuyères will be
discussed to determine whether these data have possible
behavioral implications. Those features that have only
several pieces of tuyère, or those whose total weight
amounts to less than 25 grams of tuyère have been
eliminated from this particular discussion because
they are samples too small to be significant. The
clearest clustering occurs in Block D where 65 percent of the tuyères from the Early Iron Age horizon
have 50 to 100 percent vitrification on the outside;
some pieces have slag and vitrification on the inside
as well. Most of these cases are confined to units
H (5400), E (5600), J (5050), and A (5075), which is
a bracketing of Feature 13 located in G (5200) (see
Figure 2). Henceforth, for clarity of narrative, the
letters outside the parenthesis will be used. For
both letter and number codes, see the code maps
accompanying each illustration. Tuyères recovered
from the Late Iron Age deposit show a 55 percent
incidence of vitrification and slag-runs covering more

than 50 percent of the tuyère fragment. These samples
are located predominantly in units G and E, areas with
high tuyère representation in the Late Iron Age midden
(Figure 3). Feature 13, located in the central portion
of controlled excavations in Block D, is one of two
features on the site with an adequate tuyère sample
to analyze. In Feature 13, 38 percent of the fragments are vitrified or display an oxidized inside and
reduced outside. While Feature 13 is not directly
functional in iron production, its receipt of refuse
from iron production is essential evidence; tuyère
evidence from Feature 13 and from the surrounding
midden confirms the subsidiary hypothesis. The Block
D areas, especially those areas surrounding Feature 13
and Feature 13 itself, provide confirmatory evidence.

Block E tuyère evidence also confirms the subsidiary
hypothesis. Sixty percent of the tuyère fragments
from the Early Iron Age have 50 to 100 percent
vitrification and slag. Many samples also have slag
on the inside. Fifteen percent of this sample has a
distinct reduction-oxidation border. A significant
concentration is located to the east of Feature 6
and contiguous with the hearth which is Feature 55;
seven of the eight vitrified fragments also have
vitrification on the inside, and two have more than
50 percent fluid slag on the inside. The other
significant cluster is located 1 meter south of
Feature 6, where three of the nine fragments have
slag flow on the inside. These two clusters agree
with the other evidence for iron production in Block
E. The bracketing of Feature 6, which lacks tuyères,
may point to refuse disposal activity, whereby tuyères
and other materials are pried out of the furnace and
broken up adjacent to the forging pit.

An iron-smelting function is most probable for Feature
100 among all features. Consequently, this feature
provides the best testing context for the hypothesis.
In this case, a more complete breakdown of the data
is necessary:

```
Feature 100:   100% vitrification   93.5 grams
               50-80%      "        16.1   "
               14-45%      "        17.2   "
               50-75%      "  and   79.2   "
               25-50% slag
    Oxidation-Reduction Boundary.......85.5   "
                                      291.5 of 755.3
                                              grams
          Total: 39%
```

The evidence from Feature 100 further confirms that
the preheating hypothesis is testable, as does the
evidence from Feature 13, and Blocks D and E. The
data from Blocks A and B and the test pits are not
significant enough to merit separate discussion, but
taken together they also fall within the range of
variability for the areas already discussed.

The evidence applied to the subsidiary hypothesis
from the Rugomora Mahe site is only a tentative,
embryonic investigation into one area of Early Iron
Age technology but ultimately has very important
implications. Actual field tests must be conducted
with indigenous furnaces. These experiments must
comparatively test furnaces in which tuyères are
embedded at varying depths with varying charcoal and
ore densities and monitored air blasts. The controls
will be furnaces with tuyères that stop in the wall.
Of primary importance will be observation of Bahaya
smelting of iron as an independent test. Finally,
archaeological investigation will continue to try to
locate Early Iron Age furnaces that are in situ, which
will hopefully provide structural evidence relevant
to the hypothesis or the generation of alternative
hypotheses.

The significance of a complex technological procedure
such as preheating in the Early Iron Age is considerable. This process was not perfected in Europe until
the mid-nineteenth century. If it existed in Africa
during the Early Iron Age, then it is a poignant
commentary that African Iron Age technology had
developed to a level of complexity much beyond what we
have heretofore thought. This very tentative evidence,
when combined with the C14 dates for the Early Iron
Age at the Rugomora Mahe site in Katuruka, suggests
a possible combination of attractive environmental,
demographic, and resource factors which, when combined
with an early knowledge of iron production, results
in the very early establishment of a complex productive
technology in Buhaya.

The spatial distribution of artifacts associated with
iron production on the site is particularly important
for determining areas associated with different
aspects of iron working. It is not yet clear if the
spatial distribution of nonvitrified or nonslag-coated
tuyères is indicative of a process other than smelting,
such as forging. We have limited direct evidence,
like a stone anvil for forging and until we do we must
work with a general category that includes all tuyères.

The following distributional study will discuss the
spatial placement of tuyères and their spatial relationship to features with a putative iron-working
function.

The density of Early Iron Age tuyères in Block A is
relatively light. This is an anomaly, given the
postulated iron-working function for Feature 20 at
-60 centimeters along the south-central border. The
sparseness of evidence is problematical for the
Feature 20 interpretation, but only if it is assumed
that tuyères are broken up and left behind as refuse.
It may be that a different smelting process was performed here. Preheating is not out of the question,
for photographs of smelting furnaces in Bunyoro
(Roscoe, 1923) show men smelting iron in underground
structures, into which tuyères could be placed—in
much the same way as in Sukur, Nigeria (Sassoon, 1964).

Figure 1 shows that Early Iron Age tuyères are located
in the center of Block A near or adjacent to Features
2 and 20. The limitation of tuyère evidence to units
B, H, I, and J confirms that these features are the
focus of iron-working activities which provide tuyère
refuse. Figure 1 also depicts the Late Iron Age
distributions that appear to be randomly scattered
in that deposit. Those located in the eastern end
in unit 0 may be associated with Feature 5 of the
Early Iron Age and may have been brought up into the
Late Iron Age deposits by soil disturbance. The
tuyères that occur in unit L immediately to the east
of Feature 20 are very probably the result of excavation for Feature 7, the bottom of which goes well
into the Early Iron Age horizon less that 30 centimeters away from Feature 20. It is highly likely
that tuyères were brought to the surface by that
activity. Certainly, there is no associated evidence
for Late Iron Age iron-working in the area, and the
tuyères have the same physical attributes as those
in Feature 20 and in unit I. The occurrence of tuyères
in units E, N, and P (the latter two in the east side
of Block A) does not appear to have any particular
association and may be considered as random
distributions.

The distribution of iron-working artifacts in Block D
is particularly noteworthy in its spatial relationship
to Feature 13, which terminally functioned as a refuse
pit. Figure 2 shows that the area to the west of
Feature 13 (located in unit G) is devoid of Early Iron
Age tuyères. This area (B, C, and D) lies between
Feature 13 and Features 28 and 29, which are putative
smelting furnaces of a bowl type. It appears that the

intermediate area was cleared of refuse including
slag, as we will see, which may then have been deposited in Feature 13. This construct is inferential and
is based on the fact that Feature 13 contains refuse
from iron production activities. Out of these
configurations a hypothesis can be generated for
future testing, i.e.: If there is a complex of smelting structures, juxtaposed to a refuse pit(s), then
the area intermediate between the two classes of
structures will be free of iron production artifacts.
It is necessary to begin to systematically test
propositions of this sort to establish the internal
structure of different types of Early Iron Age settlement sites or special activity sites. Patterns in
structure will thereby be more easily defined and
will be accepted in the future with confidence rather
than be based on inference alone.

The area to the east of Feature 13 has a very heavy
density of tuyères. Especially in units H, J, and K
there are heavy densities of tuyères, which are found
in association with concentrations of charcoal, slag,
and burned clay. Feature 10, located in G, was a
collection of slag and charcoal situated on clay
that showed signs of burning. It is my tentative
hypothesis that this is a forging area, as the slag
is shattered—not fluid—and collected in the midst
of charcoal pockets that may be the remains of forging
hearths. The empirical structural evidence suggesting
this hypothesis is admittedly slight, but it is
buttressed by other evidence: (1) the tuyères in the
area lack vitrification and slag deposits and this may
be associated with forging, and (2) the slag is
angular and shattered, which indicates that it has
probably been hammered in order to separate it from
bloom. In this regard, it is distinctly different
from the fluid slag of, say, Feature 20 in Block A.

The Late Iron Age distribution of tuyères in Block D
is uniformly low in the southern portion of the block,
with the exception of unit G. It may be that this
finding results from disturbance of Feature 13, the
top of which had many tuyère fragments. The
northernmost units have a high density of tuyères,
but the source is not clear. It may be that there
have been recent forging activities to the north
that were not defined by observation of the surface.
At this time, there is no evidence in the Early Iron
Age or Late Iron Age deposits that might help to
explain this occurrence.

The densest distribution of tuyères is found in Block
E. The Early Iron Age horizon in the eastern portion

of Block E (Figure 3) is the area of greatest density.
The Early Iron Age cultural material began at -80 to
-82 centimeters and is marked by a transitional brown-
orange soil. The heaviest density of tuyères is
found at this level. In fact, there is a distinct
cultural discontinuity at this level, with heavy
densities of other iron-working artifacts from the
Early Iron Age also plentiful. The area of greatest
density surrounds Feature 6 on three sides, with
the northcentral side free of tuyères. Excavation
did not extend far enough north to determine if there
might be a refuse pit into which refuse may have been
placed from the area north of Feature 6. The other,
southcentral area of concentration, in units U, DD,
W, and N is not associated with any archaeologically
defined structures, but it was delimited at the same
depth as the eastern cluster.

When the southcentral Early Iron Age tuyère cluster
is viewed in conjunction with the Late Iron Age
distribution of tuyères, it will be seen that there
is a circular configuration, with the center of the
block (units A, O, P) devoid of tuyères. No suggestion
about the configuration of this distribution is offered
at this time, but it may be related to the heavy distribution of ironstone at the -82 centimeter level in
units H and O. The fragmentation of ironstone into
small pieces and a limited tuyère distribution may
mean that this area was an ore preparation area,
which would have prevented or removed refuse
accumulation. This area had no particularly distinct
definitions, and the possible significance of what once
appeared to be a noncultural phenomenon is pointed
out by the tuyère distributions and ironstone concentrations.

Based on the physical inspection of the tuyères, it is
my judgment that many of the fragments in the Late
Iron Age deposit in fact originated from the lower
horizon. Because of root disturbance (up to 30 centimeters in diameter), human disturbance, and rodent
activity, the tuyères have probably been transported
upward; in all except one case, all the tuyères were
found below -30 centimeters in the western part of
Block E. There also appears to be a similar relationship manifest in units E and test 9100 in the northern
part of the block. The materials in the north-north-
west sector have no apparent below-surface association.

The remainder of tuyère fragments on the site have no
particularly significant spatial distribution. There
are several pieces in Block B and in the test pits.
Test C1 to the east of Block A had sufficient tuyère

fragments from the Early Iron Age horizon to suggest
that another iron-working complex may be nearby.

Most tuyères vary in thickness from 5 to 8 millimeters,
and the diameter of the opening varies from 4 to 7
centimeters, with most close to 5 centimeters. In most
cases, it is difficult to determine the exact diameter
because of the highly fragmentary state of most of
them.

Some of the slag evidence for features has already
been presented in the discussion of smelting temperatures. Slag has a lighter density than the bloom
to which it is usually attached. A heat-retaining
furnace, good flux, ore of high iron content, high
temperature, and correct gas balance will result in a
more consolidated bloom. The furnace that Pleiner
(1969) built for his experiments had a bottom, horizontal shaft through which draught could be regulated
and the bloom tapped periodically. Furnaces arranged
in this way, where the bloom descends and can be
removed during smelting, can receive a continuous
charge for an extended time. But bloom in the bowl-
type furnace at the Rugomora Mahe site would have
settled to the bottom amid slag. After the bloom is
removed from the furnace, the task is to chip off
slag and then beat out most of the remaining slag in
the forge.

Areas with the greatest slag densities are associated
with freeing the bloom by either or both processes.
We do not yet know where the smelters removed most of
the porous slag before forging; it may have been in
one of the two task areas or in both. The argument
suggested previously, that fluid-looking slag is
associated with smelting and that angular, porous
slag is the possible product of bloom extraction
and forging, is only an argument by inference and must
be verified by extensive observation and experimentation in the field. Until confirmation is obtained,
the argument will no longer be employed in analysis
of slag distribution.

The spatial distribution of slag in Block A bears
close affinities to that of tuyères. Figure 4 shows
that the southcentral area, especially unit I where
Feature 20 is located, has the highest Early Iron
Age representation. These slags are undoubtedly a
part of Feature 20 (which had 2.38 kilograms of slag),
as they were recovered immediately above the feature.
Units G and J in the northcentral area also have a

concentration of slag, with densities dropping off slightly. The densities in the three units to the west and one unit to the north of Feature 20 are relatively even—all within 4 grams. The distinctiveness of the northcentral area and southcentral areas with a low-density distribution on their peripheries corresponds to the tuyère configuration, and it suggests that a structure with functional characteristics similar to Feature 20 may exist to the north or east of unit J. Unfortunately, these subtleties in the data were impossible to catch in the field and therefore could not be used in modifying a research strategy.

The Late Iron Age slag (Figure 4) is surprisingly dense in Block A. Two units, H and E in the center of the block, have slag concentrated in the top 20 centimeters, and in unit I over Feature 20, most of the slag is within 30 centimeters of the surface. Therefore, it is not certain that it can be attributed to Feature 20. The dense slag in the southwest corner is immediately above the Early Iron Age horizon, but it is associated with exclusively Late Iron Age artifacts. The remainder of the slag appears to have little pattern.

The lack of associated structural features with slag from the Late Iron Age deposit in Block A creates problems for formulating propositions for explaining these phenomena. If the area was once a Mukama's nyaruju house and later his gashani house, and if blacksmiths resided in the king's court, as they usually did on a rotational basis, then their forging activities may well have distributed slag in the vicinity of the king's residence. This analogy is suggested by ethnographic evidence and by the structure of forging remains in the inner court of the Mukama of Karagwe at Bweranyange, where an iron forge was excavated very close to where informants claimed the Mukama had his royal residence. The same behavior may very well have been associated with the king's court in Kyamutwara.

The slag evidence for Block D also agrees with the tuyère evidence from the same area. Figure 5 shows that the area of highest concentration is in the southeastern part of the controlled block excavations. Feature 10 with 0.84 kilograms in unit G and Feature 13 in the same unit with 2.43 kilograms of slag, when combined with a density from the Early Iron Age horizon of 1.13 kilograms, contribute to a total of 4.4 kilograms of slag concentrated in this space. Immediately to the south, there is a density of 0.32 kilograms and to the east, 0.16 kilograms.

Significantly, there is no Early Iron Age slag in
the western section, which is also true for tuyères.
The exception is unit A in the northwest with 0.10
kilograms, which also agrees with the tuyère data.
This finding may suggest that the northern area
borders another iron-working area and may possibly
be a litter-free area surrounding and related to
putative smelting activity in Feature 29 to the west.
I believe that the particularly heavy density of slag
in G and H can be linked to the same functional complex
as suggested in the analysis of tuyères and features.

The Late Iron Age deposit in Block D is limited to the
top 22 to 24 centimeters. Below this level are increasing densities of Early Iron Age pottery, but
recent disturbances have reached to -35 centimeters.
Nonetheless, there is a clear change in cultural
stratigraphy in the -20 to -25 centimeter zone, as
there are significant increases in Early Iron Age
artifacts, especially artifacts related to iron production. The distribution of slag in the Late Iron Age
deposit appears to be inversely related to the Early
Iron Age distribution of slag (Figure 5). In the
eastern area, there is a decrease from the Early Iron
Age levels in units I and K. The proximity of these
units to Features 61 and 62, Early Iron Age features
possibly associated with iron working, may explain
why such high densities exist in the eastern portion
for the lower horizon. In the other Early Iron Age
high-density area, the southcentral area in units G
and H, there is also a significant decrease. In the
western area, however, the inversion is manifest by
very high concentrations of slag in units B and C,
where there was no slag in the lower horizon. It is
not clear why this inversion occurs.

The most extensive concentration of slag on the site
is located in Block E, as Figure 6 indicates. The
northeastern sector has the heaviest concentration,
with a total of 1.25 kilograms located in test unit
9100 and unit C. This space is the same as occupied
by Features 6 and 48, both of which have been interpreted as iron production structures. If an argument
had been formulated from the tuyère densities in
Block E, on the assumption that both artifact categories represent similar technological behavior, then
it might be expected that slag in Block E would
correspond to the tuyère distribution. There is a
correspondence in test unit 9100 and in unit R just
to the south. Also, we can see that the area to the
north and northeast of Feature 6 is relatively free
of slag, as it was free of tuyères.

The low density of slag to the east of Feature 6 does
not correspond to the tuyère evidence. However, most
of the slag evidence in the Late Iron Age midden
that appears in this area was recovered only 4 centimeters above the Early Iron Age midden level and may
very well belong to the earlier deposit. Most slag
from the Early Iron Age midden occurs in a vertically
discontinuous cluster. At -82 to -90 centimeters,
there are suddenly much heavier concentrations of slag
associated with Early Iron Age pottery. Hence, there
is a definite cultural horizon marked by artifacts
associated with iron production in Block E. The
spatial differences in slag and tuyère distributions
adjacent to Features 6 and 48 may point to different
behaviors associated with iron working.

Another area with a distinct spatial distribution of
slag in Block E is the central, heavy density that
runs north to south from unit I to units U, M, CC, and
DD. This particular phenomenon appears to be unrelated
to features, unless they remain unexcavated to the
southeast. Distributions of this kind, when removed
some distance from the production area, may be
associated with another behavior related to preparing
slag for forging away from the smelting area, but
propositions of this sort must await further empirical
evidence before they can be tendered. As mentioned
earlier, the low-density area in units H and O may
be associated with a putative ore preparation activity
area.

The concentrations of slag in the northeast area are
further evidence for the hypothesis that Features 6
and 48 are associated with iron production. The
central densities are not as clear, but they may
possibly be the result of simple refuse activity
tied to the production of iron at Features 6 and 55
(see Figure 7).

Slag from the Late Iron Age deposit in Block E is
more difficult to interpret. The basic pattern
obvious in Figure 6 is that the northeastern sector
bears close affinities to the Early Iron Age pattern.
There is a heavy density in test 9100, over Feature 6,
in C over Feature 48, and also the west and immediately
to the south of Feature 6. At approximately -98
centimeters in both units J and R, there are two
intrusive Late Iron Age Features, 49 and 56. It
therefore seems reasonable to suppose that much of the
slag found in Late Iron Age deposit in units I, J,
and R is the result of intrusive activities that would
have brought much of the Early Iron Age material to
the surface and redistributed it throughout the Late

Iron Age deposit. It is significant that very little
of the Late Iron Age slag is found within the first
15 centimeters (with the exception of unit R in
Block E). It is unassociated with recent activities
on the site. However, like Block A, the complete
absence of Late Iron Age structural features in
association with the slag is problematical. From
physical inspection of the material, I am convinced
that much has been pulled up from the Early Iron Age
horizon. Verification of disturbances in some places
in Block E suggests this process. At this point it is
impossible to know if this is sufficient interpretation. The tentative proposition, then, is that if
there exist Early Iron Age iron production and
associated artifacts, evidence of intrusive activity,
and no structural evidence for Late Iron Age iron
production, then the occurrence of iron production
artifacts in the Late Iron Age deposit is the result
of disturbance and redistribution of Early Iron Age
cultural materials.

Slag in Block B is predominantly Late Iron Age, with
the exception of 10 grams removed from the top of the
subsoil in test unit 3100 (Q). As Figure 8 demonstrates, the slag is limited to the periphery of
Feature 4. The heaviest concentration of stones in
Feature 4 is in units G, H, I, and L. The heaviest
concentration of slag lies outside the organic soil
border of Feature 4. This may mean that the space
including Feature 4 may have been separated from
activities associated with iron production. The
activity interpretation for Feature 4 offered by the
Bahaya—a house for cows or a cow shed—excludes
cultural activity associated with iron technology,
and this interpretation agrees with the distribution
of slag in Block B.

Block C slag is very limited, with 0.38 kilograms in
unit A at -10 centimeters and a much smaller amount
(26 grams) from the Early Iron Age midden in unit B
(see Figure 9). The significant slag concentration in
Block C is located directly above Early Iron Age
Feature 21 in unit D. There, 0.21 kilograms was
recovered from the Late Iron Age deposit, and 2.34
kilograms immediately above Feature 21 at -28 centimeters. This slag undoubtedly belongs to Feature 21,
which may have an iron production association. (For
a discussion of Feature 21, see Chapter 9.)

The fired bricks associated with slag in Feature 100,
the brick pile mnemonic, are found throughout the

site. The contextual evidence from Feature 100 and
the comparative evidence provided by Hiernaux's and
Maquet's observations suggest that fired bricks
are associated with iron smelting and possibly other
aspects of iron production. This evidence indicates
that a hypothesis for the association of bricks with
other artifacts from iron production is appropriate:
If fired brick is associated with tuyères and slag
such as in Feature 100, then bricks will be distributed
on the site in a close spatial relationship to iron
production features and with high densities of iron
slag and tuyères.

The distribution of brick fragments in Block A shows
a very heavy density immediately above Feature 20
and a small fragment just to the north in unit H.
This agrees with spatial evidence for Early Iron Age
tuyère and slag evidence. Feature 20 has twelve
pieces of brick, seven of which have flat or curved
sides. This finding indicates that they are formed
and are not merely hunks of fired former surface
clay. These fragments weigh 1.21 kilograms.

Although the Block D brick evidence is relatively
sparse, it also confirms the hypothesis. Most of
the brick from the Early Iron Age midden comes from
the same unit where Feature 13 is located and in units
K and H, immediately to the east and south of
Feature 13. There is only corresponding tuyère
evidence for unit H, but the slag distributions (see
Figure 5) closely agree, especially for the previously
mentioned units bordering Feature 13. It is highly
probable that the high density of bricks in the unit
containing Feature 13 comes from the top of the
feature as the brick fragments were recovered from
that level. Feature 13, as a refuse pit, contains
0.15 kilograms of brick fragments, most of which are
very small but which nonetheless display signs of
differential oxidation-reduction. These signs
indicate that one side has been subjected to a reduction atmosphere. The Late Iron Age distributions
are random, but the one large fragment in unit B at
-10 centimeters may be related to Feature 13.

The distribution of brick fragments in Block E also
confirms the hypothesis. There is a clustering
of brick around Feature 6 (which itself has only
54 grams of brick), especially to the north, west,
and south but not in the east. This configuration
agrees with the slag distribution but not as
significantly with the tuyère distribution, which has
a different spatial arrangement. The only major
anomaly in Block E is the location of five brick

fragments in four separate spits in unit G, at depths
varying from -90 to -120 centimeters. This location
was free of tuyères and had a very low density of
slag. However, the unit to the northeast (A; see
Figure 6) also had a high density of brick, which may
mean that these border excavations may be near a
feature with a high brick concentration, namely, an
iron-smelting furnace. The more southern brick
locations are unclear, although generally they tend
to agree with the slag evidence for the southern
part of Block E.

The remaining areas of interest are test B-1 and the
southeastern unit of Block F, where there was a concentration of brick in an area with evidence of burning activity, but no direct evidence of smelting. In
retrospect, it is possible that the heavy densities
of slag and the presence of brick in tests A-1 and
B-1 indicated the presence of a smelting area in
the immediate proximity. The distribution of fired
brick on the site confirms the hypothesis. . The
presence of brick on the site is also a good marker
for iron-working activity and has the same spatial
distributions and proportional densities as slag.
But it does not have spatial affinities to tuyères.
This lack suggests that hypotheses about tuyère
association with a related activity in iron production
(for instance, bloom retrieval) can be entertained
in the future.

The archaeological recovery of iron tools or implements, which are the final products of the entire
sequence of iron production, thrusts the archaeologist
of Iron Age Africa directly against the problem of
insufficient ethnographic data for functional interpretation. It may appear that the form of an iron
implement suggests a clearcut function. These basic
assumptions are fraught with difficulties, for the
intuitive categories the archaeologist inevitably
works with provide synchronically limited functional
interpretations, if he is dependent on personal
experience with functional empirical data. The
fundamental drawback is that we have insufficient
evidence of a diachronic sort for functional interpretations of iron tools and implements. Binford
(1964) has addressed this point very lucidly in his
discussion of examples of functional change through
time while form remains constant.

A little less than two years of exposure to iron
tools in Buhaya revealed, for instance, an astoundingly

wide variation in function for the chopper or <u>muhoro</u>
knife (see Figure 10a). In precolonial days, <u>this</u> was
an all-purpose tool: it was used to cut down the
stems of banana trees; in warfare during close battle;
and as a utility knife. Its use today is principally
limited to chopping down banana stems. There has been
a distinct change from a technic to an ideotechnic
function for the chopper knife, as it has been widely
replaced by the panga or machete and is today kept
in many homes as a relic, as a reminder of the old
days. So, too, most spears have lost their original
function—hunting and warfare. A Muhaya occasionally
may use his hunting spear if he attends the community
hunts into the swamplands, but he is more likely to
leave his spears resting on the special post in his
house reserved for spears. It is not unusual to see
a large repertoire of unused spears, many of which
are inherited. In this manner, they function as
sociotechnic items, because they may demonstrate the
social status of a successful ancestral warrior, or
sometimes as ideotechnic items because they serve as
reminders that the old days were less peaceful and
more disruptive than today. One man said:

> These are the spears of my grandfather and
> father. These days we have no use for these
> things, for we have peace. In the old days
> there were many wars and many people killed.
> I keep these spears here because they belong
> with me, but I will not use them.

With the introduction of many European and Asian metal
goods, there has been an increasing tendency to replace
traditional iron goods as they wear out with imported
items. Less frequently the form and function of an
iron implement are transformed. I encountered this
phenomenon once in Kitobo village in Kiziba, where a
man brought a large spear butt to a blacksmith and
requested that it be made into a chopper knife. He
did not have the money to buy a new panga, but he
could afford to pay a smith to change the spear butt
into a knife.

It is therefore difficult to know the exact function
or range of functions of a specific form. Rapid
change in function and form during the last 100 years
is not indicative of the degree of change in the
past, but certainly the same capacity for change
existed previously. By necessity, then, the categories
used to describe iron working on the Rugomora Mahe site
are taken from the ethnographic present circa 1900,
when Rehse's and Kollman's early observations caught
the material culture of Buhaya before it had been

extensively changed. The categories are limited
and should be taken not as firm functional categories
but rather as arbitrary analytical devices.

Most of the iron artifacts date to the Late Iron Age.
This numerical bias is in good part the result of the
rapid oxidation of iron. The same processes that lead
to the oxidation of soil and transform it into ironstone also affect iron. As a consequence, most Early
Iron Age iron has disappeared. We would often come
across oxidation stains that were so faint that form
could not be determined. A number of Early Iron Age
pieces were recovered in protected contexts, such as
under a piece of slag. In most instances, the early
artifacts appear to be of possible ornamental function,
or else they appear as unidentifiable lumps, which
because of their advanced oxidation were not cleaned
by electrolysis.

Five pieces of identifiable iron are found in an
Early Iron Age context, of which three and possibly
four belong together. The three pieces illustrated
in Figure 11a were together in Feature 13A, 3 centimeters from the topmost level of the feature. The
piece in Figure 11b, while located lower in the same
feature, may be a part of 11a. The form appears to
be a bracelet, very similar to one illustrated by
Rehse. It is possible that the illustrated pieces
are sections of wire. We know that the Bahaya had
tools for wire drawing in the late nineteenth
century. If they possessed this aspect of iron
technology along with much more complex aspects of the
tool kit, then it would appear to be possible that
wire-drawing techniques developed during the Early
Iron Age. Certainly, this inference can only be
confirmed by the actual recovery of a wire-drawing
tool from an Early Iron Age context. The 4 centimeter
long piece in Figure 11d also appears to be part of a
bracelet, which is a most provisional interpretation
based on shape. The fragment is severely oxidized,
but its rounded cross-section suggests that it is
not a curved tool like the sickle knife (see Figure
10b), which is hafted to a pole of 2 to 3 meters and
used to cut down dead banana leaves and bunches of
bananas.

The putative bracelet fragment (11d) was recovered
2 centimeters above the delimitation of Feature 6 in
Block E. It can be considered part of the feature
complex, as it was found in association with slag
and charcoal. Several centimeters deeper, there was

another piece of iron in the form of a lump similar
to that illustrated in Figure 11c. Block E with its
plentiful evidence for iron working also has the
highest representation of iron from the Early Iron
Age. The occurrence of two lumps of iron weighing
21 grams from the Early Iron Age midden 3 meters to
the south of Feature 6 in the northwestern part of
unit R may be further evidence of a forging function
for Feature 6.

Knife blades with a tang for hafting to a long handle,
such as in Figure 12a, are the most common iron objects. The tang is affixed to the handle with a
resin and is driven into a hole smaller than the
diameter of the tang. The upper side of the blade
is much thicker and is blunt; the tang is located
on the upper, thicker side. All the examples
illustrated in Figure 12 are blades of this type.
The distribution of these blades on the site is
limited to Block excavations A, B, C, and E. The
three from Block E are from the central portion of the
block. This is a particularly utilitarian tool; its
presence on the site may be the result of use there
in agricultural activities. Stratigraphically, this
type of tool is limited to the more recent Iron Age.

The variety of spear blades on the Rugomora Mahe site
encompasses virtually the whole range of spear blade
types extant in contemporary Bahaya material culture.
It is significant that of seven whole or partial spear
blades, four were found in the gashani house area,
Block A excavation. All were recovered within 17
centimeters of the surface. The Ankole-type spear
(13a) found in unit E, Block A, is a particularly
well-preserved example, while 13b and 13e are in a
highly oxidized state. The spear shown in 13f almost
appears to be an arrow point. Its relatively recent
stratigraphic association, and its lack of a tang
for hafting, which Bahaya arrow points have, would
place it within the spear blade category.

Rehse provides illustrations of hafted spear blades
that are relatively rare today in Buhaya. Figures 13
b and 13c with a central tang resemble 14a and 14b,
which are spear blades whose tangs are placed in the
end of a pole and then bound up with fiber or wire.
Type 14b is most uncommon today in Buhaya. The
indentation on the left side of 13c appears to be the
result of oxidation rather than the lower indentation

of 14b.

The putative functional ascription of bracelet for
the curved iron objects recovered from an Early Iron
Age context can be challenged by other evidence
available at the Rugomora Mahe site. The alternative
evidence, when combined with the contextual evidence,
suggests the necessity for a new proposition about
an alternative function. The other evidence is a
hanging chain for a bell. Figure 15a is a bell with
a clapper, open bottom, and a ring through the top.
The bell comes from unit P in Block E at -67 centimeters. The bell is definitely from the Late Iron
Age deposit. The shape of the ring on the bell
suggests that a variety of iron goods were made in
circular form. This example well illustrates some
of the interpretative difficulties archaeologists
encounter when they rely on intuitive analogies rather
than on analogies based on tested functional
equivalencies between ethnographic data and
archaeological evidence.

The bell illustrated in Figure 15a is very similar
to one described by Rehse. During his visits to the
Mukama's palace in Kiziba, he noticed that most
doorways through the series of enclosures that
protected the king's residence (rwensinga) had a
bell: "Most of the entrances through the king's
palisade have a doorbell, which is fastened on a
long stick, and is made in the same shape as our bow-
bells" (Rehse:13). The illustration provided by Rehse,
15, is exactly the same as the bell recovered in Block
E. Rehse does not mention if this type of bell (there
are other, round bells in Buhaya) had a universal
distribution, or if it was confined to the king's use.
Based on present evidence, it is impossible to argue
that the bell is exclusively a royal artifact.

The recovery of the remaining circular objects, 15c
and 15d, also in an area of high density of iron
production artifacts tends to confirm the testability
of an hypothesis about a functional association with
iron working.

Ethnographic data on the material culture of the
Bahaya show that the Bahaya had finer knives that
were also hafted to short handles. Figures 16a and
16b are examples of the finer, smaller blade that
has either lost its tang or that was hafted directly
to the handle without a tang. The former is the
more likely, as each has a thicker, nontapered edge

on the top; this means that they are similar in form
to the chopper knife. Type 16g is a good example of
a fine blade. The ones shown in 16c, 16e, and 16f
may also be of the same type, but these are ambiguous
cases. The function of 16d and 16h is not clear.
There are no analogous forms from which an argument
might be made, though 16d and 16h may be tangs from
knives, such as 16g supports.

The stratigraphic placement of these forms is noteworthy. Excluding form 16h, all the knife blades
were recovered from below -20 centimeters and ranged
in depth from -20 to -55 centimeters. The smoking
pipes on the site also had a similar stratigraphic
delimitation. This, when viewed in association with
the distribution of Late Iron Age iron artifacts on
the site, points toward a special function for Late
Iron Age objects. They may have been associated
with ceremonial life at shrines where goods were
brought as offerings to the Bacwezi and Bakama spirits.

One particularly notable artifact which appears to
be associated with ceremonial life is an unusually
large spear butt (an iron socket attached to the
bottom of the wooden shaft) which was recovered at
-45 centimeters in G of Block E. Measuring 30 centimeters in length, 16.5 centimeters in circumference,
and weighing 603 grams, this large spear butt once
belonged on a spear of exaggerated proportions. The
large ceremonial spears of Buganda kingdom immediately
come to mind as a comparative model. The presence of
a king's bell only two meters to the southeast along
with what appears to be part of a large, royal
ceremonial spear adds further credence to the interpretation that the site was directly controlled by
the Bahinda and that the Kaiija shrine was an important
focus for later ceremonial activities. This latter
interpretation is also buttressed by a heavy density
of ceramic smoking pipes around Kaiija tree.

The head of an iron hammer/anvil was recovered from
the top 15 centimeters of unit H in Block A (Plate 2).
Unit H is in the center of the gashani area delimited
by the thorn trees. This hammer weighs 1.45 kilograms;
thus, if it was made in precolonial times, it represents a sizable investment in iron and labor. The
hammer head in horizontal cross-section is square, and
each of its four sides is concave. In this respect,
it differs somewhat from the roundheaded or six-sided
enyondo traditional hammer still used today by smiths
in forging. The form of the hammer head suggests that
it is a miangata hammer similar to the one illustrated
in Kiziba, Land und Leute (Rehse:87).

The deposition of the hammer in the gashani indicates
that relatively precious (but broken?) items were
brought as offerings to the area. That the iron
hammer was an offering seems to be confirmed by oral
tradition. One example among many is: "I saw pieces
of iron as thick as my leg during the 1920s beneath
Kaiija, but these pieces have been removed to forge
with" (Paulo Kagasheki, 10/22/69, in Kanyangereko-
Nkimbo). The large heaps of iron or bloom, not slag,
under Kaiija tree until fifty years ago suggest very
strongly that in precolonial days the tree was an
enormously important shrine associated, perhaps, with
the prosperity and welfare of iron production in
Buhaya. One can only speculate that Rugomora Mahe's
adoption of mythemes associated with the shrine and
his control of iron-working clans might have elicited
offerings to his spirit in the same material medium.
There are also oral traditions that describe the
hammer planted by Rugomora Mahe in Kahororo village
upon his return to Buhaya; it was square like the
hammer found in the gashani (Mzee Kaijage, 10/24/69,
in Maruku).

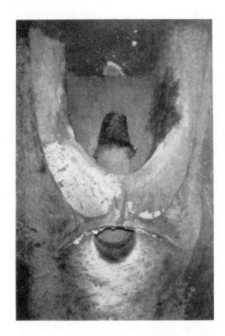

Plate 1: Preheating of a tuyère in a Sukur, Nigeria, smelting furnace.

Plate II: The head of a *Miantaga,* and iron hammer used by smiths; recovered in the center of the *gashani* in Unit H, Block A.

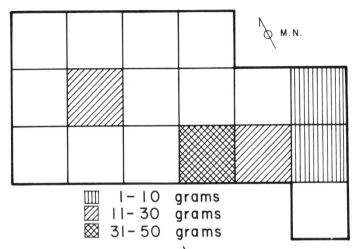

DENSITIES OF TUYÈRE DISTRIBUTION
IN LATE IRON AGE MIDDEN, BLOCK A,
GASHANI HOUSE

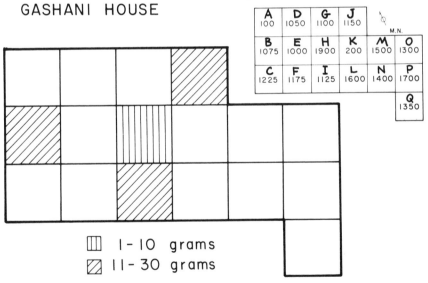

DENSITIES OF TUYÈRE DISTRIBUTION IN
EARLY IRON AGE MIDDEN, BLOCK A,
GASHANI HOUSE

Figure 1: Block A tuyère densities.

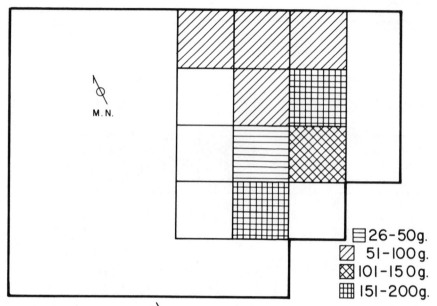

DENSITIES OF TUYÈRE DISTRIBUTION IN
EARLY IRON AGE MIDDEN, BLOCK D

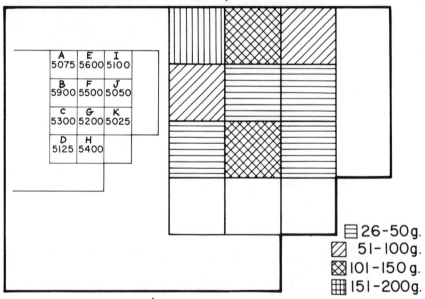

DENSITIES OF TUYÈRE DISTRIBUTION IN
LATE IRON AGE MIDDEN, BLOCK D

Figure 2: Block D tuyère densities.

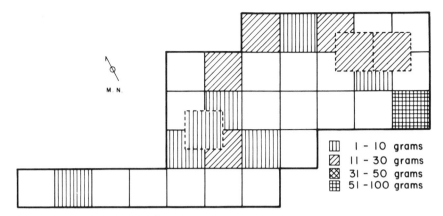

DENSITIES OF TUYÈRE DISTRIBUTION IN LATE IRON AGE
MIDDEN, BLOCK E, NEAR KAIIJA TREE

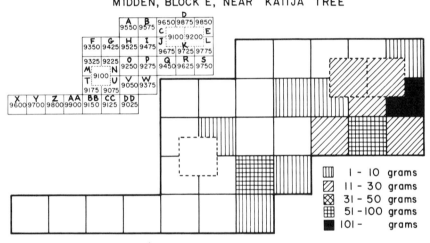

DENSITIES OF TUYÈRE DISTRIBUTION IN EARLY IRON AGE
MIDDEN, BLOCK E, NEAR KAIIJA TREE

Figure 3: Block E tuyère densities;
note the heavy density near the
putative Early Iron Age furnace,
Feature 55, to the east of the double
test units.

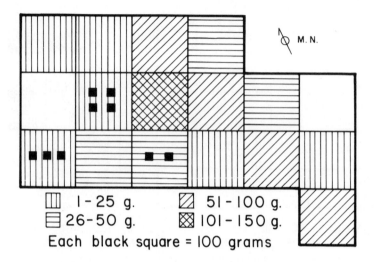

DENSITIES OF SLAG DISTRIBUTION
IN LATE IRON AGE MIDDEN, BLOCK A,
GASHANI HOUSE

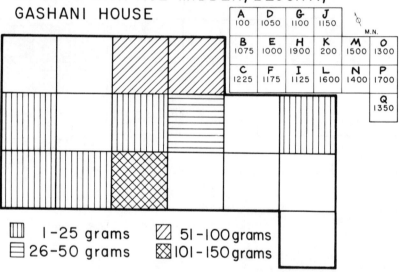

DENSITIES OF SLAG DISTRIBUTION
IN EARLY IRON AGE MIDDEN,
BLOCK A, GASHANI HOUSE

Figure 4: Slag densities in Block A.

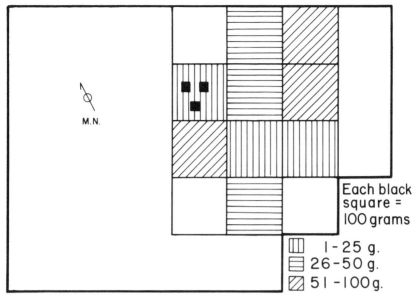

DENSITIES OF SLAG DISTRIBUTION IN
LATE IRON AGE MIDDEN, BLOCK D

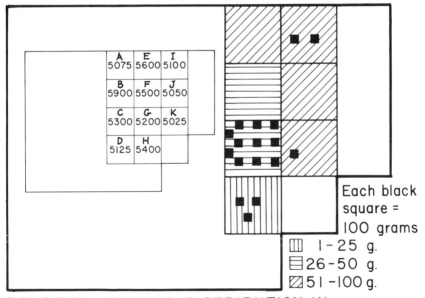

DENSITIES OF SLAG DISTRIBUTION IN
EARLY IRON AGE MIDDEN, BLOCK D

Figure 5: Block D slag densities; note the very dense concentration of slag overlying and adjacent to Feature 13, an Early Iron Age refuse pit.

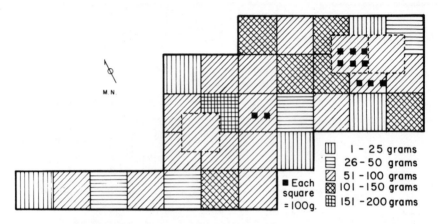

DENSITIES OF SLAG DISTRIBUTION IN LATE IRON
AGE MIDDEN, BLOCK E, NEAR KAIIJA TREE

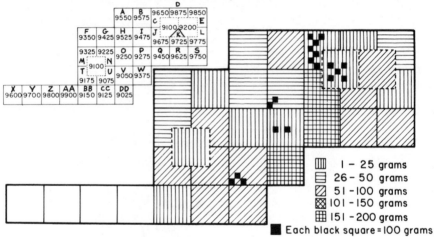

DENSITIES OF SLAG DISTRIBUTION IN EARLY IRON
AGE MIDDEN, BLOCK E, NEAR KAIIJA TREE

Figure 6: Block E slag densities; note
that the heaviest concentration of slag
is to the west of Feature 6, the
probably Early Iron Age forging pit in
the left of the double test. This side is
the front of the forge.

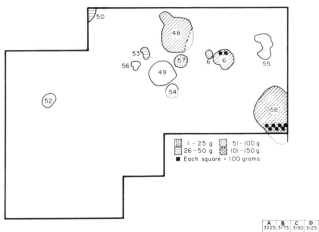

Figure 7: Slag densities in Block E Features; Early Iron Age Features such as 6, 48, and 58, which make up part of the iron production complex beneath Kaiija tree, supported the heaviest densities of slag among features in Block E.

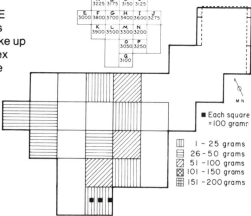

Figure 8: Block B Late Iron Age slag densities are very low in the central area, or the area where cattle were possibly housed.

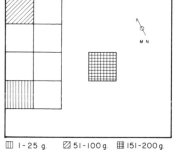

Figure 9: Densities of slag in the Late Iron Age midden of Block C.

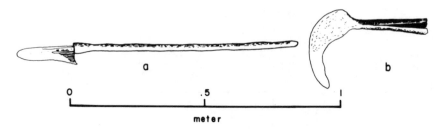

Figure 10: (a) Chopper knife; multi-purpose; now used primarily in *Kibanja* tasks; from Rehse, p. 36. (b) A sickle knife used for cutting bananas, attached to a 2-3 meter pole; from Rehse, p. 52.

Figure 11: Early Iron Age iron artifacts.

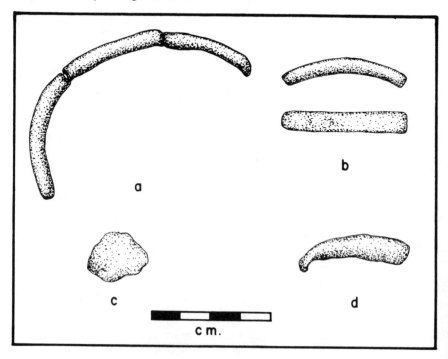

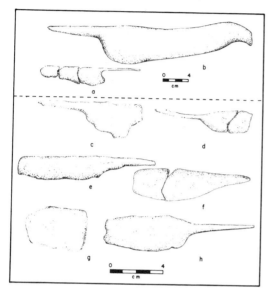

Figure 12: Late Iron Age chopper knife blades: a (unit A, Block B), d (unit I, Block E), and g (unit O, Block B) were recovered from the first excavation unit or the first 15 cm., while c (unit I, Block C) and e (unit G, Block E) were located at −20 cm., h (unit P, Block A) was at −24 cm., and f (unit P, Block E) was located at −35 cm.

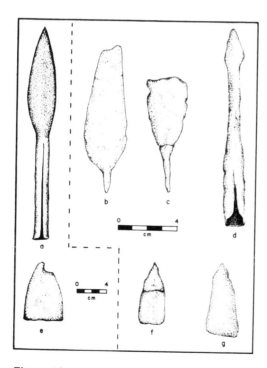

Figure 13: Late Iron Age spear blades.

Figure 14: Bahaya hafted spear
blades; from Rehse, p. 33 and p. 52.

5 cm

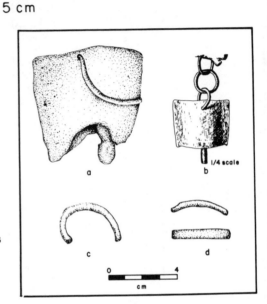

Figure 15: Late Iron Age, Block E; b is
bell described by Rehse.

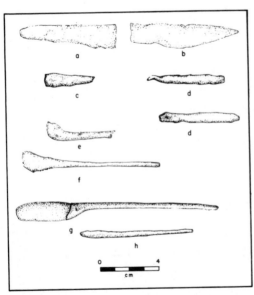

Figure 16: Late Iron Age knife blades
and possible shafts.

11
Tentative Conclusions and Future Directions

The previous discussion helps to demonstrate some of
the problems faced by archaeologists who work in
previously uninvestigated areas where published,
documentary evidence for history and premodern
technological life are minimal. Buhaya, when compared
to many other technologically advanced cultures around
the world, is relatively close to its traditional period. This is a distinct advantage to the archaeologist
who does his own social-cultural anthropology in the
field. Most archaeologists have to rely on published
accounts of earlier ethnographic observations which,
when it comes to complex phenomena such as technological systems, can be fraught with error. Most ethnographic analogs used in interpreting excavated cultural
materials and features in this study came from ethnohistoric investigations about iron production conducted
over several months.

Even though first-hand observations of the technological process await ethnoarchaeological work during
future investigations, it is possible to determine the
range of variability in furnace forms, say, by studying the oral history of twentieth-century smelting in
Buhaya. The descriptions of this phase of the technological process are more reliable than the one published record, Herman Rehse's account of iron smelting in
his Kiziba, Land und Leute. This account includes excellent illustrations of Baziba material culture in the
early twentieth century. For the most part, however,
it is a highly confused description that reflects
Rehse's inadequate knowledge of iron technology, and
it is an idealized account with posed, inaccurate
pictures. It offers few reliable guidelines for
interpreting similar phenomena in the archaeological

record. Hence, the necessity for ethnoarchaeological
studies that concentrate on the form and function of
the technological process and an associated social
and ritual behavior.

The working hypotheses set out in Chapter 8 were confirmed by the archaeological data obtained during four
months of excavations at the Rugomora Mahe site.
Their viability as hypotheses are clear, and they will
continue to be useful tools in subsequent investigations, along with the host of subsidiary hypotheses
generated by analyses of features and data from iron
production activities. Subsequent to the Rugomora
Mahe excavations, however, it became clear that a
more general hypothesis was necessary in order to
test the methodology on other sites. Of particular
importance in this regard was the tie between mythology
and a prehistoric occupation, which was eventually
dated to three occupational periods, 500 B.C., 100
A.D., and about 1700 A.D. Thus far, the investigation
had employed a rigorous scientific method; continuation
of testing based on a hypothetico-deductive model was
imperative for supporting the Rugomora Mahe results.

The next step was to formulate a hypothesis that could
be applied to other sites. It became apparent that
any attempt to move toward a strict deductive-nomological approach at this time would have been unrealistic
and inappropriate. The explanandum would be difficult
to subsume under a general law that addressed the tie
of prehistoric sites to mythological phenomena without
research in areas outside Buhaya. It is very possible
that the phenomenon may be culture-bound. Only future
research elsewhere can determine the appropriateness
of a deductive-nomological approach to this case. It
was decided that the phenomenon was sufficiently
exciting and complex that the Bahaya generalities had
to be worked out first. Thus, the hypothetico-
deductive proposition: If myth and folklore about the
Bacwezi and Rugomora Mahe are tied to the Early Iron
Age, then other physical sites tied to similar myth
will be Early Iron Age (occupation/special activity)
sites.

The first test of this hypothesis was conducted in
the milieu of other Rugomora Mahe myths and folklore
at a site called Nkimbo. Plans were made to test-
excavate near the Kya Rugomora tree in Nkimbo,
Kanyangereko, approximately a mile from Katuruka. The

Kya Rugomora tree at Nkimbo (see Chapter 7, Figure 3)
is a mnemonic object associated with the mythology
of Rugomora Mahe (Figure 1). One version of the myth,
when obtained at Kya Rugomora tree, maintained that
one of the iron supports or legs of the iron tower was
located at the tree. The tree is also mentioned in
other accounts as a place where iron was produced to
build the iron tower.

Two test pits were placed immediately to the west
of the tree. One meter to the west of Kya Rugomora
tree at -72 centimeters, we encountered an Early Iron
Age pot burial (Figure 1). One particularly fine
example of a "classical" Urewe-type pot was recovered.
This globular, necked pot had a 2.5 centimeter wide
dimple in the base along with bevelled rim and decorative elements that included grooving and incising,
the grooving in a scroll motif similar to those
illustrated by Posnansky (1961:184) and Leakey (1948:
22). The feature also included an open bowl with a
carinated rim, along with grooving and incising. The
primary significance of these finds, which happen to
be two excellent examples of Early Iron Age pottery,
is that they were discovered beneath Kya Rugomora
tree through the testing of the primary hypothesis.
These results help confirm the hypothesis.

Testing of the hypothesis continued at Korongo tree
in Maruku village. Korongo tree is one of the two
magical trees given to Rugomora Mahe by Mugasha and
later planted in Kyamutwara kingdom (see Figure 2).

The confirmation of the hypothesis in these cases is
an auspicious beginning to the working out of relations
among myth, folklore, and archaeologically recovered
prehistoric remains. Explanations provided in
mythology about activities performed on sites are
incredible, unexpected sources of information for
interpreting prehistoric life. There appears to be
a very strong relationship between explanation in
myth and prehistoric lifeways, which the archaeologist
attempts to interpret and explain. The question of
what constitutes an adequate test in this case and
in archaeology is problematical. Results thus far
obtained in Buhaya during testing of the primary
hypothesis are exciting and encouraging. But further
testing and modification of hypotheses are necessary
and will continue, so that we can hope to understand
the processes of continuity in Buhaya that tie extant
oral tradition so explicitly to prehistoric times.

As work continues, it is important that the methodology
not be bounded by the reconstructed logic. Hypothetico-

deductive propositions probably will continue to be
developed by a complex process which Kaplan called
observations, shrewd guesses, (inductive generalizations?), and scientific intuition. For instance, during tests of the main hypothesis, it was observed that
very large trees, which sometimes function as shrines
to the Bacwezi gods, are possible markers of Early
Iron Age sites. This observation, as well as the
observation that Bacwezi myth may be associated with
large shrine trees, should be employed in formulating
an alternative hypothesis for testing the linkage
among ancient tree shrines, mythology, and Early Iron
Age sites.

The formulation of alternative hypotheses is an
integral part of a hypothetico-deductive approach and
in no way presupposes disproof of the original
hypothesis. Instead, it allows the development of
logical arguments and tests that are complementary to
and flow from the testing of the original hypotheses.
It is hoped that the methodology herein described
will encourage an understanding of the demonstrated
value of an explicit, conscious approach to archaeological inquiry and explanation. What is practical in
the Buhaya context may not be so elsewhere. It may
be dangerous to advocate a particular methodology in
archaeology or attempt to establish that any one
approach must work. Scientific archaeology is in
an incipient state and that sensitive embryonic
condition can only tolerate a flexible, open, experimental approach.

The Rugomora Mahe site provides an experimental model
in archaeology that is of considerable importance to
the African historian. The site is tied to oral traditions that provide accurate and detailed descriptions
of prehistoric activities performed there. Hence, it
is more than simply a shrine at which an archaeologist
might expect to find ceremonial artifacts. The
archaeological investigations show that myth about
ancient technology is accurately preserved to the present day. There is also a correlation between the
location of ceremonial activities during the last 300
years and the underground location of Early Iron Age
structural features. Wherever there is a heavy density
of ceremonial pottery, coins, cowries, spear blades,
and bones dating to the Late Iron Age, then immediately
below there are structural features dating to the Early
Iron Age.

These high correlations between Early Iron Age

structural features and Late Iron Age ceremonial
life are not coincidental. They appear to be phenomena
that are similar to the extant iron tower mytheme
and its relationship to prehistoric activity areas.
The iron tower mytheme has survived manipulations and
borrowing, whereas other localized myths that may have
been associated with the other areas on the site do
not survive today. The gashani house (a ceremonial
structure) was located directly over one of the
densest concentrations of Early Iron Age features
on the site. This find suggests that the Bahinda may
have known about former local myths similar to the
iron tower episode.

The Rugomora Mahe site is also a phenomenon that
belongs to the history of political and religious
conflict in Kyamutwara. According to the oral
traditions, the occupation of the site was accompanied
by a close alliance between the Bahinda dynasty and
the spirit mediums of Mugasha, who attempted to
wrestle political power from opposition forces, the
indigenous clans led by Bacwezi spirit mediums. The
Rugomora Mahe site was a strategic locus first for
the Bacwezi opposition and then for the Bahinda.
As an ancient place, it appears to have had an
associated mythology that was aetiological for an
advanced technological system, which was the source
of power for the indigenous clans. Those who controlled the essential shrines associated with the
productive economy held the means to power and
authority.

Bahinda adoption of mythemes already associated with
the site also might have provided a direct historical
tie to the site and a kind of legitimacy. At first
sight, it might appear that the use of a Bacwezi
mythological structure in royal Bahinda genealogies
could be a similar legitimizing device. But this
possibility is negated by our comparative texts
which show that the Bacwezi structures are more
thoroughly employed by Bacwezi spirit mediums who
belong to indigenous clans. They continue to preserve
local myth about prehistoric iron working, but they
use royal genealogies to do so. However, this is
far from passive acquiescence, as the history of the
Bahinda king, Rugomora Mahe, is rendered with a
traditional Bacwezi structure. In another sense,
then, the Bacwezi opposition might still function at
a symbolic level, for the spirit mediums may have
been successful in transforming royal history with
impunity. Another alternative is that royal sanctions
might have been employed (for reasons of obtaining
a legitimate tie to the past) to insure that the

Bacwezi spirit mediums rendered the traditions
according to the mixed format. The modification of
royal history might have occurred in Kyamutwara because the history of Kyamutwara is much less regularized and codified than that of Kiziba, where sanctions
against divergent interpretations appear to have been
much stronger. The consequence of these subtle
cultural differences is that today the Bakama in Kiziba
are characterized as the safe, civil force in the
Culture/Nature opposition, while in Kyamutwara the
Bahinda continue to be characterized as wild, untamed,
and dangerous in the myth about Rugomora Mahe. The
persistence of the Rugomora Mahe myth might be
partially related to historical causes such as the
continued, real threat to the Bahinda dynasty in
Kyamutwara by clans such as the Bankango. In other
words, opposition to the throne in recent times has
been much more prevalent in Kyamutwara. Sanctions
could have failed to touch significant portions of the
Kyamutwara population, and, consequently, alternative
oral traditions might have flourished.

In Kiziba kingdom before the consolidation of Babito
power, the dynasty is represented in oral tradition
as associated with the Bacwezi. In fact, the Bakama
become putrid flesh and belong to the same category
as Bacwezi spirit mediums when they are possessed
by Bacwezi spirits. But the Babito eventually
developed a royal cult of spirit mediums possessed
by the spirits of dead kings who opposed the Bacwezi
spirit mediums. This allowed the Babito to successfully consolidate their rule. From the time that the
royal cult was developed, the Kiziba oral traditions
have displayed highly regulated characteristics.
Since the development of a ritual and religious
opposition between Bakama and Bacwezi embandwa,
religious belief in Kiziba has emphasized the
dangerous aspects of Bacwezi spirit mediums. The
royally sponsored cults and official sanctions against
divergent oral traditions have prevented a characterization of Babito rule since Burungu I (the eighth
king) as anything but legitimate and desirable.

The Bahinda claim that the Rugomora Mahe site was a
royal kikale and later a gashani of the Mukama appears
to be verified by late seventeenth-century cultural
features that may be related to ceremonial life. The
correspondence between the C14 dating of these
features and the genealogical distance from the
present for Rugomora Mahe would also suggest that
Bahinda rule in Buhaya was firmly established only
some 200 years before the arrival of Europeans, not
some 400 years as historians have previously

speculated. The dating of the Early Iron Age features,
which falls between 500 B.C. and 200 A.D., proves
that mythology in Buhaya is capable of continuity
through thousands of years without distortion of its
core truth when it is tied to physical features of the
landscape. If mythology is an explanatory system that
details exactly what activities or associated activities occurred in prehistoric times, then it is also a
symbolic commentary on the impact of iron technology
in Bahaya culture.

The symbolic aspect of the iron tower episode is
especially significant, for it is accompanied by
another mytheme about insufficient agricultural goods
followed by great agricultural plenty. When Rugomora
Mahe returns from Isheshe with magic trees and an iron
hammer (which is in fact an anvil used in iron forging),
great plenty results from the crops he brings. He
also changes the clan name of those who smelt iron
because they do not pay homage to him. In other words,
he directly controls the clans that do the iron working. The mytheme about the lack of and subsequent
surplus of crops, as well as its inclusion with episodes that stress the control of the chief forging
tool and the control of iron-working clans, not only
suggests the inclusion of another earlier myth, but
also a linkage between control of iron working and
increased agricultural productivity.

The symbolic thrust of the myth is that crop surplus
accompanied the mastery of iron technology but that
it was preceded by famine and uncontrolled iron working. The myth then shows that mastery of iron
technology leads to a cultural fluorescence—the
building of the iron tower—which ultimately ends
in disaster, the collapse of the tower to the west.

This myth provides a symbolic, allegorical model for
the history of resource exploitation in Buhaya. This
statement might appear speculative, but it has been
demonstrated that some mythologies about economic
life in Buhaya have great historical accuracy and
astounding continuity through time. Accordingly, the
mythemes about the iron tower, surplus crops, and
control of iron working probably are generalized,
symbolic commentaries about the Bahaya mastery and use
of iron technology in the area. The following discussion will point out the congruence between the
archaeological construct for the history of resource
exploitation and the possible value of mythology as
a historical model for the history of resource
exploitation in Buhaya.

The data from the survey of mining sites indicate that
well-developed and well-organized mining operations
were conducted by indigenous clans who depleted the
iron ore resources of some areas and had to move
elsewhere to find continuing supplies of iron ore.
The large slag heaps in places such as Kangantebbe—
the vestiges of which are said to have been large slag
heaps in Bwanjai and Kikukwe, Kiziba kingdom—and the
oral traditions about slag heaps that have since disappeared all suggest that a large-scale, prosperous
iron technology was based in the coastal Buhaya kingdoms. The Bahaya were known to the Banyambo in the
nineteenth century as people who traded their iron
goods to the north. In addition, the Bahaya have
extensive oral traditions about the trade of their
iron goods to the north in return for salt and ivory.

The highly productive iron technology in the Buhaya
region appears to be associated with a highly efficient
technological procedure, preheating, which is further
enhanced by a high grade haematite ore. This highly
productive iron technology would have far-ranging
ramifications for agricultural production, increasing
population density, and overexploitation of the
forests. These consequences are suggested by
(1) the exploitative economy of today and in the
past, (2) the history of settlement, and (3) the extant mythological symbolism. These aspects need to
be discussed more fully, for they suggest hypothetical
constructs that can be formulated in more specific
form for testing.

First, the production of iron tools would have made
possible faster and perhaps more extensive forest
clearance. Kendall's ecological data for the region
(Chapter 2) do in fact show widespread dimunition of
forest at the same time that iron was being produced
at the Rugomora Mahe site—approximately 500 B.C.
The dating without the ecological evidence would
appear very early, but it is made credible by Kendall's
data. Furthermore, iron working is known at least a
millennium before in Egypt (Goghlan, 1956) and Meroe
at 514 B.C. ± 75 (Willett, 1971:358). Charcoal from
the Nok culture site of Taruga in Nigeria had been
obtained from a sealed context in a furnace and
dated to 300 B.C. ± 100 (Fagg, 1969; Willett, 1971).
Charcoal has also been associated with slag in the
Taruga midden dated to a century earlier.

It is entirely possible that knowledge of iron working
spread to sub-Saharan Africa during the early part of
the first millennium, or perhaps even earlier.
Experimentation may have taken place in widely

scattered places. But in order to justify continued
production, the correct conditions were necessary:
an adequate supply of charcoal, a good grade iron ore,
and a supply of labor. The Buhaya area, with its forested lands and good ore, as well as reliable rainfall
and healthy climate, would have been ideal for the
formulation of a productive iron technology and for
the development of a population base sufficient to
maintain the complex technology.

Once iron is available, then preparation of cleared
forest land for agriculture can be accomplished more
rapidly. Forest clearance for agricultural production
during the Early Iron Age may have been a long fallow
system such as slash-and-burn, with land returned to
fallow after several years in production. It is very
difficult to document the evolution of agricultural
systems, but we do know that, as population density
increases, there is a tendency away from shifting
cultivation toward more intensive systems such as bush
fallowing and annual cropping.

As Boserup (1965) emphasizes, the arguments heretofore
posed for agricultural production are basically
Malthusian. The basic Malthusian argument in regard
to iron tools and agriculture can be summarized as
follows: iron allows for more successful use of soil
nutrients, which means surplus crops, which in turn
means an increased capacity for population growth;
the sequence then results in more intensive
agricultural systems, which repeat the surplus cycle
and end in soil exhaustion and population dispersion.
Boserup suggests that original causality can be
attributed to increased population density, which
may be unrelated to increased agricultural productivity.
If there are variables that cause increased population
density outside of increased agricultural capacity
or productivity, then it is necessary to isolate them.
In the Buhaya area, the production of iron seems to
have led to concentrations of populations, usually
in areas where iron ore was available.

High-density population is linked to iron production
because of the need for a large, reliable labor force
(maximal lineages), which then would have led to expanded need for higher agricultural productivity.
The causality sequence in this case works from iron
production to localized population densities recruited
from maximal lineages to more intense exploitation of
the environment to obtain more foodstuffs. If a more
intense agricultural system develops, then tropical
soils are endangered by leaching and laterization.
That danger, however, can be avoided by allowing a

mature secondary forest to reclaim the land.

It is my hypothesis that the areas where iron ore has
been mined and iron produced support the densest
populations in Buhaya, as well as the oldest settlements. Survey has shown that the Kikukwe-Kigarama
area in Kiziba, the Kangantebbe-Kanazi area in Kianja,
Maruku and environs, Bugabo, and Itawa-Kabare are
some areas where early iron-working clans and mining
production areas were located. The results from
regional surface survey indicate that these areas
are also areas of Early Iron Age occupation. While
the different survey data do not exactly correspond,
they do fall within the very same zones. The first
two ridges along the shore of Lake Victoria are the
most intensely exploited areas for iron produced in
northern Buhaya and the most heavily populated
areas in Buhaya (Tanzania Census, 1971). The site
in Katuruka thus far is the only documented iron
production site in the Early Iron Age, but it is
significant that it is located in an area with very
dense settlement.

Concentration of iron-producing communities on the
ridge tops in the Early Iron Age would have led to
two demands on the forest resources: (1) increased
demand for agricultural goods—or a trend away from
long-term fallow, and (2) demand for charcoal. As
mentioned previously, the demand for charcoal may
have contributed to even more intense exploitation
of the forests in the vicinity of the iron production
centers. Exploitation of the forests for charcoal
could have easily disrupted a long-term fallow system
by preventing secondary forest regeneration.

The hypothesis, then, is that the causal variable for
change to an intense, multicrop agricultural system
in Buhaya is iron production. It leads to the
limitation of population to specific areas, overexploitation of the forests, interference with
regeneration of long-term fallow systems, and
laterization of soils. As Boserup (1965:21) notes,
given these circumstances, a neo-Malthusian argument
would postulate that upon destruction of the soil
a people either starve or move on to new land where
they presumably repeat the process.

However, the prehistoric peoples in the Buhaya area
continued to occupy the area and did not starve. Why?
The extant agricultural practices in Buhaya in part
explain some of the adaptive devices that developed
as a consequence of possible overexploitation of the
land. If iron production took hold at a very early

date because of ideal conditions, it is reasonable
to believe that some of those conditions continued
to predominate and, therefore, kept people tied to
the area.

The development of deep mulching practices (Chapter
3) may be related to the possible interruption of
long-fallow agriculture, the overexploitation of
the land by intensive agriculture and charcoal
production, and the development of intensive agriculture. In Buhaya, multicrop plantings, the presence
of beans, coffee trees, and banana trees, make up a
multiple canopy cropping that in form resembles a
gallery forest. Under these conditions, there is
virtually no rain bombardment of the soil. These
crops, especially beans and bananas, are adaptive
crops given the above conditions. When combined with
the mulching and manuring practices previously
described, they help maintain high fertility on a
basically poor soil and are instrumental in reclaiming
land that has been lost to overexploitation in the
past. Settlement patterns in Buhaya have been
oriented toward a highly proudctive iron technology.
This pattern results in depredation of the land and
eventually in the development of adaptive agricultural
practices that lead to intensive agriculture on a
naturally low-fertility soil.

Part of this discussion began with the suggestion
that aspects of the Rugomora Mahe myth provided a
symbolic, interpretative model for the economic
history of Buhaya. One of the primary themes of the
myth is that food resources were inadequate before
the arrival of Rugomora Mahe. He then controls iron
working, plants trees to establish forests, and builds
an iron tower. The themes suggest that iron production needs control, that there are insufficient food
and forests. Once the iron-working clans are
controlled, forests reestablished, and food increased,
iron technology is once again given a free reign—so
that an iron tower is built. This ends in disaster—
the destruction of the tower—or a repetition of the
previous technological/ecological cycle. Iron
technology may have been so highly productive in
Buhaya that, even under the centralized control of
the Bahinda and Babito dynasties, its high
productivity became its fundamental attraction,
despite its ecological drawbacks. Iron evidently
became an essential commodity controlled by the
state and supported by the state. It assumed a
place of paramount importance in the redistributive
system as a partial substitute for agricultural goods.
Of course, the demand for iron generated by the

political system may have been a repetition of a
previous destructive cycle. It might very well be
that agricultural goods assumed less importance in
the redistributive system because continued high
rates of iron production sufficiently intensified
pressure on the land that agricultural surplus was
eliminated; thus, a change toward iron as a more
essential redistributive commodity was necessitated.
Eventually, the forests came under the control of the
Bakama, whose permission had to be obtained to cut
wood or charcoal, even though specific clans had to
be approached for rights to charcoal production in
the same forests. The interference of the
Mukama in charcoal production for iron production
appears to be a regulatory device of considerable
importance for a balanced ecology in Buhaya.

The same causality sequence for economic problems as
suggested above, uncontrolled iron production, is
strongly implied in the Rugomora Mahe myth. The conjunction of these symbolic themes with the hypothetical
construct suggested by archaeological investigations,
and the previously demonstrated conjunction between
archaeological data and mythology, suggest that
mythology about the history of economic life must
be taken seriously. It may well help to explain
the history of resource exploitation in the Buhaya
area.

The constructs set out above have been suggested by
the history and location of iron production, survey
results for prehistoric settlement, and the
characteristics of contemporary agriculture. For
the moment, many of the ideas fall within the purview
of testable but as yet untested hypotheses. They
show the possible dynamics of prehistoric interaction
with the natural environment. Archaeological research
in Buhaya will attempt to test these propositions
in the future through the acquisition of further subsistence and settlement data and through the study
of the development of sterile grasslands and intensive
agriculture. Central to future studies will be the
further study of iron production, its distribution,
and its contribution to other aspects of culture,
particularly change in the agricultural system.

The conjunction of mythological evidence with
archaeological evidence for explaining prehistoric
life in Buhaya is most significant for the study of
African history. Most historians of Africa who
have been concerned with prehistoric periods have
addressed themselves to chronological problems.
Rather than pose questions that seek to explain

developmental processes in African cultures, there
has been a preoccupation with dating migrations of
peoples and the dispersion of linguistic groups.
These orientations have neglected questions of
development and change through time in major regions.
The result has been a sequence of constructs that tie
together random C14 dates on maps and that claim
direction of migrations based on the apparent sequence
of the dates. These problems will be discussed in
the following chapter. It is hoped that they will
illustrate the greater potential and need for higher
priority for problems reviewed in this chapter.

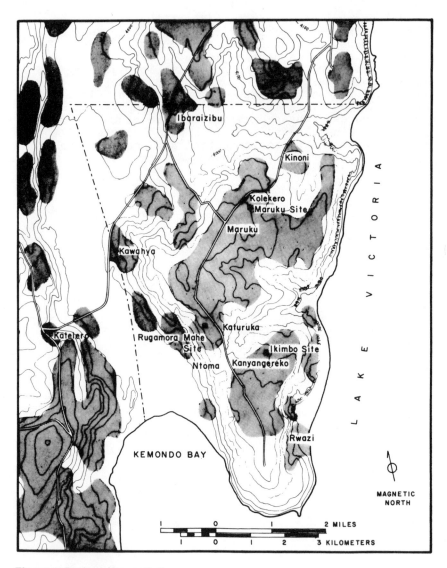

Figure 1: Pot burial beneath *Kya
Rugamora* tree in Ikimbo.

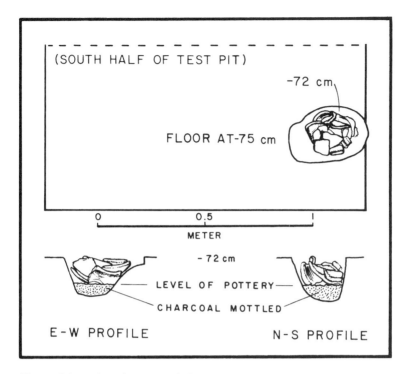

Figure 2: Location of excavated sites associated with Rugamora Mahe oral tradition in Maruku, Buhaya; shaded areas indicate areas of present settlement.

12____Implications for African History

Since the publication in English of Jan Vansina's
Oral Tradition (1965), historians of Africa have been
increasingly concerned with developing methods that
will confirm the historical value of oral traditions.
Independent proof for the historicity of oral traditions is often lacking; consequently, the historian
is usually left with comparative analysis as his
primary analytical method.

The Buhaya research, however, now suggests that the
concept prehistoric must be questioned, particularly
in cases where there is a demonstrated tie between
archaeological evidence and oral traditions. When
archaeology affirms the accuracy of oral traditions
that explain, comment on, interpret, or locate
activities and sites predating a literate tradition,
then the germaneness of the concept must be critically
questioned. The position taken here is that, when
archaeological evidence confirms the historical value
of oral traditions about preliterate life, those
cultural phenomena in that time period should be
considered historic rather than prehistoric. To
retain "prehistory" as a concept in this context
ignores and even militates against the historiographies
and historical concepts of other cultures. The
ramifications of this relativist perspective are considerable both for the study of history and prehistory.
Given this logic, historians must begin to reassess
and expand their concepts of what history is, and
prehistorians must prepare to forfeit part of the
temporal domain previously considered as prehistory.

Attempts to link oral traditions to archaeological
finds have been sparse, primarily because of the

lack of adequate methodologies. It also results from
the assumptions that it is probably not possible and
that oral traditions, if they have any utility with
archaeology, are most useful in constructing migration
routes of peoples in the past. This attitude has been
realistically summarized by Vansina, who said:
"Archaeology can throw light on certain aspects of
the past, especially on migrations and on material
culture. It is, however, often impossible to link
the information obtained from oral traditions with
any definite archaeological finds" (1965:174).

Vansina, while keenly recognizing the importance of
archaeology as a complementary form of evidence for
oral traditions, wrote from a perspective that
reflected the limited development of methodologies
linking the two forms of evidence in the early 1960s.
The argument here is that archaeological evidence
used to construct schemes about migrations is often
misused and, furthermore, that it is misdirected. It
is misdirected in that the current emphasis on
migrations ignores more important archaeological
questions, such as the need to seek explanations
for changing adaptations of Iron Age cultures on a
regional basis.

A scientific approach too often is lacking in historical literature about Early Iron Age Africa. This is
a matter of great concern to those who, in their
attempts to provide substantial documentation,
incidentally provide data for the creation of
incautious hypotheses by other historians of Africa.
There has been a tendency in the writing of African
history, as Huffman (1970) has correctly observed,
to elevate hypothesis to fact. This is especially
true in the continuing discussion about Bantu "migrations" and the coming of iron technology to sub-
Saharan Africa.

Some of the archaeological evidence used in constructs
about migrations—in particular Bantu migrations—will
now be examined. Central to this discussion is an
assessment of the scientific quality of such attempts,
for the problems inherent in such constructs are more
profound than Huffman's criticism suggests. My
position here is that hypotheses in historical writing
about Bantu migrations have been based on isolated
empirical data, or even on a single datum, and have
usually sought to explain the direction of a migration
by Bantu-speaking peoples. The hypotheses are usually
stated as interpretive positions; logical problems
arise when "interpretive" hypotheses are not
explicated as hypotheses per se, hence their ready

transformation to "fact." Collingwood (1946) noted
that once a notion gains popularity it becomes fact,
for it becomes part of the historiography. In this
process of transformation, the crucial logical error
is that the "hypotheses" usually are not justifiable.
That is, the empirical data indicate that the "hypotheses" cannot be tested adequately, and if this is so,
then they are not justifiable. In terms of logic,
then, many of the ideas heretofore advanced by
African historians are neither valid nor logical.

The previous discussion can be illustrated with
several case studies of historical writing for the
East African Iron Age. Oliver (1966) provides a good
example of a reasoning process that stressed direction-
ality to population movement from random C14 dates.
He points out that at that time (i.e., 1966) it became
known that Machili in Zambia had iron in the first
century, that there were widespread sites in Rhodesia
by the fourth to ninth centuries, that there was an
Early Iron Age occupation in Kalambo Falls from the
sixth to sixteenth centuries, and that Uganda had iron
by the eleventh century. He questions those who
previously claimed a north to south movement of Bantu
peoples based on the same evidence. He then concludes:
"To me they [the dates] seem to indicate a movement
spreading north and south from the Zambezi. The
clear implication would seem to be that it was
the Bantu who brought the Iron Age to Rwanda and
Uganda and western Kenya, and that they brought it
from the south." (1966:375)

Oliver called this statement a hypothesis, but it
was hardly that. At that time, it was simply the
drawing of lines between dates on a map and adding
directional indicators from earlier to later dates.
The point is that it attempts to infer population
movement and the direction of population movements
from isolated archaeological dates. It ignores the
fact that the available data are archaeological
phenomena, not prehistoric phenomena. In short,
Oliver's statement reflects the areal interests of
archaeologists and the embryonic stage of research
on the Early Iron Age; it does not reflect, by any
stretch of the imagination, the settlement patterns
of Early Iron Age peoples. As a consequence, data
on the Early Iron Age are geographically and
temporally limited. Oliver's commentary, like those
of others (e.g., Posnansky, 1968a), is based on
extremely sketchy data that are the function of
limited research, not thorough archaeological knowledge of prehistoric Iron Age peoples in East and
Central Africa.

Thus, Oliver's position is speculation and not hypothesis. A hypothesis needs to be justifiable; there
has to be some indication that empirical data can be
retrieved to test it. In this case, there is only
random archaeological information and no substantial
evidence in the prehistoric record that suggests
movements of peoples or directions of possible
cultural diffusion. One may conclude, then, that for
now Oliver's speculation cannot be converted into
convincing hypothetical form. Oliver did, of course,
intend to perform a service for African history by
suggesting possible alternative interpretations for
the development of Early Iron Age cultures. In this
regard, a stimulating, although not always accurate,
picture emerges. However, historians are not alone
in their advocacy of propositions based on insufficient
groundings. The same propensity has been demonstrated
by archaeologists.

Posnansky (1968a) denied Oliver's charge that
archaeologists (including Posnansky) claimed a north-
south migration of Bantu-speaking peoples. Yet,
Posnansky, too, created propositions based on insufficient evidence. For example, he regarded Soper's
third century A. D. dates for Kwale ware in eastern
Kenya as problematical, for they necessitated a new
migratory construct:

> The early date is problematical and suggests a
> movement from the south of agricultural peoples
> different from the Rift Valley pastoralists.
> Similar pottery was also found by Kohl-Larsen in
> central Tanzania which may indicate, if the
> ancestral ware had a western origin, a movement
> around the drier already occupied Rift Valley
> area to the wetter hill country of the Usambaras
> and Pare mountains perhaps at a time before the
> Dimple-based settlements of Uganda and western
> Kenya had begun (1968a:9; emphasis mine).

As can be seen, new archaeological discoveries in
Early Iron Age Africa have tended to be regarded as
problematical because they distrupted previous speculation about the migratory movements of Bantu-speaking
peoples. Inevitably, the new data are employed to
create new migratory speculations; often these
speculations are based on yet another level of speculation. For instance, in Posnansky's argument that
there may have been an earlier movement toward the
Usambaras, "if the ancestral ware had a western
origin," we have two levels of untested proposition
(1968a:9).

Another major theme that emerges from a reading of
historical writings about the Early Iron Age is what
may be called isolated speculations that confuse
archaeologists' attempts to elucidate developmental
processes and change during the Early Iron age. A
case in point is Oliver's (1966) discussion of possible
migratory paths suggested by C14 dating of sites. He
does not suggest that channel-decorated pottery (a
term which he also mistakenly applies to the more
northerly pottery complex) is a regional variation
or decorative technique common to one co-tradition
(Huffman, 1970). "They [the C14 dates] suggest to
me that the nuclear Bantu learnt the typical designs
of channel decoration from some intrusive, possibly
Indonesian group in Southeast Africa, and carried it
north in the later phase of their expansion, when they
occupied the northern sector of the lake region"
(1966:375).

There is absolutely no evidence to suggest that this
proposition is either testable or legitimate. It
is this kind of speculation by nonarchaeologists that
tends to confuse those less familiar with the
archaeological literature. This level of speculation
militates against the propagation of archaeologically
based hypotheses, for it siphons off attention from
much more substantial positions. This matter is
substantially more serious than hypotheses being
converted into facts, for it is apparent that legitimate hypotheses have not yet been formulated and that
many interpretative positions presently rest on
successive levels of previous speculations.

The pitfalls of speculation can be avoided by generating only those hypotheses that are allowed by the
data and that are testable. It would be appropriate
to adopt a methodological approach in historical
writing on the Iron Age that reflects the rigors of
developing scientific approaches in archaeology. In
this sense, the approach taken in the Buhaya research
can be used as an example. It is, of course, necessary
to expand interpretation of the actual development of
Early Iron Age peoples, but this need not be achieved
at the expense of sound historical explanation.
Posnansky (1968a) warned that before firm conclusions
can be reached about the settlement histories of Early
Iron Age peoples, it is essential first to fill in
the geographical gaps. The development of more
demanding methodologies will more adequately help fill
these gaps than has been done previously.

The basic problem in historical interpretation can be
identified as a preoccupation with migrations, the

routes for which have generally been decided from
random dates. The worthiness of attempts to explain
migrations is not in question, but such goals should
not at this time have priority in research or in the
writing of African history. The priorities need
ordering so that there is an increasing emphasis on
the development and changing adaptations of Early
Iron Age cultures on a regional basis. Fagan's
(1967a) research of the Kalomo culture in Zambia is
a superb example of the basic, fundamental subsistence-
settlement evidence we need in order to build better
explanations for change in the Early Iron Age.
Attempts to explain the routes of Bantu migrants, if
they existed at all, are premature at this time.

Regionalized programs of study will help to determine
causal factors for change in culture thorugh time
in each area. These programs will allow, for instance,
more opportunity to study ceramic styles and functional
types as local cultural forms tied into more generalized processes of adaptation and change. Again, the
tendency in East and Central African history in the
use of ceramic evidence has been to see gross
similarities in decorative style (the reduction of
all East and Central African Early Iron Age pottery
to the channel category is a good example) as evidence
of migration or diffusion. Considering the limited
evidence available to the historian, this tendency
is perhaps understandable. But now that sufficient
regional studies have been performed, reductionist
arguments founded on ceramic evidence are no longer
suitable.

Much of the speculation in African history about Bantu
migratory routes is related to the differing linguistic
data provided by Guthrie and Greenberg. Oliver and
others have made some very persuasive attempts to
reconcile the position of Greenberg (who claims that
Bantu is a linguistic subgroup related to the Benue-
Niger group of languages and hence has its origins
in the Cameroun-Nigeria border area) with Guthrie's
hypothesis that Bantu languages dispersed from a
central core area in northern Zambia. It is not
necessary to recapitulate specifics of the arguments
here, but suffice it to say that Oliver has attempted
to reconcile the linguistic argument by pointing out
that Guthrie's core gorup may have been founded by
pre-Bantu speakers from West Africa. It is when
Oliver attempts to construct a map of population
dispersion in stages according to the available
archaeological information and Guthrie's linguistic
construct that problems begin to emerge. Basically,
Oliver argues that the Bantu peoples, such as the

Kamba, who today display the lowest affinity of root words to the core group represent the fourth stage of dispersal—at the beginning of the present millennium.

A basic assumption of the Oliver construct is that the fourth stage of population dispersal represented surplus populations that left their parent populations (those who resulted from the stage three expansion) because of overpopulation. Earlier, stage three developed because of the introduction of Asiatic crops such as the banana which allowed "colonization" of humid areas after consolidation in the core area (stage 2). These arguments, however ingenious, never have been buttressed by substantiating evidence. Today, sufficient evidence is available to justify a completely new start in our attempts to explain the development of Early Iron Age cultures in East Africa and to review some of the basic assumptions that have colored past attempts to explain the development of Iron Age culture.

The first point to reevaluate is the dating evidence. In eastern Kenya and Tanzania, the Early Iron Age complex defined by Kwale ware has been dated as predominantly the second and third centuries A.D. The dates for Urewe ware in the Kavirondo Gulf fall in the third and fourth centuries A.D. (Soper, 1969), and Soper's recent (1971d) excavation at Chobi in northern Uganda is dated to 290 A.D. $\pm$ 125. As noted above, the relevant dates from the Rugomora Mahe site in Buhaya are:

$$
\begin{array}{lll}
\text{N - 890 :} & 450 \text{ B.C.} \pm 115 \\
\text{N - 895 :} & 550 \text{ B.C.} \pm 115 & \\
& & \text{1st} \\
& & \text{Occupation} \\
\text{RL- 405 :} & 610 \text{ B.C.} \pm 100 \\
\text{RL- 406 :} & 520 \text{ B.C.} \pm 110 \\
\\
\text{N - 891 :} & 60 \text{ A.D.} \pm 115 \\
\text{N - 892 :} & 120 \text{ A.D.} \pm 110 & \text{2nd} \\
\text{N - 898 :} & 170 \text{ A.D.} \pm 100 & \text{Occupation}
\end{array}
$$

Three dates from the Makongo site are also relevant to the discussion:

$$
\begin{array}{ll}
\text{N - 902 :} & 40 \text{ A.D.} \pm 100 \\
\text{N - 900 :} & 985 \text{ A.D.} \pm 100 \\
\text{N - 901 :} & 910 \text{ A.D.} \pm 100
\end{array}
$$

The first date at Makongo falls within the standard deviation obtained for the second occupation period at Katuruka. N-900 and N-901 appear to date much later, perhaps terminal Early Iron Age occupation of the Makongo site, located on the Lake Victoria shoreline. Finally, Van Noten's excavations in Rwanda of supposed royal graves tied to oral tradition have yielded Early Iron Age pottery and dates of 295 A.D. + 50 (GrN-5735) and 230 B.C. + 60 (GrN-5752) (Sutton, 1973).

These recent datings of the Early Iron Age in East Africa overturn the construct offered by Oliver, who in his map (1966:369) puts the Buhaya coast, the Kavirondo Gulf, and eastern Kenya and Tanzania within the second millennium A.D. dispersal area. The date for Chobi, which is outside the stage 4 perimeter on Oliver's map, means that iron production was established in the northern part of the lacustrine area by the third century. The dates for western Kenya, eastern Kenya and Tanzania, northwestern Tanzania, and Rwanda indicate that there were well-established groups of iron-producing peoples, perhaps Bantu speakers (though this possibility is, of course, impossible to determine) by the first and second centuries A.D. The Buhaya investigations have demonstrated that iron producers in East Africa were much earlier, 400 to 500 B.C., although these peoples may have been limited to specific environments. It is also possible that it might have taken several centuries for iron working to develop fully and to saturate a geographical area completely. Once that happened, sites for later periods would be much more plentiful. In sum, a host of technological variables can influence the successful practice of iron technology.

It is clear that the archaeological phenomena cannot be tied to generalized linguistic phenomena, and certainly not in terms of dispersal of language groups over the terrain. The Oliver construct does not seek to explain how or why iron production takes root and prospers in some areas very early—nor does it point out the implications for later population expansion. Oliver connects population growth and expansion to a Malthusian notion that new food crops ipso facto created surpluses and that surpluses led to growing populations:

> Where rainfall is distributed throughout the year, the banana can become not merely a seasonal luxury but a staple food. It can support a relatively dense population and requires practically no labor. The lake region provides ideal conditions for its culture, and it would be

> entirely logical to suppose that a population
> explosion in the lake region occurred as a
> result of its introduction (Oliver, 1966:369;
> emphasis mine).

Oliver's argument continues with the suggestion that
the surplus population generated by the surplus of
crops then went on to colonize other areas.

There is a good reason to look for other causal
linkages. A working hypothesis based on research in
Buhaya suggests that the history of settlement in
the Buhaya area is related to dense, localized populations that gathered together to operate a complex and
highly organized productive technology demanding
significant manpower. This highly productive economy
and concentrated population led to the depletion of
natural resources and to the development of adaptive
changes in the agricultural system to maintain dense
populations. Thus, the availability of new food
crops does not appear to have been a significant
causative factor in population growth. However, the
arrival of Asiatic food crops in East Africa during
the Iron Age may have provided a means of adapting
to an overexploited and quickly diminishing supportive
habitat.

The above proposition is suggested not only by the
settlement history of Buhaya but also by the oral
traditions of the Haya. Most of the Haya predynastic
myths stress the importance of millet to the early
cultural period. According to oral tradition, the
Basita clan sold its control over the royal drums
(political power) for millet while on its way to
Buhaya. Myths about the coming of the banana to
Kyamutwara kingdom, for instance, suggest that the
banana came some time after the indigenous clans had
settled in the area. These oral traditions certainly
do not provide a chronology of crop introduction, but
the mythological emphasis that bananas helped allevi-
ate a condition of great hunger suggests that the
coming of bananas might have enhanced agricultural
productivity and the maintenance of the population
base, as well as fostered the development of intense
multicrop agriculture. It is also possible that
overexploitation of the natural environment led to a
partial dispersal of population from the Buhaya
area to other areas in East Africa. However, this
is only a logical argument and has not yet been
substantiated by evidence.

The complex hypothesis stated above has been
generated from empirical evidence gathered during oral

tradition and archaeological investigations in Buhaya.
As such, it is grounded in data and is testable.
Therefore, if we study the growth of iron production
among Bantu-speaking peoples through a series of
testable propositions such as are set out above, we
can develop explanations that will elucidate causal
factors for culture change related to population
growth and iron production. The alternative is to
continue to follow dates on maps, which results in a
never-ending series of pulsating migratory patterns
tied to notions of agricultural surplus and its
effects on population size. Explanations for change
obtained through regional research will, therefore,
lead to the recognition of common development patterns.
After this groundwork is established, African historians will have substantial data from which to draw
in attempting to write syntheses of Early Iron Age
development.

The role of iron as a catalyst for Bantu expansion
has also been widely assumed (Davidson, 1959; Oliver,
1966). The idea is an attractive one, for it seeks
to link capability for expansion to iron production.
However, as Posnansky has pointed out, no substantiating evidence for the position exists, for it is just
as reasonable to propose that Bantu populations were
already in East and Central Africa before knowledge
of iron working arrived. Certainly, Greenberg's
evidence for the antiquity of the Bantu linguistic
subgroup allows for such a possibility. Until sites
are located in the forests of the Congo watershed
that predate the East African and Central African
Early Iron Age, there will not be sufficient evidence
to formulate a testable hypothesis about the possible
role of iron production in the settlements and movements of Early Iron Age peoples. The Buhaya research
may shed some light on this particular problem, for
it is probable that prior to Iron Age settlement in
the Buhaya area, it was covered by high evergreen
forest (McMaster, 1960). The settlement of the
west coast of Lake Victoria might have been affected
by peoples passing from the west through similar
forested areas. The Rwanda evidence might also
suggest this possibility, but there is insufficient
ecological or settlement evidence from either area
to warrant further speculation. Perhaps regional
research to the west in Zaire will establish more
substantial possibilities for hypothesizing.

One of the primary questions in this whole complex
of interrelated problems is the origin of iron
working. Posnansky (1966) believes that the knowledge of iron production did not come from Meroe, but

his position, like Oliver's, was based on evidence
available in 1966. Shinnie's dates for the production
of iron at Meroe—third to fifth centuries B.C.—and
evidence from Ethopia dating to the fourth to fifth
century B.C.—are approximately the same as the
Katuruka dates (Willett, 1971; Posnansky, 1968a). The
location of a major iron production center at Meroe
on a primary waterway—the Nile—and the ease of
passage on a major waterway, regardless of the Sudd,
support the possibility that iron production was
transmitted from north to south. In his discussion of
dates for the Nok culture in Nigeria, Willett (1971)
suggests that iron production could easily have come
from Meroe via trade routes across the Sudanic belt.
Certainly, the possibility for transmission of iron-
working knowledge from the south also exists, but it
seems less likely. Moreover, it is an argument that
proposes the most improbable and most difficult
routes by which this complex technological information might have been conveyed and practiced.

My previous argument stresses that it is fruitless
to speculate that there were migrations of people
or a diffusion of technological knowledge in certain
directions on the basis of isolated dates and their
affinities or differences. If there are similarities
in dating and in formal attributes of the artifacts,
however, a tentative proposition can be offered to
test the relatedness between the two phenomena.
Consequently, a justifiable hypothesis for the Buhaya
area evidence is as follows: given the similarities
in time period for the Early Iron Age at Meroe and at
Katuruka (the Rugomora Mahe site), and given the
similarities in furnace brick form and smelting
furnace type, these similarities indicate other
relationships in the technological processes in the
two areas resulting from diffusion between Meroe and
Buhaya.

As it stands now, this proposition cannot be taken as
interpretation, for it is set up only to test
rigorously what may or may not be a relationship
between formal attributes in iron production
materials. It will be tested in the future and the
greater the complexity of the test, the greater
confidence the results will inspire—if they confirm
the hypothesis. In this way, we can move toward a
writing of African history that will eschew speculation and will espouse the demonstration of relationships and the development of explanations concerned
with change in cultures.

Finally, the Buhaya research addresses a problem

discussed in detail during the analysis of oral tradition, namely, the determination of historicity in mythology. While some historians-anthropologists such as de Heusch (1968) have attempted to deal with the historical value of myth through structural studies, they have worked with myth as a discrete body of data, that is analytically unrelated to other sources, such as archaeology. It is hoped that this present study has suggested some viable uses for mythology. Further revision of historical interpretation can proceed as historians devote themselves to further study of mythology, especially the historical content of myth in different African cultures.

As attempts to link oral traditions to archaeological evidence are initiated, it will be necessary to develop rigorous, replicative methodologies. This development will lead to greater credibility for demonstrated relationships; it will avoid the pitfalls of arguments based on single occurrences; and it will lead to more general propositions that may have cross-cultural relevance. With the added power of oral traditions to explain lifeways during the Iron Age, it should be possible for historians and archaeologists to formulate hypotheses that seek to explain cultural change caused by exploitation of the natural environment as well as interaction with the social environment. Regional coverage with these goals will then lead to more comprehensive data, which in turn will allow the generation of hypotheses about such events as migrations, which are justifiable and which can be tested by subsequent research.

Appendix A—Origins
of Rugomora Mahe:
Augustine Kaindoa

Omukama Kalemera was the son of Nyarubamba, who before his death had two children; his successor was
Kalemera, and the other son was Ruhinda, who went to
rule Ihangiro. When Nyarubamba died, he was
succeeded by his son Kalemera. Kalemera ruled and
had one child named Kimuri and another named Mwehozi.
The wives of Kalemera observed that Kimuri was highly
favored, as he was first born. In their jealousy,
they devised ways to kill Kimuri. These women
gathered lumingo (or elephant grass) and scratched
off fine spines on the top of the grass and then put
these into the milk pot of Kimuri. After Kimuri drank
milk from the pot, he coughed and coughed, and
eventually died.

When Kalemera learned of Kimuri's death, he called
Kayango, his Katikiro, from Kyanyoni to see what had
happened to Kimuri. Kayango was unable to determine
the cause of death, so Kalemera requested him to call
all the Bafumu [witch doctors]. When the Bafumu had
arrived at the Magango kikale, Kalemera instructed
them to make medicine and to divine what had killed
his son, saying to them, "If you don't discover what
killed him, I will kill all the people in this
kingdom." The Bafumu found that Kimuri had not died
from a disease, but that he was murdered by the
jealous wives who didn't want Kimuri to become Makuma.

Kalemera was extremely angered by this news and said,
"It is best that I kill all my wives," but the
Bafumu advised him against this course, warning him
that if he did so he would not have another wife until

*Provided July 28, 29, 30, 1970, in Bukoba.

the time of his death. They said that prison would
be better, so Kalemera built a fenced-in compound at
Kaboya, where he kept his wives. Kalemera then
killed the remainder of his children with the exception
of one, Mwehozi, whom he also wanted to kill but was
prevented from doing so by Kayango. He killed them
in great anger, for he did not see the use of having
children that his wives would kill. Kalemera had
Mwehozi brought to him and ordered that he be blinded;
Kalemera was then satisfied that Mwehozi seemed to be
dead, for he was then something less than a man. He
said, "I don't want to see this child again. Take
him to my wives at Kaboya." Mwehozi was then
accompanied to Kaboya, but not before Kayango inquired,
"Who is going to cook for Mwehozi?" In response,
Kalemera sent a Muzana. (A Muzana is a woman who
worked for the Mukama after her father had offended
the Mukama and had been forced to send his daughter(s)
in payment of the fine; as a group, they cleaned out
the manure, gathered fodder, and house grass, and
cleaned surroundings of the kikale. If the Mukama
favored a Muzana and took her as a concubine, then
she became a Nshoreke, got her own house and increased
status. He would then call her Babonaninsheka, which
means "they see me laughing," to which she would
repeat Bamanyankebwa, which means "they think I have
forgotten." All this is a reference to a time when
some people were abusing the Mukama—and he became
aware of it.)

After Kalemera had sent the Muzana to stay with
Mwehozi, his anger again rose and he started to kill
people and cows. He killed people and cows to make
a river of blood flow from Magango to the River
Muleleizi; he announced that when it reached the
Muleleizi, he would stop the killing. And when the
blood reached the Muleleizi, the Mukama stopped the
slaughter, but then he seemed to be mad or not in
possession of all his senses. While Babonaninsheka
lived with Mwehozi, he slept with her and got her
pregnant. Babonaninsheka bore a male child.

Twelve years after the boy's birth, a man named
Kasindo went to Kalemera to report that Mwehozi-Kiume
(the blind one) had a child. Kalemera became extremely
angry to learn this, as he did not want an heir. He
ordered people to send all the children of one Muteko
(from different villages—Maziba, Kimbugu, Iguruibi,
and Itoju); Kashana was ordered to bring him all
these children. Kashana told the parents of the
children in all those villages that the Mukama wanted
to see their children. The Mukama also ordered that
the son of Kiume should accompany the other boys of

the Muteko. Kiume feared that Kalemera would kill
his son, but Kashana assured him that none would be
killed and that perhaps the Mukama wanted to appoint
one as leader of the Muteko.

The children were then taken to the kikale at Magango.
Kalemera then had two wives at his kikale, Itunire
and Mabuye. They knew of the Mukama's plan to gather
all the children in order to get Kiume's son, Mahe,
to the kikale to kill him. As the children were
being brought to the Mukama, the wives sent their
housemaid with a knife and sewing needle to meet
Mahe and to warn him not to go to the Mukama, who
was planning to kill him. The girl was to explain,
"This is the needle which will blind you, and if you
are not blinded, then this is the knife which will
kill you." The girl spoke to Mahe as she was instructed and warned him to flee in order to avoid
either possibility. Nonetheless, Mahe accompanied
his friends to Nyakabuga (past the outside area
called Nyarulembo, past the first fence into
Nyarubuga, and then into Nyakabuga) and danced with
the other boys in front of Nyaruju. But Mahe then
left his friends and passed through a small side
entrance through which manure was removed, until he
got to the outside fence where he removed poles to go
through. Kalemera then asked if Kiume's son was
there and when he learned that the boy was, he said,
"Bring him here for me to see." But Mahe was not
found and a general search was started. Kalemera
had his wives' quarters searched, but without success.
He then ordered, "Find that child, because before I
die I will see him and have him killed."

After escaping from the kikale, Mahe passed across
the Muleleizi River to Makongora, then to Luhanga
(in Kianja), past the Kamanywabake River to Bushumba,
Izigo, and finally Kimbugo in the late evening. There
he was asked why he was alone. He explained that
his father had left him with a friend who abused him,
so he was returning to Ihangiro. The villagers took
him to Kashana, the Mukungu who had gathered together
the boys for Kalemera. Mahe was not known to these
villagers and his air impressed them, so they requested that Kashana send someone to accompany Mahe
when he wanted to leave.

Knowing that someone would escort him, Mahe departed
very early in the morning to leave his escort behind.
He crossed bush country until he reached Kagoma
village in Ihangiro. There he slept in caves known
as Nyanga za Bashuma (the caves of thieves). The
next morning he passed via Muleba to Itungo where he

entered the house of Byolugana, who was ruling
Ihangiro with the Mukama, Ntare Mugamira, as Kayango
did with the Mukama in Kyamutwara.

There Mahe stayed for three months. In Byolugana's
home there lived a Mufumu named Nyakifunu, who upon
seeing Mahe prophesied that Mahe would become a
Mukama.   After three months, Mahe informed Byolugana
that he would depart; Mahe accompanied other Bazinza
children, who had come to barter coffee beans, back
to Buzinza. Mahe did not go into the Buzinza interior
but stopped somewhere near the lake where he stayed
for two years. In this village, Mahe came to know
two brothers who were fishermen. They eventually
accompanied Mahe in their boat to Bukwaya Island,
where he stayed for two days before deciding to
report his presence to the chief of the island. He
then visited the chief, Machunda. By this time
Mahe was fully matured. When Machunda saw Mahe, he
said to himself, "Hmmm, this child might be a Mukama
or from my clan, Bahinda." He called his daughter
and instructed her to put milk in her milk calabash
for Mahe to drink. But the daughter, Nyamata, displayed her distaste of Mahe and his unkempt appearance
by spitting at her father's suggestion (thus showing
that she thought it a worthless suggestion).

When Machunda observed Nyamata spitting, he became
very annoyed and explained that Mahe would be a chief
in the future. He demanded an explanation. When Mahe
saw Machunda's annoyance, he explained that it did
not matter for he did not drink milk and so Machunda
should not be disturbed.

Machunda then affirmed his hospitality by telling
Mahe, "If you need anything to eat or anything else,
just come here and I'll give it to you." Mahe
stayed on Bukwaya Island for two years before he
departed for the Isheshe (Sesse) Islands. Mahe
went with fishermen to the Isheshe Islands, where they
stayed on the lakeshore but without anything to eat.
While he was on the lakeshore, he heard someone in
the forest cutting wood. He followed the sound of
the cutting, until he came upon Mugasha who was
cutting firewood. Mugasha never encountered anyone
where he stayed, and he was astonished to see Mahe
approaching. Mugasha asked Mahe who he was, why he
had come, and from where he had come. Mahe said, "I
have come with fishermen, but I do not have food,
for they are only fishing. So, when I heard someone
cutting wood, I came to ask him to take me to a
village where I can get food." Mugasha said, "Yes,
my son, you have come here, but no one comes here to

see me. However, I will take you to a village where
you can get help." (This is because Mugasha always
lives in the water, but when he leaves the water he
goes to stay only with his wife, Nyakalembe.) Mugasha
told him not to worry, that he was a chief but a
chief whom no one saw and that he would take Mahe to
his home to care for him. Again, he repeated how
surprised he was to see someone. Then Mugasha cut
firewood enough for eight men; Mahe offered to help
him carry the load, but Mugasha said, "No, they are
too heavy." But Mahe lifted them and carried them
off. Mugasha was astonished to see someone as strong
as himself.

Mugasha took Mahe to his home. There Mahe met
Mugasha's wife Nyakalembe and his daughters, Nyamilimo
and Mbandame. Mugasha introduced Mahe by explaining
that Mahe could do work as Mugasha himself. The women
then happily received Mahe. Early the next morning,
Mugasha started to build a fence. While Mugasha dug
holes for his fence, he also dug holes in rocks for
the poles. Mahe offered to help him, but Mugasha
refused, saying, "Only I can do this work." But Mahe
insisted that he was like Mugasha and therefore
could also do it. And he did so by also digging holes
in the rocks for the fence poles. When Mugasha observed Mahe digging holes in rock, he ran to his wife
and told her of Mahe's feat. His wife advised Mugasha
to make blood friendship with Mahe, and if he rejected
this, she advised that Mugasha should give a daughter
to Mahe to marry.

But when Mugasha offered Mahe his daughter in
marriage, Mahe refused and explained that he had been
sent out from his home and could not marry, but, "When
I am settled, I will come and marry your daughter."
Mugasha did not offer Mahe blood friendship, but he
did offer to show Mahe how to leave the place where
he was, so that Mahe could easily return when he
wanted to marry Mugasha's daughter.

Eight years had now passed from the time Mahe had
departed Kyamutwara. During Mahe's absence,
Kalemera had died. Kalemera was succeeded by his son
Mwehozi-Kiume, who was the only possible successor.
Bwogi was the name given to Mwehozi-Kiumi; he built
his kikale at Katonge.

Before Mahe left Mugasha's home, Mugasha gave Mahe a
dog. He said, "Take this dog. It will bring you
back here." Mahe left Mugasha's home while Mugasha
stood on a hillside and directed him to a river called
Nyarimbika where he could meet fishermen. These

fishermen then accompanied Mahe to Lukungu (in Uganda but near Kanyigo), from which place he went to Kanyigo where he met the chief, Kyosamugongo (Chief of Nshumba).

Mahe went to visit Kyosamugongo in the evening (Kyosamugongo had been Mukama for years at that time); the Mukama was happy to see Mahe, with whom he entered into a wrestling match called ekigwo or nture. People did not want the Mukama to do this, but the Mukama insisted. Immediately after beginning, Mahe threw the Mukama to the ground. The Mukama lay there unconscious while the people thought that Mahe had killed the Mukama and therefore should himself be killed. Mahe immediately escaped, evading all searchers. He ran to Kishaka, Kihororo, and on to Mitaga. He then went on to the Kagera River at Mashangano. He talked to the fishermen who told him that the drums they heard were sounding about the man who lived to kill the chief, and that was to warn the boat pilots on the other side not to take anyone across the river. Once across the river, Mahe announced that it was he who had killed the Mukama and if anyone came for him they should turn back. Then Mahe started to run—through Kagamba village to Burembe. There he found the Babwongu clan and Njoju, the Mukungu [chief] there. Njoju asked, "Where are you going, young man?" Mahe said, "I don't know yet where I'm going. But I have come to ask for a place to sleep and then to start my journey again tomorrow." Njoju wanted to take Mahe to his mother, Kyanyuzi, but Mahe refused and said he wanted to stay with Njoju.

Before Mahe departed the next morning, Njoju went to his brother Muchumaile to ask his advice about why Mahe spent the night at his house without eating. Muchumaile told Njoju that he would personally visit Mahe. At about twelve noon, some men came from Mutakula to ask Njoju for some medicine for divining. Njoju had a divining instrument called Kagwi (the name for sticks used to get banana juice) in which medicine was kept and which had never been touched. After Njoju had made divining medicine for these people, Mahe asked to hold the Kagwi, but Njoju said, "No! No son and no brother holds this Kagwi, only me who got it from my father." Muchumaile, when he heard Mahe insisting, said, "Alright, let him touch it, and we'll see what happens to him." Mahe then sat on Njoju's chair and took the Kagwi from Njoju. Mahe said, "You, Kagwi, maker of divinations, if you are the one which does so, let me use you" (Iwe, Kagwi, lukeya ondagulire Nkeila). When Njoju saw that Mahe

was holding Kagwi without its doing anything to him,
he became very pleased and took it from Mahe to hold
himself and told Mahe to sit in front of him. Njoju
addressed Kagwi, "You have been held by this man and
you did nothing to him. I want you to show me what
kind of man this is." Kagwi then beat Mahe's face,
and Njoju told Mahe, "When you complete your journey,
you will be a chief somewhere." Mahe answered,
"When I return home and become a chief, I will call
you and give you a kibanja, but do not forget to come
with your Kagwi." Mahe stayed on with Njoju for three
days before resuming his journey. From there he want
to Ishango, where he spent two days before going to
Hoima, Bunyoro. From there he traveled to Bunyagueu
and on to Igara, where he stayed for seven years
milking and herding the cows of chief Kabura.

Makama Kabura gave Mahe a house and a widow to live
with during his stay in Igara. During the seventh
year of Mahe's stay with the widow Nkanyize, she told
Mahe, "You have come here to Kabura to obtain divinations about your life." She want on to tell Mahe
that the Mukama would never make divinations for Mahe,
unless Mahe wronged him in some way and aroused
Kabura's anger; only then would Kabura perform
divinations, she explained. Nkanyize then planned a
way for Mahe to offend the Mukama. She instructed
Mahe to run cows through Kabura's tobacco patch. The
next morning Mahe ran the cows through the tobacco;
this was immediately reported to Kabura, who asked
that Mahe be sent to him.

Mahe was taken to Kabura, who told Mahe, "I know you.
You have left your kingdom and have passed (then he
named all the places) and by now your grandfather and
father have died and people are starving and there is
no Mukama. I am not going to accuse you in Kiziba
when you threw down the Mukama. So return to your
kingdom (omwiyanga) and become a Mukama as your
father and grandfather and give people food to eat.
When you go home, do not pass directly, but go via
Isheshe to see Mugasha and tell him that you have
been at my home. Leave now." Kabura then went into
his house, but he left his magic or divining stick
behind; Mahe picked it up and secreted it in his
clothing. He then went to the widow's place where
he collected his belongings and his dog, and then he
started to run from Igara. Kabura soon discovered
that Mahe had taken his stick and he said, "Oh, my
stick has been taken by Mahe who left here and was
born in the Kingdom of Kyamutangata. His kingdom
will not be called Kyamutangata, but will be known
as Kyamutwara which means 'they will steal things.'

He has taken my stick, and he will return and become
a Mukama. When he dies, his sons and grandsons will
rule, but strangers will come and take over the
kingdom."

Mahe eventually reached the home of his friend Njoju,
to whom he said, "I have passed here to tell you that
I am returning home to become a Mukama, and when I
do I will call you to make divinations for me." Mahe
passed on to Mashagano where he met fishermen who
took him to Isheshe. He found Mugasha there and
explained his entire journey before asking Mugasha
to make blood friendship with him. It took four
days for the blood pact to be concluded, and then Mahe
told Mugasha that we wanted to return home. Mugasha
informed his wife, Nyakalembe, to prepare medicines
for Mahe so that he could grow crops in his kingdom—
where there wasn't any food. Mugasha then said, "I
will make the other medicines myself." Nyakalembe
then gave Mahe every medicine for growing crops, such
as ebitoke [bananas cooked by boiling], sweet
potatoes, enkuku (like beans, eaten before the marriage ceremony; it is Swahili), finger millet (buro or
ulezi), and everything else grown today in Buhaya.
(The women in Buhaya praise Nyakalembe [Mugasha's
wife] as the goddess of agriculture. They are led in
this praise and offering by men who behave as women—
greeting as women do. He [a Muharambwa] is the one
who disposes of dead animals and snakes. He is called
to throw away bad juice if it comes during pombe
[beer] production; he removes burned bodies or the
ashes of bodies when houses burn.)

After Nyakalembe had given Mahe everything she had
prepared, she told Mugasha to give Mahe the remainder.
Nyakalembe told Mahe, "When you go home, you will
find a man who will be called Muharambwa who will be
leading the women, behaving as a woman and cultivating
with the women. He will be eating grasshoppers and
the meat of goats (which are not eaten by women) with
women." Then she gave Mahe a oluyondo (of cowries
and entembe, which are banana seeds, and large beads
called enkoshole) and said, "Give this to the man you
appoint as leader of the women and name him
Muharambwa." Mugasha gave Mahe a hammer, a piece of a
tree named [not remembered], and other kinds of trees.
He then told Mahe, "When you return, plant this hammer
and these trees, so when I come I will know where
you are staying." Mugasha then cut three (hard)
branches from the Muhunge tree and made a raft from
them for Mahe, the dog, and the basket of medicine.
Mugasha pushed the raft into the water with his foot.
Mahe finally arrived at Kyamurange, Bugabo, in the

evening. He left his trees behind and passed through
elephant grass until he came to the house of Ndwano,
whose wife, Nyabuoro (Mukamakazi), was present. The
woman was very surprised to encounter a man with long
fingernails and long hair. But she welcomed him
in. He told her, "I have come here to sleep, for it's
too late to go home. I will go home in the morning.
Where is your husband?" She explained that he had
gone fishing but was wasting his time, as there were
no fish in the lake. When Mahe asked why there were
no fish, Nyabuoro said, "We have no Mukama. Our
Mukama has died and the one who was to succeed him
has disappeared, so we have no one to ask for food."

Mahe explained that he had made a long journey and
had no food, but that he wanted only juice to drink.
She said, "There is nothing here; people are starving
and dying from hunger. There is no juice, and that
is why you are so strange, because you do not know
what is happening in this country." Mahe said, "But
as I passed through your kibanja, I saw a ripe juice
banana. Can you not make juice from that?" The
disbelieving woman had to be directed by Mahe to the
place where he had seen the bananas. Nyabuoro went
with him into her kibanja, discovered the ripe bunch
of bananas, and cut it down. Mahe asked her why she
was not preparing food, for he had observed ebitoke
(bananas) outside. Nyabuoro did not question Mahe
further, but went outside and cut the ebitoke.
After she had brought the ebitoke, Nyabuoro prepared
juice for Mahe, and then she prepared the ebitoke
for her husband. Mahe asked her, "Will you please
hide me so that your husband does not know that I am
here, and then in the morning when you open the house,
I will slip out quietly so no one will know of my
presence."

Nyabuoro did as he requested and made a bed concealed
by an ekitala (large basket divider). When the food
was ready, Nyabuoro's husband arrived but without
fish. He was welcomed with juice, which caused him
to ask where she got it. The woman was evasive in
her answer, so her husband did not pursue it as he
was so astonished about the presence of food he had
not eaten for so long. When his wife put down the
ebitoke, he was so joyful that he began to dance and
praise God and then Kazoba.

Ndwano again asked, "My wife, where did you get this
juice and food?" She replied, "Do not worry, I did
not steal it but I have gotten it and cannot hide it
from you." After eating, Nyabuoro asked Ndwano to
escort her to the latrine. Instead, she told her

husband that inside there was a man who had instructed
her to cut the bananas which Ndwano had eaten. When
they returned to the house, Ndwano praised Mahe,
saying, "Habuka Ishewanga habuka Rugaba" (a praise
reserved for only Bakama and truly important men on
the level of gods, for Ishewanga was a Mucwezi,
successor to Wamara).

When Mahe realized Nyabuoro had broken the secret to
her husband, he said that never again would he trust
a woman, adding, "When I go home, I will tell all men
that they must never share secrets with women." Mahe
then left his hiding place and asked Ndwano to give
him a fish to take to his wife, so she could cook
it for his dog. Ndwano said, "There is no fish in
the lake because we don't have a Mukama. People are
looking for the Mukama, but he has not been seen.
There are no fish in this kingdom." Mahe told him
that if he was not leaving the next day, Ndwano would
have found a fish for his dog, but that he was returning home the next day. Ndwano asked Mahe not to
leave, but Mahe said, "I could stay, but if I did I
would fear that you'd tell your neighbors and they
would catch me. I will not go, but do not tell them
as your wife has told you. If you do, I will never
remember you." The next morning Ndwano left for
fishing after Mahe reminded him to bring a fish for
his dog. Ndwano caught many fish and filled all the
boats. Ndwano returned with fish for Mahe's dog
and found that his and his neighbors' kibanja were
filled with bananas. Mahe asked Nyabuoro to get sweet
potatoes. She did not protest, but went with a basket
and dug up many sweet potatoes.

Meanwhile, Kayango had learned that there were many
bananas in Bugabo. He instructed that divinations
be made by his Bafumu, who told him that the Mukama
could be found in Bugabo. The Bafumu also determined
from what clan the Mukama would come, that is, the
Mushosi clan. Kayango had three separate groups of
Bafumu—Abafumu B'empyaula (using water, butter, and
medicine called olwihura and a seed named entobotobo
Iwasha), Abafumu F'enkoko (using the entrails of
chickens), and Abafumu Ab'emya (using burning hot iron;
those not burned are not clans with the chief). All
divined the Mushosi clan.

A Mushosi clan member was then selected, given coffee
beans to pretend to sell, and told to go to Bugabo to
find the Mukama. When the Mushosi arrived at Ndwano's
house, Mahe saw him and asked Ndwano to bring the man
so he could buy some coffee. When the Mushosi saw
Mahe and sold him the beans, he brushed himself with

banana leaves and returned immediately to Kayango.
He told Kayango, "I have seen the Mukama and have
left him at Kyamurange."

Kayango did not know how to catch Mahe in order to
make him Mukama. So he asked the Bafumu for advice,
and they instructed Kayango to send men to the area
under the pretense of hunting emondo and engonge (a
cat). Kayango informed Karoya, Mukama of Kanyangereko,
and Mate, Mukama of Kianja, that they must go hunting
on the lakeshore for engonge and bring it to him.
And he told other hunters to go to the forests and
catch emondo and bring it to him alive. Several days
later Kayango had received the emondo and engonge.
Then he told the hunters to go with the Mushosi and
the animals to the lakeshore where the Mushosi had
seen Mahe.

Mahe did not stay in the house during the day; instead,
he stayed in elephant grass. When the hunters reached
Ndwano's house, they freed the animals according to
Kayango's instructions, which held that Mahe's dog
would chase the animals and reveal Mahe's hiding place
to the hunters. The animals were then freed, Mahe's
dog followed them, and Mahe pursued his dog, trying
to stop it. Once disclosed, Mahe was quickly
captured by the hunters. Mahe told the hunters that
they should release him as he had nothing to do with
them. But the people said, "No, this is our Rugaba,
this is our own Mukama. Let us take him." When
Nyabuoro heard people shouting, she went to see and
saw Mahe being lifted from the ground. She asked,
"What has that man done wrong? If he has done something wrong, Ndwano will pay for it. This man is
Rugomora (he who satisfied hunger), who gave food to
us when we were hungry." Mahe said to all those
gathered, "Stop, I want to tell you something before
you kill me. I have been called Mahe, but now I
am called Rugomora—as this woman has named me.
Wherever you take me, call me Rugomora." Mahe told
the woman, "I don't know where I am going, but
wherever I settle, I will call you to stay with me."
While being held by the people, he asked one man, a
Mujubu by clan, to go into the house and get his
basket of medicine and care for it during the journey.

As Rugomora and his captors started their journey,
they first passed the Mwiga River. Then Rugomora was
taken to Buheza (close to the lake and east of
Kishange), then to Kishange, Iruya, Bishaka, Kaagwa,
and Biyonga, where he found people catching lake
flies. He asked what the people were doing, and he
was told they were catching lake flies. He then

asked their clan and was told it was Bazigu. Rugomora
replied, "It is not good to call them Bazigu. It is
better to call them Babini (which means foolish or
ignorant people). I call them this because they do
not care to see their Mukama after being without one
so long." (To this day, these people are called
Babini Ba Biyonga. From Biyonga, Rugomora traveled
to Iyanda (south of Mugeza and north of Kahororo),
where he asked the Mujubu to bring his basket. There
he planted a tree called Mpangwakinyomo (which means
no one will interfere except ants) and said, "This
tree will not move and will not produce another tree,
but will remain one, as I will not move and never
leave my kingdom." He planted the tree in the
kibanja of a Muhinda whom he told to leave the kibanja,
so his man, the Mujubu, could care for the tree. Then
Rugomora traveled through Burugo and on to Kahororo
(near Makongo), from where he could see Makongo, and
to Kyaya, where he wanted to see a Muyango named
Ireba, who was the man who named Bakama. When Ireba
arrived, he told Rugomora that he, his father, and
grandfather had named Bakama. Rugomora told him he
had gotten the name Rugomora from a Mukamakazi.
Ireba agreed that the name was acceptable but told
Rugomora that after Rugomora became Mukama, he would
visit Rugomora, discuss the name, and then Rugomora
would be assured of a good rule.

Rugomora left ensimbi [cowries] for Ireba and told
Ireba to come to his kikale after he was settled.
Then Rugomora went on to Bukoba, where he planted
the hammer Mugasha had given him in the kibanja of
Kauza, a Muziba. When he entered the property of
Rutakwa, son of a Munyankole, he found Rutakwa making
juice with other people. Rugomora Mahe said, "I see
you are making clean juice and I would like some to
drink." After Rugomora Mahe had taken juice without
water, he told them that in the future they would
bring him juice. "You will no longer be called Bakoba,
but you will be called Bakoba abo mwa Munene" (Bakoba
who make pure juice).

Rugomora Mahe then traveled on to Busimbe and then
to Kabashaga, Kibuye (now Ntungamo), where he found
the Bamanyi making iron tools. Rugomora Mahe saw
them carrying baskets, and he asked them what they
had. They told him it was charcoal. When he asked
them their clan, they said it was Bamanyi. Rugomora
Mahe replied, "No longer are there Bamanyi, for they
will now be called Bahuge" (which means the forgetful
ones). For Rugomora Mahe felt that they were not as
they were called, "the clever ones," for they had not
left their work to pay respect to him. From Kibuye,

Rugomora Mahe passed to Irunhurura and Kyansozi (near
Rubale), where he found the Bahimba clan, whom he
told, "When I arrive to where I am going, I will
appoint you to an office." Rugomora Mahe had been
told by Kabura in Igara that when he reached home and
found a daughter of the Bahimba, it would be she who
would prepare his bed the first day at the place
where he settled. Rugomora Mahe gave ensimbi to the
Bahimba, so they could take it to Mushambwa in Rubale
Forest (a place for offerings to wild animals).

Rugomora Mahe traveled on to Luija where he gave a
tree called Karongo to the Basingo and told them to
plant it in Maruku-Nkaraba in the shamba of a Musingo.
In Luija number two, he sent ensimbi to Kibunga, a
Matundu. (He did this as a reward to people who
helped keep his kingdom in his absence, and the
Batunda were among the first rulers.) Rugomora
Mahe then passed to Rugege (to the east of Maruku),
on to Lwamuyonga, crossed Kigona stream to Ibainjo
(near the lakeshore) where he sent some ensimbi to
Kyema Forest (to appease the leopards), went on to
Byabumba, Isikira (village), where he entered the
house of a Mulama clansman, Machumu, to spend the
night. [Today Damain Tibergira lives there.]   The
next morning, Rugomora Mahe passed through the
present shamba of Bwana Tebelotera to a nearby field,
where he sowed the seeds from Isheshe—seeds for
trees called Emizinda and Emicwezi—saying to the
people, "When I settle, come here and cultivate and
many trees will grow to become a forest called
Ilemera." Then Rugomora Mahe passed through Kakoko
to Kazi, where he took a stone, sat on it, and said,
"This is my chair, where I will sit." He moved on
to Kyemizinga and to Omulutungalwa Mukara, where he
called all the drums together and told people to beat
them so people would know that he was there. The
place where this was done is called Gagaulira, or
"the place where they heard him."

When Rugomora Mahe left this place, he continued on
to Byamawa Kashoro-Burambizi, where he built his first
kikale, which faced in the direction of Mugasha at
Isheshe. A few days after he had settled, he instructed people to slaughter cows and their meat at the
Nyarulembo of his kikale. He told people to watch
the meat until a bird came and took some, and then
they were to follow the bird to the place where it
landed and dropped the meat. Then a Marere bird
came, picked up some meat, and flew to Katuruka,
where it dropped the meat. After the meat had been
dropped, people went to inform the Mukama that the
meat had been dropped at "The Place." Rugomora Mahe

left his kikale then, and just outside he observed
Nyango ants; he told people to follow the ants, which
he said would stop in his shamba. "Where they stop,
I will build my nyaruju house," he said. Rugomora
Mahe followed the Nyango with his people until the
Nyango entered Rwihura tree. There he told his people
to build the nyaruju house. Then he took one of his
trees, Muturuka, from his basket and plantęd· it, and
announced: "This village will be called Katuruka,
which means "The place where I've arrived." Once
Rugomora Mahe had settled at Katuruka, all of
Kyamutwara was aware that there was a Mukama. Rugomora Mahe made four entrances to his kikale. The subchiefs after Rugomora Mahe became Mukama were Mate
of Kianja, Kateite of Bugabo, and Karoya of
Kanyangereko. By the time these men had come to
Katuruka, Rugomora Mahe had already made three
entrances to his kikale. The first entrance faced
Kianja; the second faced Katoma (or small Kyamutwara);
the third faced Kanyangereko; the fourth faced
Mugasha at Isheshe and was the main entrance.

Once established in his kikale, Rugomora Mahe called
iron workers to make iron for him at Luija where
Kaiija tree is located. He instructed his workers
to make only iron bars and told them that he would
describe to them iron tools he had seen so they could
make them. As the iron workers continued with their
work, Rugomora Mahe explained to people that, when
he left his kingdom, he went to Ihangiro, Businza,
and Bukwaya, where he met the daughter of Machunda
and that she had spit at him. Rugomora Mahe said,
"I would like to go and get engaged to that girl, but
before marrying her I will neglect her." Rugomora
Mahe sent his men, the Ntumwa (his most trusted
friends from among the Abalamata), to Bukwaya to
contract the engagement witn Nyamata. Machunda was
told that Rugomora Mahe wanted to marry Nyamata,
but Machunda refused and claimed that it was too far
for his daughter to go. The Ntumwa returned with the
negative response. Rugomora Mahe said, "No, tell
him that it is not far, for I can beat drums here and
he will hear them there." Then Ntumwa informed
Machunda of the drums, and Machunda agreed that he
would try to hear them. The Ntumwa then returned
to Rugomora Mahe and took the drums to Giziba
Island (near Muchunda) where they beat the drums.

Machunda later agreed that Rugomora was very close by
and that he had no objection to his daughter marrying
Rugomora Mahe. Rugomora Mahe prepared nine times
three cows, which were taken to Machunda, who was
very pleased. When Machunda's party left Bukwaya,

the Ntumwa moved to Kerebe Island where they beat
the drums. As the Machunda party continued to move,
the Ntumwa moved on to Ilemera where they continued
to beat the drums. Eventually, Nyamata reached
Kigoma on the lakeshore. There they prepared themselves nicely to be received by the Mukama. They
went to Ilemera, and when the Mukama learned this, he
sent a messenger to Ilemera telling the party not to
move further. Then Rugomora Mahe gave a spear to one
man, told him to take it to Nyamata and say to her,
"When I was at your home, you neglected and abused
me, so I have sent this spear for you to sleep with
as your husband. I will not be your husband." He
instructed his people to take Nyamata to Kakoko's
house, where she should be married to the spear.
(This spear can be seen at the heir's house in
Ishekira.) He also sent a message that Nyamata's
party should return with the message that Rugomora
Mahe would not marry her, but that she would be
married to a spear and not sent home to Machunda.
And so, Nyamata stayed together with the spear until
she died.

Rugomora Mahe told his smiths that he wanted to build
an iron tower high enough to see where the clouds
ended. Rugomora Mahe built the tower both in Katuruka
and Nkimbo, Kanyangereko. At Nkimbo there is a tree
called Kya Rugomora which marks the place where the
tower was built. The iron workers and smiths made a
tower so high that the top could not be seen, and then
it collapsed, killing many people. Parts of the
tower fell as far as Katerero-Omunyoma. Rugomora Mahe
was very disappointed about this, and because of the
danger, be began making bricks. From the bricks,
Rugomora Mahe constructed houses.

By this time, Rugomora Mahe had grown children, whom
he appointed to rule different villages. His first-
born son, Mugasha, he sent to rule Bugabo; his second
son, Kiro, he sent to Katoma; to Ikenga he gave all
parts of Bukara; Kibaje, he sent to Muraiya (lower
Kianja); his successor, Rutairwa, was not given an
appointment. Eventually Rugomora Mahe died of old
age and was succeeded by Rutairwa who became
Omukama Kahigi of Ibwera-Omurubungo.

Appendix B___Myth
of Rugomora Mahe:
A Royal Version

After Kalemera had blinded his son, advisors took
Kayango, or Kiume as he was called, into their care
out of concern about a successor to Kalemera. Kiume
was taken to Kaboya near Kabalinda where there was
a house constructed for him; after he made his home,
the old, unmarried women, Ngunge, were moved there.
Kayango and the other elders also supplied Kiume
with a young girl to see to his needs. This girl
was a Munkango-Mushamata (or Mushamata Ihiga and former Bankango, not included in more recent immigration).
Kiume had intercourse with her frequently, so that
she was impregnated and gave birth to a child. But
people held the birth of Kalemera's grandson a secret.
Yet, the secret leaked to Kalemera, when Kiume's son
was about twelve years old. Kalemera ordered the
boy brought to him. But the people close to the boy
prevented the boy's final arrival, for they knew
Kalemera's tendencies. So the child was hidden,
but before he could be hidden, Kalemera had a stick
cut to the height of the boy Mahe. When all of the
young boys came before Kalemera for inspection, he
tried to see which one most nearly fit the proportions
given him, but without success.

Gradually, people had stopped coming to the kikale
of Kalemera. He started dancing in his kikale at
night. One time he called a Muzigu man whom he
appointed Mulangira; the first two confided to him
that he was behaving as a mad man. (Both of these men
were cooks.) At this time, there were messengers
from Kiziba, Karagwe, and Ihangiro present at the

*Version by Bayekela Rusinga, 10/22/69, 10/25/69, and
10/29/69, in Maruku.

court. It was during this confidential advising that
it was decided it would be better for the Mukama to
die than for him to continue to make a fool of himself, and it was decided that the Muzigu would get
his appointment. That night the Mukama was left with
the Muzigu and a girl. The three of them disappeared
with a dog and were never seen again.

Their footprints were followed to the River Muleleizi,
and they continued on the other side of the river and
went on to Kamanywabake. When they got there, the
trackers assumed that the Mukama had gone to Bwigura,
where there was a house for Mugasha's spirit. The
Abaraguzi (diviners) saw things this way. When
Kalemera was not found at Bwigura, people then went
to Rubale-Lwa Mayondwe. (The seachers were Kayango
and his cohorts.) They then went on to Kashekele
on the Kianja-Ihangiro boundary, thinking that
Kalemera may have gone to make war on neighbors.
When he was not there, Kayango ordered the people
to return to their homes. When Kayango returned,
he beat drums to call the people. He announced that
he had seen Kalemera elsewhere and that he had died,
for he feared that the truth would act as an invitation
for attack from other kingdoms. He then also announced
that he had buried Kalemera in his Magango kikale.

As only Kiume existed, Kayango appointed Kiume as
successor to Kalemera. After nine days, Kiume was
named Bwogi. (Before he was called Kiume, his name
was Lukambya.) He was quite old when appointed.
There was great famine in the chiefdom during his
reign, but he did not reign long before dying. During
this time, chiefs wore skin cloth smeared with butter.
Even though Kiume was blind, he was very cruel.
However, his blindness allowed abuse. For example,
once his people put a skin of a freshly killed cow on
the Mukama. The young men could get away with this,
as Kayango lived in Engarama. After two days, when
it became obvious that he was becoming cold from the
skin, the Mukama was taken into the sun and a drum
was beaten to announce his sunning. However, the
Mukama soon felt the skin shrinking and becoming
tight on him. When he asked what the trouble was,
those around him explained that the sun was affecting
it. Finally, the skin became very tight, and when
Bwogi complained and asked why again they again told
him it was shrinking. Bwogi then asked for elders to
come and advise him, but he was told that all the old
men had been killed by his father. Thereupon, Bwogi
asked them to cut him out of the skin. But his
tormentors refused, saying that they feared they
might cut him. But one man called an old man for

advice; the man found the Mukama nearly squeezed to
death, so he ordered some water in a boat. After
the boat was filled, Bwogi was carried to the boat
and placed inside. The old man then cut the skin
open and removed it. Afterwards, the Mukama gave his
helper a large shamba. This man advised Bwogi to
stop cruel practices such as those done by his father,
for he had once almost been killed for his intolerance.
Bwogi eventually died during the time of the famine.
Kayango was then left as chief of the kingdom, as
the people fruitlessly looked for a legitimate
successor. People began to complain because of
Kayango's rule rather than Bahinda rule. So Kayango
sent some people to see Bafumu in Igara, for he had
heard that Mahe was thereabouts and he wanted to discover Mahe's presence. The people who were sent
encountered Mahe in Igara and traveled with him until
Ishango. (Mahe had first gone to Karagwe and from
there on to Ankole and up to northern Toro where
Igara is.) In Igara, Mahe had been a cattle herder.
While a cattle herder, he passed his cattle through
a tobacco shamba and had been abused by an old woman
sorcerer who told him he had better go home to his
chiefdom where there was a famine and to cut his hair
and fingernails. This irritated Mahe, so he left
Igara for Koki. While in Koki, he stayed with a man
who had goats. When he departed, he took two goats
with him. To this day, a new Mukama always takes two
goats from this place. His departure from Koki
was precipitated by abuse, for the people there said
that he had been chased from his own chiefdom, that
he had long hair and nails, and that he had better
leave and go home. They were treating him as if he
was an embandwa or muzimu.

From Koki, Mahe crossed Ishango to Isheshe where
Mugasha was the first man he met. He brought two
dogs with him, one called Galinunda and the other
called Galibahaga. The first means "Magic to make me
die will be finished," and the second means "News
about me will be finished." He stayed with Mugasha
in Isheshe. He made friendship with Mugasha, who gave
him bunches of magic sticks to help him rule in
Kyamutwara, for his previous travel companions had
already returned home. Mugasha gave him all sorts
of seeds in a basket (Kitwalo basket) which would grow
crops. Mugasha escorted Mahe to the lake and put him
on a branch of the Muhunge tree along with his dogs
and then pushed him off with his foot. Mahe traveled
as far as Rubafu in Bugabo. There he went to the home
of a man of the Mulama clan. He found only the man's
wife, while the husband was away fishing. Too much
sunshine caused Mahe to take refuge in the house with

his dogs. He asked the woman where her husband was
and she explained. He then asked for food for his
dogs, but she said no one had food because there was
no chief. Mahe told her to cut bananas which he had
seen on the edge of her shamba. She protested, but
he insisted she go to cut what he had seen. When she
went outside, she was surprised to find the bananas
Mahe had spoken of. She cut them and prepared them
for food. Mahe then asked for juice; again she protested but received instructions from Mahe, which
proved to be correct. So she cut the banana and prepared the juice. Mahe left the house in the evening
to spend the night in the bush. The man of the house
returned with three small fish and found his wife with
food. He asked her where she had gotten the food,
but she did not answer. She spent the night without
telling her husband, who left at 3 A. M. to go fishing.
Mahe entered the house the next morning to again
ask for food for his dogs. She got the food, and
from that moment all the people of Bugabo had many
bananas. The husband returned early to see where
his wife was getting food and discovered Mahe. His
wife welcomed her husband and explained Mahe's presence. The man greeted him. Mahe asked the man for
fish for the dogs, but the fisherman said there
were no fish. But Mahe insisted that there were many
fish and said he would go the next day to see for
himself. The dogs got some fish, but early the next
morning Mahe went with him. In the meantime, some
people had gone to report to Kayango that the Mukama
had to be in Bugabo, as they had suddenly received
great plenty in food. They explained that they had
not seen Mahe because Mahe stayed in the bush.

Kayango therefore came from Engarama with hunters
and dogs along the lakeshore. When they reached
Bugabo at Kyamalange (near Rubafu), Kayango came
across Mahe in the bamboo trees sitting as usual.
He was found by the hunters and their dogs which
followed the scent of Mahe's dogs. Kayango had
instructed his people not to kill anything, so Mahe
was taken unharmed. Kayango already knew Mahe, so he
announced that Mahe was their long expected chief.
Mahe was clothed in new skins, and a woman proclaimed
that Mahe was Rugomora, for he had given them food.
This is how the name Rugomora started.

Rugomora and his triumphant party traveled to Bujonga
where Bazigu clan people were catching lake flies
but chose to ignore the passing of the Mukama Rugomora. Rugomora said to leave them be and renamed
them Babini (those who are dull). They went on to
Iyanda in Bugabo where Rugomora planted a tree in

order to show that he was established and not to be
chased (again) from Kyamutwara; this tree is named
Lwachundi Kaine and is there to this day. From Iyanda
they went to Kahororo where Rugomora planted a
hammer as a symbol of his chieftainship. Bukoba
was his next stop (Bunena side) where he left a
Musaizi who had been with him. The Bakoba made
banana juice for Rugomora, and he appointed them to
make juice for the Bakama. From there he went to
Kibuye, where the Bamani or Batundu were making iron.
They ignored Rugomora, who then renamed them Bahuge
(the forgetful ones). Rugomora then went on to spend
nine days at Ilungami before he went on to Katuruka;
for he had magic made while in Ilungami to find a
place for his kikale. Ndagu medicine was used by
the Bafumu to determine the place of the kikale;
the intestines of chickens and sheep were inspected.
Rugomora first had a temporary house or Ikumbi made
at Katuruka, and then his big house of Nyaruju
Rwesinga was constructed. Before he departed his
temporary house, he told a Musaizi companion, "They
have called me Rugomora, so I call you Mahe." And
he left this man in his temporary house. The Mukama
then ordered all the Bahinda to look after Mahe and
all his descendants. To this day, a new Mukama must
call a descendant of the lineage of Mahe to stay
with the Mukama and be renamed Mahe by the Mukama.
Rugomora gave him a spear called Ntinakalija for
executions and a rope for tying people up.

Rugomora's kikale was constructed in Katuruka. Three
roads were made from the kikale—one from the left,
one from the right, and one to the front. One road
went toward Bugabo, one toward Engarama, and one
toward Kanyangereko. These were made to facilitate
access of his subjects. At the Musaizi's home, he
planted medicine called muturuka, which kept Rugomora from leaving his kingdom. (Perhaps the medicine
came from Isheshe.) This place can be seen to this
day.

The sons of Rugomora were Kahigi Komulubugo Ibwera,
Luhima who was chief of Bugabo; Mugasha, chief of
Kyarakyengo (Nyakato area); Kiro, chief of Katoma;
Nyamitwe, chief of Bukara who had his home at
Ijuganyondo; and someone in Bujanangoma and all parts
of Buhaya except Kiziba. During his reign, Rugomora
built a house of mud bricks, but after some time
these collapsed [the witness says he knows of people
who have found these in Katuruka while they
cultivated]. It was within the walls of this house
that Rugomora had an iron tower built. When it became
very high, it collapsed killing many workmen and

falling as far as Omunyoma near Katerero. (One old
man says he saw the tools used to build it in 1911.
Katori may have the tools.) One came from Kanyangereko,
Byandilima, Kyembale (near the tea estate). After
this failure, Rugomora did not attempt to build the
tower again.

Until Rugomora's death, his kingdom remained in peace,
for he had successfully dispersed his sons throughout
the kingdom. When Rugomora died, the elders gathered
together to nominate Kahigi as Rugomora's successor.

Appendix C
Rugomora Mahe: A Text

Kiume eventually impregnated the girl, who bore a
child named Mahe. When Kalemera learned a number
of years later of the boy, he desired to kill Mahe.
(Kalemera was still in a rage against the Bahinda—
who had killed his son Kamuli). However, again Kayango interfered and warned Mahe of his sure death.
Mahe escaped to Goziba Island (near Mwanza). The
local ruler was Machunda. Mahe wanted to marry
Machunda's daughter, Ilemera, but the girl refused
to marry him because of his dirty condition. After
this abuse, Mahe left Goziba by boat to Isheshe
Islands. After his stay there, he went on to Igara.
While in Igara, Mahe became a cattle herder for
Nyamizinda, the chief (or subchief) of Igara. People
told Mahe that if he wanted to have his future divined
because of Myamizinda's interference, it would be
necessary to wrong Nyamizinda in order to have him
consult sorcerers. Mahe then took his cows through
the shamba of Nyamizinda, who abused Mahe, saying,
"You fool! You had better go home to your own
chiefdom to take the throne, for people are experienc-
ing famine there becasue they have no chief."

When Nyamizinda spoke this way, Mahe left and passed
through Kiziba where he found Magembe on the throne
[the witness insists that this is Magembe II, but he
is not absolutely sure]. Magembe and Mahe entered
into a wrestling match in which Mahe was the victor.
The Baziba then started asking for Mahe's death, as
he had beaten their Mukama. But Magembe prevented
his death, as he had originally initiated the sport.
Mahe left Kiziba to travel again to Isheshe. There

*Mzee Kaigage, 10/24/69, in Maruku.

he met Mugasha, whom he asked for help to return home, and Mugasha gave him a branch of the Muhunge tree on which to ride back to Kyamutwara.

Mugasha pushed the branch off into the water while Mahe sat on it. Mahe traveled as far as Bugabo. Mahe had two dogs accompanying him. He landed in Bugabo between Rubafu and Kyamalange villages. There the people were suffering from severe famine. At the first home he reached, he asked the woman for juice and then for food for his dog. When she said there was nothing, Mahe directed her where to go to get bananas in her shamba and told her to make juice from the beer bananas she would cut. She doubted him, but she found the bananas as he said she would and returned with them. She made food for the dog and juice for Mahe after her return. When the woman's husband returned from fishing with new fish, she went outside and enjoined him to enter and greet their visitor. Mahe asked him for the fish to feed his dog, but the man refused, explaining that there were too few fish available. But Mahe told him to give them up and the next day he would go to fish with success. The next morning, the man had a great haul of fish, so many men went to get their nets. They filled more boats so that they finally had to give them away to people. So many fish came that they suspected the presence of the Mukama, so some men were sent to report to Kayango that they had seen the Mukama. When Kayango learned the news, he immediately dispatched hunters to find Mahe. He instructed them that anything in Bugabo that they found in the forest should not be harmed. When the hunters reached Bugabo, Mahe took flight to the bush [the witness says in order to find the hunters]. Mahe and his dog followed the hunters' dogs until he came on them and was taken by them. The first woman Mahe had met then proclaimed, "This is not Mahe, but Rugomora (he who satisfied us)." Rugomora was brought chiefly skins, and celebrations were held.

As Rugomora traveled into his kingdom, he discovered people in Biyonga (Bugabo) hunting lake flies and paying him little heed. Disturbed, Rugomora changed their clan name to Babini (those who care nothing or are ignorant). He then went on to Kahororo where he planted a hammer and said, "Anyone who is a mulogi, or sorcerer, or son of a mulogi will not be able to lift this." [The witness says he saw it in 1928 at Kahororo in the bush and that it was a square type.] He then went to Bukoba where he planted a tree, Mujuju, which started growing immediately. He also met a Bukoba clansman who gave him sweet juice and honey.

He appointed this clan to thenceforth give juice to
the Bakama and named the Bakoba ba Kahinda bomwa
Munene, or "Bukoba of Kahinda who made Munene juice."

Rugomora then arrived at Kibuye where the Babango were
making iron. They failed to welcome Rugomora who
then, out of pique, changed the clan name to Bahuge
or the dull ones. The next step was Kyansozi (near
the forest reserve in Maruku), where he spent the
night with a man named Mishaguru, a Muhinda. He
then went on to Irungami village and finally to
Katuruka where he built his kikale. After this,
people started making many iron tools, whereupon
Rugomora drew up a plan to build a tower to the
heavens to see what they looked like. When the tower
was very high, so that the man on the top could
barely see a man on the ground, the tower fell on a
place called Omunyoma Katerero. [The witness says
he knows the place where the iron was smelted for
the tower, near the present palace.]

Some time after, as Rugomora Mahe was going to Rwagati,
people asked him for water at Kigabiro where there
was none. Rugomora was put down and beat the ground
with his stick and water came forth. To this day
that well may be seen. Rugomora lived several years
thereafter before dying.

Rugomora was succeeded by his son Kahigi. His other
sons were appointed as subchiefs: Miuyugi at
Kanyangereko; Kyana at Bukara; Kiro at Katoma;
Torongo in Bugabo; Kyoya in Bugunangoma; and one
at Kyarkyangoi.

Appendix D
Dimensions
of Bricks in Feature 100

a	9 x 6 x 5.5 cm.	1	10 x 9 x 6 cm.
b	9 x 7 x 6	2	9 x 6 x indetermin.
c	7 x 6 x 5	3	12 x 9 x 7
d	10 x 9 x 5	4	16 x 9 x 6.5
e	12 x 10 x 6	5	10 x 9 x 5 (est.)
f	10 x 7 x 6	6	7 x 7 x 6
g	9 x 9 x 6	7	13 x 8 x 6
h	9 x 6 x 6	8	9 x 7 x 9
i	15 x 10 x 6	9	13 x 9 x 6.5
j	17 x 10 x 7	[10]*	18 x 9 x 6.5
k	11 x 9 x 6	11	14 x 9 x 6
l	14 x 7 x 6.5	[12]	11 x 9 x 7.5
m	11 x 8 x 6	13	10 x 8 x 5.5
n	8 x 8 x 6	[14]	12 x 9 x 7
o	10 x 9 x 6	15	9 x 6 x 5
		[16]	10 x 9 x 9
		17	10 x 9 x 5
		18	9 x 8 x 5.5
		[19]	17 x 9 x 7
		20	16 x 9 x 6.5
		21	10 x 7 x 7
		[22]	10 x 9 x 6.5

*Those enclosed in brackets are unbroken examples.

Appendix E — Early and Late Iron Age Slag Densities

	Provenience No.	Early Iron Age	Late Iron Age
Block H	100	0	6 g
	200	29 g	88 g
	1000	0	423 g
	1050	0	2 g
	1075	0	10 g
	1100	91 g	38
	1125	35 g	227 g
	1150	48 g	35
	1175	13 g	28
	1225	9 g	309
	1300	5 g	0
	1350	0 g	72
	1400	0 g	70
	1500	0 g	43
	1600	0 g	17
	1700	0 g	6
	1900	12 g	132
Block B	3000	0 g	36
	3050	0 g	58
	3100	10 g	323
	3125	0 g	98
	3150	0 g	4
	3200	0 g	146
	3250	0 g	23
	3300	0	26 g
	3600	0	9 g
	3800	0	46 g
	3900	0	33 g
Block C	1200	2 kg 95 g	222 g
	1375	26 g	0

	1525	0	377 g
Block D	5025	158 g	2 g
	5050	60 g	67 g
	5075	102 g	37 g
	5150	65 g	66 g
	5200	1131 g	12 g
	5300	0	59 g
	5400	318 g	34 g
	5500	35 g	49 g
	5600	52 g	41 g
	5900	0 g	303 g
Block E	9000	231 g	0
	9025	142 g	13 g
	9050	380 g	179 g
	9075	136 g	13 g
	9100	278 g	0
	9125	127 g	0
	9150	21 g	0
	9175	31 g	0
	9200	60 g	0
	9225	53 g	0
	9250	16 g	0
	9275	80 g	0
	9325	39 g	0

Feature Density

Feature No.	Weight in grams
6	73.7
6 B	175.5
10	838.2
13	2425.85
14	107
19	20
20	2375
22	30
30	87
31	29
34	65
36	13.5
37	76.2
38	12
41	47
48	767.7
51	31.2
53	43
57	6
58	125.5
60	62
61	7
63	22.6
100	10.351 kg

Appendix F — Tuyères

	Provenience No.	Early Iron Age	Late Iron Age
Block A	1000	12.3 g	9.9 g
	1075	0 g	13.6 g
	1125	176 g	0
	1150	12 g	0
	1300	3.6 g	0
	1400	0	18 g
	1600	0	44 g
	1700	0	4 g
	1900	3 g	0
Block B	3500	0	9 g
Block D	5025	49 g	5 g
	5050	56 g	5 g
	5075	26 g	87 g
	5150	5 g	12 g
	5200	9 g	28 g
	5300	0 g	10 g
	5400	53 g	0
	5500	11 g	6 g
	5600	10 g	38 g
	5900	0 g	9 g
Block E	9000	0	3 g
	9025	6 g	0 g
	9050	78 g	7 g
	9075	0	23 g
	9100	22 g	26 g
	9150	1 g	2 g
	9200	22 g	16 g
	9225	2 g	9.6 g
	9375	18 g	0 g
	9425	0 g	20 g
	9450	18 g	13 g
	9475	7 g	0

9550	0 g	13 g
9575	0 g	4 g
9625	71 g	0 g
9725	23 g	6 g
9750	5 g	67 g
9775	117 g	0 g
9850	4 g	0 g

Extra Block
Lists   1125   18 g   3 g

Feature Density

Feature No.	Weight in grams
12	41
13	564.2
16	4.7
20	12.5
21	24
29	23
40	17
41	3
48	2
58	12
59	6
60	21.5
62	15.6
100 A + B	655.4
100 C	99.9

Bibliography

Allen, William L. and Richardson, James B., III.
1971 "The Reconstruction of Kinship from
Archaeological Data: The Concepts, Methods, and
the Feasibility," American Antiquity, Vol. 36,
No. 1; pp. 41-53.

Ascher, Robert.
1961 "Analogy in Archaeological Interpretation."
Southwestern Journal of Anthropology, Vol. 17,
No. 4; pp. 317-325.

Banerjee, N. E.
1965 The Iron Age in India. Munshiram Manoharlal,
Delhi.

Beattie, J.H.M.
1957 "Initiation into the Chwezi Spirit Possession
Cult in Bunyoro," African Studies, Vol. 15;
pp. 150-161.

1960 Bunyoro: An African Kingdom. Holt, Rinehart
& Winston, New York.

1963 "Sorcery in Bunyoro," in J. Middleton and
E. H. Winters, eds., Witchcraft and Sorcery in
East Africa. Routledge & Kegan Paul, London;
pp. 27-55.

1964a "Divination in Bunyoro, Uganda," Sociologus,
Vol. 14; pp. 44-61.

1964b "The Ghost Cult in Bunyoro," Ethnology,
Vol. 3; pp. 127-151.

1968 "Aspects of Nyoro Symbolism," Africa,
Vol. 38, No. 4; pp. 413-442.

1971 The Nyoro State. Clarendon Press, Oxford.

Beidelman, T. O.
1970 "Myth, Legend and Oral History," Anthropos,
Vol. 65; pp. 74-97.

Bernhard, F. O.
1965 "Two Types of Iron-Smelting Furnaces on Ziwa
Farm," South African Archaeological Bulletin,
Vol. 17; pp. 235-236.

Bikunya, Petro.
1927 "Ky'Abakama ba Bunyoro. Sheldon Press, London.

Binford, Lewis R.
1962 "Archaeology as Anthropology," American
Antiquity, Vol. 28, No. 2; pp. 217-225.

1964 "A Consideration of Archaeological Research
Design," American Antiquity, Vol. 29; pp. 425-441.

1965 "Archaeological Systematics and the Study of
Culture Process," American Antiquity, Vol. 31;
pp. 203-210.

1967 "Smudge Pits and Hide Smoking: The Use of
Analogy in Archaeological Reasoning," American
Antiquity, Vol. 32, No. 1; pp. 1-12.

1968a "Some Comments on Historical Versus Processual
Archaeology," Southwestern Journal of Anthropology, Vol. 24; pp. 267-275.

1968b "Methodological Considerations of Archaeological Use of Ethnographic Data," in R. B. Lee
and I. DeVore, eds., Man the Hunter. Aldine,
Chicago.

Binford, Sally R. and Binford, Lewis R.
1968 New Perspectives in Archaeology. Adline,
Chicago.

Boserup, Esther.
1965 The Conditions of Agricultural Growth. The
Economics of Agrarian Change under Population
Pressure. George Allen & Unwin, London.

Burridge, K.O.L.
1967 "Lévi-Strauss and Myth," in Edmund Leach, ed.,
The Structural Study of Myth and Totemism.

Tavistock Publications, Edinburgh; pp. 91-118.

Chapman, Susannah.
1967 "Kantsyore Island," Azania, Vol. 2, pp. 165-191.

Clarke, David L.
1968 Analytical Archaeology. Methuen & Co. Ltd., London

Cohen, Ronald.
1966 "The Dynamics of Feudalism in Bornu," in Boston University Press Papers of African History, Vol. 2, ed. by J. Butler; p. 98.

Cole, Glen H.
1965 "Recent Archaeological Work in Southern Uganda," Uganda Journal, Vol. 29, No. 2; pp. 149-161.

Collingwood, R. G.
1946 The Idea of History. Clarendon Press, Cambridge.

Cory, Hans.
n.d. Historia ya Bukoba. Mwanza.

Cory, H. and Hartnoll, M. M.
1945 Customary Law of the Haya Tribe. International African Institute, London.

Cunnison, I.
1951 History on the Luapula. An Essay on the Historical Notions of a Central African Tribe. Rhodes-Livingstone Papers, Lusaka.

Davidson, Basil.
1959 Old Africa Rediscovered. Little, Brown, Boston

Deetz, James.
1967 Invitation to Archaeology. Natural History Press, New York.

1970 "Archaeology as a Social Science," Current Directions in Anthropology, Vol. 3, No. 3, Part 2; pp. 115-125.

Doran, James.
1970 "Systems Theory, Computer Simulations and Archaeology," World Archaeology, Vol. 1, No. 3; pp. 289-298.

Fagan, Brian.
    1965 "Two Soli Smelting Furnaces from Lusaka,
    Northern Rhodesia," South African Archaeological
    Bulletin, Vol. 17; pp. 27-28.

    1966 "Early Iron Age Pottery in Eastern and Southern
    Africa," Azania, Vol. 1; pp. 101-110.

    1967a Iron Age Cultures in Zambia. Chatto & Windus,
    London.

    1967b "Radiocarbon Dates for Sub-Saharan Africa,"
    Journal of African History, Vol. 7, No. 3;
    pp. 513-527.

Fagan, B. M. and Lofgren, Laurel.
    1966 "Archaeological Reconnaissance on the Sese
    Islands," Uganda Journal, Vol. 30, No. 1; pp. 81-
    86.

Fagan, B. M. and Willett, F.
    1967 African Studies Bulletin, Vol. 10, No. 1;
    pp. 43-50

Fagan, Brian M. and Yellen, John E.
    1968 "Ivuna: Ancient Salt Working in Southern
    Tanzania," Azania, Vol. 3; pp. 1-44.

Fagg, Bernard.
    1969 "Recent Work in West Africa: New Light on
    the Nok Culture," World Archaeology, Vol. 1,
    No. 1; pp. 41-50.

Fisher, Ruth.
    1970 Twilight Tales of the Black Baganda. Second
    edition; Frank Cuss, London.

Fritz, John M. and Plog, Fred.
    1970 "The Nature of Archaeological Explanation,"
    American Antiquity, Vol. 35; pp. 405-412.

Gilsenan, Michael.
    1972 "Myth and the History of African Religion,"
    in T. Ranger, and I. Kimambo, eds., A Historical
    Study of Religion. University of California
    Press, Berkeley and Los Angeles.

Goghlan, H. H.
    1956 Notes on Prehistoric and Early Iron in the
    Old World. University Press, Oxford.

Gould, Richard A.
    1973 "Australian Archaeology in Ecological and

Ethnographic Perspective," Warner Modular Publications, No. 7; pp. 1-33.

Hammel, Eugene A.
1972 "The Myth of Structural Analysis: Lévi-
Strauss and the Three Bears," Addison-Wesley
Module, No. 25; pp. 1-29.

Harris, David R.
1972 "Swidden Systems and Settlement," in Peter
G. Ucko, Ruth Tringham, and G. W. Dimbleby, eds.,
Man Settlement and Urbanism. Gerald Duckworth
& Co. Ltd., London; pp. 245-262.

Hempel, Carl G.
1965 Aspects of Scientific Explanation and Other
Essays in the Philosophy of Science. Free
Press, Glencoe, Illinois.

Hempel, Carl G. and Oppenheim, Paul.
1948 "Studies in the Logic of Explanation,"
Philosophy of Science, Vol. 15; pp. 135-175.

Heusch, Luc de.
1966 Le Rwanda et la civilisation interlacustre.
Université Libre de Bruxelles.

Hiernaux, Jean.
1968 "Bantu Expansion: The Evidence from Physical
Anthropology Confronted with Linguistic and
Archaeological Evidence," Journal of African
History, Vol. 9, No. 4; pp. 505-515.

Hiernaux, J. and Maquet, M.
1960 "Cultures prehistoriques de l'âge des metaux
au Rwanda-Urundi et au Kivu (Congo Belge), l'ère
partie," Bulletin des Seances de l'A.R.S.C.,
N.S., 2; pp. 1123-1149.

Hill, James N.
1970 "Broken K Pueblo: Patterns of Form and
Function," in Sally R. Binford, and Lewis R.
Binford, eds., New Perspectives in Archaeology,
pp. 103-142.

Huffman, Thomas N.
1969 "The Early Iron Age and the Spread of the
Bantu," South African Archaeological Bulletin,
Vol. 25; pp. 3-21.

Hyden, Göran.
1969 Political Development in Rural Tanzania.

East African Publishing House, Nairobi, Kenya.

K. W. (Sir Tito Winyi).
    1935 "The Kings of Bunyoro Kitara," Uganda
    Journal, Vol. 3; pp. 155-160.

Kendall, Robert L.
    1969 "An Ecological History of the Lake Victoria
    Basin," Ecological Monographs, Vol. 39; pp. 121-
    176.

Kimambo, I. N. and Temu, A. J.
    1969 A History of Tanzania. East African
    Publishing House, Nairobi, Kenya.

Kirk, G. A.
    1970 Myth: Its Meaning and Functions in Ancient
    and Other Cultures. University Press, Cambridge.

Lanning, E. C.
    1966 "Excavations at Mubende Hill," Uganda
    Journal, Vol. 30, No. 2; pp. 153-163.

    1970 "Ntusi: An Ancient Capital Site in Western
    Uganda," Azania, Vol. 5; pp. 39-54.

Leakey, M. D., Owen, W. E. and Leakey, L.S.B.
    1948 "Dimple-based Pottery from Central Kavirondo,
    Kenya Colony," Coryndon Memorial Museum
    Occasional Papers, No. 2; pp. 9-51.

Lévi-Strauss, Claude.
    1963 Structural Anthropology. Doubleday & Co.,
    New York.

    1970 The Raw and the Cooked. Harper & Row, New
    York.

Levin, Michael E.
    1973 "On Explanation in Archaeology: A Rebuttal to
    Fritz and Plog," American Antiquity, Vol. 38,
    No. 4; pp. 387-395.

Livingstone, Daniel A.
    1965 "Sedimentation and the History of Water Level
    Change in Lake Tanganyika," Limnology and
    Oceanography, Vol. 10, No. 4; pp. 607-610.

    1971 "Speculations on the Climatic History of
    Mankind," American Scientist, Vol. 59, No. 3;
    pp. 332-337.

Livingstone, D. A. and Kendall, R. L.
   1969 "Stratigraphic Studies of East African
   Lakes," _Mitt. Internat. Verein. Limnol._, Vol.
   17; pp. 147-153.

Longacre, William A.
   1968 "Some Aspects of Prehistoric Society in
   East-Central Arizona," in Sally R. Binford and
   Lewis R. Binford, eds., _New Perspectives in
   Archaeology_; pp. 89-102.

Lwamgira, F. X.
   1949 _Amakuru ga Kiziba na Abakama Bamu._

Malinowski, Bronislaw.
   1948 _Magic, Science and Religion._ Free Press,
   London.

Maranda, Elli Köngäs and Maranda, Pierre.
   1971 _Structural Models in Folklore and Trans-
   formational Essays._ Mouton, The Hague.

McCall, Daniel F.
   1964 _Africa in Time Perspective._ Boston University Press, Boston.

McMaster, D. N.
   1960 "Change of Regional Balance in the Bukoba
   District of Tanganyika," _Geographical Review_,
   Vol. 50; pp. 73-88.

McNeil, Mary.
   1964 "Lateritic Soils," _Scientific American_,
   Vol. 211, No. 5; pp. 96-102.

Middleton, J. and Winters, E. H.
   1963 _Witchcraft and Sorcery in East Africa._
   Routledge & Kegan Paul, London.

Milne, G.
   1938 "Bukoba: High and Low Fertility on a
   Laterised Soil," _East African Agricultural
   Journal_, Vol. 4, No. 1; pp. 13-24.

Morgan, Charles G.
   1973 "Archaeology and Explanation," _World
   Archaeology_, Vol. 4, No. 3; pp. 259-276.

Morris, H. F.
   1957 "The Making of Ankole," _Uganda Journal_,
   Vol. 21, No. 1; pp. 1-15.

1962 A History of Ankole. East African Literature
      Bureau, Nairobi, Kenya, Dar es Salaam.

Morrison, M.
      1969 "Report on Palynological Research in Uganda
      and Kenya," Palaeoecology of Africa and of the
      Surrounding Islands and Antarctica, Vol. 4,
      Capetown, South Africa.

Needham, Rodney.
      1967 "Right and Left in Nyoro Symbolic Classifica-
      tion," Africa, Vol. 37, No. 4; pp. 425-452.

Nenquin, Jacques.
      1967 Contributions to the Study of the Prehistoric
      Cultures of Rwanda and Burundi. Musee Royal
      de L'Afrique Centrale, Tervuren, Belgium.

Netting, Robert McC.
      1968 Hill Farmers of Nigeria. University of
      Washington Press, Seattle.

      1971 "The Ecological Approach in Cultural Study,"
      McCaleb Module; pp. 1-30.

Nyakatura, J. W.
      1970 Abakama ba Bunyoro. Godfrey N. Uzoigwe, ed.,
      and T. Mugana, trans. Entitled Anatomy of an
      African Kingdom. Anchor Press/Doubleday, New
      York.

Oliver, Roland.
      1966 "The Problem of Bantu Expansion," Journal of
      African History, Vol. 7, No. 3; pp. 361-376.

Pender-Cudlip, Patrick.
      1972 "Oral Traditions and Anthropological Analysis:
      Some Contemporary Myths," Azania, Vol. 7;
      pp. 3-24.

Phillipson, D. W.
      1968 "The Early Iron Age in Zambia—Regional
      Variants and Some Tentative Conclusions,"
      Journal of African History, Vol. 4, No. 2;
      pp. 191-211.

      1970 "Excavations at Twickenham Road, Lusaka,"
      Azania, Vol. 5; pp. 77-89.

Pleiner, Radomir.
      1969 "Experimental Smelting of Steel in Early
      Medieval Furnaces," Poḿatky archeologické
      Vol. 60; pp. 458-487.

Posnansky, Merrick.
1961 "Pottery Types from Archaeological Sites in
East Africa," Journal of African History,
Vol. 2, No. 2; pp. 178-198.

1965 "The Iron Age in East Africa," in Walter W.
Bishop and J. Desmond Clark, eds., Background to
Evolution in Africa. University of Chicago,
Chicago & London; pp. 629-649.

1966a Prelude to East African History. Oxford
University Press, Oxford.

1966b "Kingship, Archaeology and Historical Myth,"
Uganda Journal, Vol. 30, No. 1; pp. 1-12.

1968a "Bantu Genesis—Archaeological Reflexions,"
Journal of African History, Vol. 9, No. 1;
pp. 1-11.

1968b "The Excavation of an Ankole Capital Site
at Bweyorere," Uganda Journal, Vol. 32, No. 2;
pp. 165-182.

1969 "Bigo Bya Mugenyi," Uganda Journal, Vol. 33,
No. 2; pp. 125-150.

Posnansky, M. and Grinrod, B.
1968 "Iron Smelting and Furnaces at North Kinangop,"
Azania, Vol. 3, pp. 191-195.

Posnansky, M. and Pierce, S.
1963 "Re-excavation of Nsongezi Rock Shelter,"
Uganda Journal, Vol. 27, No. 1; pp. 85-94.

Rackerby, Frank.
1973 "A Statistical Determination of the Black
Sand Occupation (T) at the Macoupin Site,
Jersey, Co., Illinois," American Antiquity,
Vol. 38, No. 1; pp. 96-100.

Ranger, F. W. and Kimambo, I. N., eds.
1972 A Historical Study of African Religion.
University of California Press, Berkeley and
Los Angeles.

Redman, Charles L.
1973 "Multistage Fieldwork and Analytical
Techniques," American Antiquity, Vol. 38, No. 1;
pp. 61-79.

Rehse, Hermann.
1910 Kiziba Land und Leute. Stuttgart.

Reining, Pricilla C.
    1962 "Haya Land Tenure: Landholding and Tenancy,"
        Anthropological _Quarterly_, Vol. 35; pp. 58-72.

Richards, Audrey I. and LaFontaine, J.
    1960 "The Haya," in A. Richards and J. LaFontaine,
        eds., _East_ _African_ _Chiefs_. Faber and Faber,
        London.

Richardson, J. L. and Richardson, A. E.
    1972 "History of an African Rift Lake and Its
        Climatic Implications," _Ecological_ _Monographs_,
        Vol. 42; pp. 499-534.

Robinson, K. R. and Sandelowsky, B.
    1968 "The Iron Age of Northern Malawi: Recent
        Work," _Azania_, Vol. 3; pp. 147-166.

Roscoe, John.
    1923 _The_ _Bakitara_ _or_ _Banyoro_. University Press,
        Cambridge.

Rounce, N. W. and Thornton, D.
    1956 "Ukara Island and the Agricultural Practices
        of the Makara," _Empire_ _C._ _G._ _Review_, Vol. 33;
        pp. 255-263.

Sassoon, Hamo.
    1964 "Iron Smelting in the Hill Village of Sukur,
        North-Eastern Nigeria," _Man_, No. 214; pp. 174-
        180.

    1972 "Early Sources of Iron in Africa," _South_
        African _Archaeological_ _Bulletin_, Vol. 18;
        pp. 176-180.

Service, Elman R.
    1962 _Primitive_ _Social_ _Organization_. Random House,
        New York.

Shinnie, P. L., ed.
    1971 _The_ _African_ _Iron_ _Age_. Clarendon Press,
        Oxford.

Smith, Philip E.L.
    1972a "The Consequences of Food Production,"
        Addison-Wesley _Module_, No. 31; pp. 1-38.

    1972b "Changes in Population Pressure in
        Archaeological Explanation," _World_ _Archaeology_,
        Vol. 4, No. 1; pp. 5-18.

Soper, R. C.
    1967 "Iron Age Sites in North-Eastern Tanzania,"
          Azania, Vol. 2; pp. 19-36.

    1971a "A General Review of the Early Iron Age of
           the Southern Half of Africa," Azania, Vol. 6;
           pp. 5-38.

    1971b "Early Iron Age Pottery Types from East
           Africa: Comparative Analysis," Azania, Vol. 6;
           pp. 39-52.

    1971c "Resemblances Between East African Early Iron
           Age Pottery and Recent Vessels from the North-
           eastern Congo," Azania, Vol. 6; pp. 233-241.

    1971d "Iron Age Sites in Chobi Sector, Murchison
           Falls National Park, Uganda," Azania, Vol. 6;
           pp. 53-88.

Soper, R. C. and Golden, B.
    1969 "An Archaeological Survey of Mwanza Region,
          Tanzania," Azania, Vol. 4; pp. 15-80.

Stanislawski, Michael B.
    1973 "Longacre: Archaeology as Anthropology: A
          Case Study," American Antiquity, Vol. 38, No. 1;
          pp. 117-121.

Steward, Julian H.
    1955 Theory of Culture Change. University of
          Illinois Press, Urbana.

Struever, Stuart
    1968a "Problems, Methods and Organization:
           Disparity in the Growth of Archaeology," in
           Betty Meggers, ed., Anthropological Archaeology
           in the Americas. Anthropological Society of
           Washington, Washington, D.C.

    1968b "Woodland Subsistence-Settlement Systems in
           the Lower Illinois Valley," in Sally R. Binford
           and Lewis R. Binford, eds., New Perspectives in
           Archaeology; pp. 285-312.

    1968c "Flotation Techniques for the Recovery of
           Small-scale Archaeological Remains," American
           Antiquity, Vol. 33, No. 4; pp. 353-362.

    1971a "Comments on Archaeological Data Requirements
           and Research Strategy," American Antiquity,
           Vol. 36, No. 1; pp. 9-19.

1971b Prehistoric Agriculture. Natural History
       Press, New York.

Summers, Roger.
    1958 Inyanga: Prehistoric Settlements in Southern
          Rhodesia. University Press, Cambridge.

Sutton, J.E.G.
    1968a "The Settlement of East Africa," in B. A.
           Ogot and J. A. Kieran, eds., Zamani: A Survey
           of East African History, Longmans of Kenya,
           Nairobi; pp. 69-99.

    1968b "Archaeological Sites in Usandawe," Azania,
           Vol. 3; pp. 167-174.

    1972 "New Radiocarbon Dates for Eastern and
          Southern Africa," Journal of African History,
          Vol. 13, No. 1; pp. 1-24.

    1973 The Archaeology of the Western Highlands of
          Kenya. British Institute in Eastern Africa,
          Nairobi, Kenya.

Sutton, J.E.G. and Roberts, A.D.
    1968 "Uvinza and Its Salt Industry," Azania, Vol.
          3; pp. 45-86.

Swartz, B. K., Jr.
    1967 "A Logical Sequence of Archaeological Objec-
          tives," American Antiquity, Vol. 32, No. 4;
          pp. 487-496.

Taylor, Walter W.
    1948 A Study of Archaeology. Southern Illinois
          Press, Carbondale.

Thompson, Stith.
    1946 The Folktale. Holt, Rinehart & Winston, New
          York.

Trigger, Bruce.
    1968 "Major Concepts of Archaeology in Historical
          Perspective," Man, Vol. 2; pp. 527-541.

    1971 "Archaeology and Ecology," World Archaeology,
          Vol. 2, No. 3; pp. 321-336.

Tuggle, H. David, Townsend, Alex H. and Riley, Thomas
R.
    1972 "Laws, Systems, and Research Designs: A
          Discussion of Explanation in Archaeology,"
          American Antiquity, Vol. 37, No. 1; pp. 3-12.

Tylecote, R. F.
    1975 "The Origin of Iron Smelting in Africa,"
    West African Journal of Archaeology, Vol. 5,
    pp. 1-3.

van der Merwe, Nikolaas and Scully, Robert T. K.
    1971 "The Phalaborwa Story: Archaeology and
    Ethnographic Investigations of a South African
    Iron Age Group," World Archaeology, Vol. 3,
    No. 2; pp. 178-196.

Vansina, Jan.
    1965 Oral Tradition: A Study in Historical
    Methodology. Aldine, Chicago.

Watson, Patty Jo, LeBlanc, Steven A. and Redman,
    Charles L.
    1971 Explanation in Archaeology: An Explicitly
    Scientific Approach. Columbia University Press,
    New York.

Wayland, E. J.
    1934 "Rifts, Rivers, Rains and Early Man in Uganda,"
    Journal of the Royal Anthropological Institute,
    Vol. 64; pp. 333-352.

Whallon, Robert, Jr.
    1972 "A New Approach to Pottery Typology,"
    American Antiquity, Vol. 37, No. 1; pp. 13-33.

Willett, Frank.
    1971 "Survey of Recent Results in the Radiocarbon
    Chronology of Western and Northern Africa,"
    Journal of African History, Vol. 12, No. 3;
    pp. 339-370.

    1973 "Archaeology," in J. O. Biobaku, ed.,
    Sources of Yoruba History. Clarendon Press,
    Oxford; pp. 111-139.

Baguma, R. (trans.)
    n.d. "Amakuru ga Bukaya Ey'eira." No author; a
    history of Kyamutwara kingdom.

Betbeder, Father Paul.
    Extensive files on ethnography of Bukoba area,
    including such topics as snakes, sorcery, witch-
    craft, marriage, birth ceremonies, government
    budget, and folk tales. Ngote, West Lake.

Betegeki.
    1949 "Utawala wa Weneji wa Wilaya ya Bukoba,"
    Rwamishenye, Bukoba.

The Committee of the Chiefs of Buhaya at Rwamishenye.
    1949 "Obutwazi Bweikanga Lya Bukoba" (The Constitu-
    tion of the District of Bukoba).

    1956 "The Landlord and Tenant Rules (Bukoba
    District)," The Native Authority Ordinance,
    from Cory file, No. 20, University Library,
    University College, Dar es Salaam; 8 pages.

Cory, H.
    1938 "The Chronology of the Bahinda Chiefs of the
    Bukoba District," from Cory file, No. 69,
    University Library, University College, Dar es
    Salaam; 19 pages.

    1955 "Report on the Nyarbanja System In Bukoba,"
    from Cory file, No. 172, University Library,
    University College, Dar es Salaam.

    n.d. Proverbs from Cory files, University Library,
    University College, Dar es Salaam. Translated
    by R. Baguma.

    n.d. "Wahima," from Cory file, No. 231, University
    Library, University College, Dar es Salaam.

Culwick, A. T.
    1939 "Land Tenure in the Bukoba District," from
    Cory file, No. 239, University Library, Univer-
    sity College, Dar es Salaam; 37 pages.

Fairclough, M. C.
    n.d. "Report on Nyarubanja System of Land Tenure
    in the Bukoba District," from Cory file, No.
    252, University Library, University College, Dar
    es Salaam; 8 pages.

Griffith, A.W.M.
    1927 "Land Tenure Bukoba," from Cory file, No.
    273, University Library, University College,
    Dar es Salaam; 24 pages.

Kakwezi, Father John.
    n.d. "Emicocozo y'Abanziba," from files of
    Mutaihwa Lubelwa, Kigarama, Kiziba.

Kuijpers.
    n.d. "History of Kiziba," from files of Father
    Paul Betbeder.

Kyayonka, Spirian. (Secretary to the Ababito History
    Committee.)
    1953 on. "Entabuko Yoluganda Lwababito Nobukama
        Bwabo." The root and origins of the Babito clan
        and their rule. From Spirian Kyayonka, Kitobo,
        Kiziba.

Lwamgira, F. X. (Files).
    1920 "Maruku." No author.

Pesha, Q. B.
    1934 "Emigani N'Enfumu," from files of Father Paul
        Betbeder, Ngote, West Lake.

Rabajo.
    n.d. "Kikukwe Kabato," manuscript held by Mzee
        Rubajo, Kikukwe, Kiziba.

Richards, A. I. and Reining, Pricilla.
    1952 "Report on Fertility Surveys in Buganda and
        Buhaya," from Cory file, No. 373, University
        Library, University College, Dar es Salaam.

Rugachwa, Mukama.
    1920 "Karema," from files of F. X. Lwamgira.

Rutamagi, Daniel.
    n.d. "The Book of Wisdom," Kitobo, Kiziba.

Samson, F.
    n.d. "The Abankango of Kabare," from files of
        Father Paul Betbeder, Ngote, West Lake.

    n.d. "Abakango ba Bugabo," from files of Father
        Paul Betbeder, Ngote, West Lake.

    n.d. "Abahinda ba Kyamutwara," from files of
        Father Paul Betbeder, Ngote, West Lake.

Bona-Baisi, Father Ignace J.
    1960 Ikani-Ngambo. Pallottine-Fathers, Limburg/
        Lahn, Germany.

Huwiler, B. and Rwinga, Modestus.
    1933 Akatabo k'emigani n'emiizo. Imprimerie des
        Missionnaires D'Afrique, Maison-Caree (Alger).

Lwamgira, Francis Xavier.
    1949 Amakuru G'Abakama Ba Bugabo Abankango.

    1949 Amakuru G'Abakama Ba Kyamutwara.

1952   Amakuru G'Abakama Ba Kibumbiro Missenyi.
       Kiziba, Buhaya.

Mupapi, Willibald P.
       Amakuru G'Abaikuzi Ba Buhaya.   Bunena, Bukoba.

Index

approach to archaeo-
logy in Nigeria, 5;
cited, 278, 296

Zither, as accompaniment
to enanga songs, 50